Other Insight Guides available:

Alaska
Amazon Wildlife
American Southwest
Amsterdam
Argentina
Arizona & Grand Canyon
Asia, East
Asia, Southeast
Asia's Best Hotels
  and Resorts
Australia
Austria
Bahamas
Bali & Lombok
Baltic States
Bangkok
Barbados
Belgium
Belize
Berlin
Bermuda
Brazil
Brittany
Buenos Aires
Burgundy
Burma (Myanmar)
Cairo
California
California, Southern
Canada
Caribbean
Caribbean Cruises
Channel Islands
Chicago
Chile
China
Colorado
Continental Europe
Corsica
Costa Rica
Crete
Cuba
Cyprus
Czech & Slovak Republic
Delhi, Jaipur & Agra
Denmark
Dominican Rep. & Haiti
Dublin
East African Wildlife
Eastern Europe
Ecuador
Edinburgh
Egypt
England
Finland
Florida
France
France, Southwest
French Riviera
Gambia & Senegal
Germany
Glasgow
Gran Canaria
Great Britain

Great Railway Journeys
  of Europe
Great River Cruises
  of Europe
Greece
Greek Islands
Guatemala, Belize
  & Yucatán
Hawaii
Hungary
Iceland
India
India, South
Indonesia
Ireland
Israel
Istanbul
Italy
Italy, Northern
Italy, Southern
Jamaica
Japan
Jerusalem
Jordan
Kenya
Korea
Laos & Cambodia
Lisbon
Madeira
Malaysia
Mallorca & Ibiza
Malta
Mauritius Réunion
  & Seychelles
Melbourne
Mexico
Miami
Montreal
Morocco
Namibia
Nepal
Netherlands
New England
New Mexico
New Orleans
New York State
New Zealand
Nile
Normandy
North American and
  Alaskan Cruises
Norway
Oman & The UAE
Oxford
Pacific Northwest
Pakistan
Peru
Philadelphia
Philippines
Poland
Portugal
Provence
Puerto Rico
Rajasthan

Rio de Janeiro
Russia
Sardinia
Scandinavia
Scotland
Seattle
Sicily
South Africa
South America
Spain
Spain, Northern
Spain, Southern
Sri Lanka
Sweden
Switzerland
Syria & Lebanon
Taiwan
Tenerife
Texas
Thailand
Trinidad & Tobago
Tunisia
Turkey
Tuscany
Umbria
USA: On The Road
USA: Western States
US National Parks: West
Venezuela
Vienna
Vietnam
Wales

INSIGHT CITY GUIDES
(with free restaurant map)

Barcelona
Beijing
Boston
Bruges, Ghent & Antwerp
Brussels
Cape Town
Florence
Hong Kong
Las Vegas
London
Los Angeles
Madrid
Moscow
New York
Paris
Prague
Rome
St Petersburg
San Francisco
Singapore
Sydney
Taipei
Tokyo
Toronto
Utah
Venice
Walt Disney World/Orlando
Washington, DC

INSIGHT CITY GUIDE
LOS ANGELES

DISCOVERY CHANNEL

APA PUBLICATIONS

L

Part of the Langenscheidt Publishing Group

※ INSIGHT GUIDE
Los Angeles

Project Editor
Martha Ellen Zenfell
Picture Editor
Hilary Genin
Art Director
Klaus Geisler
Cartography Editor
Zoë Goodwin
Production
Kenneth Chan
Editorial Director
Brian Bell

Distribution

UK & Ireland
GeoCenter International Ltd
The Viables Centre, Harrow Way
Basingstoke, Hants RG22 4BJ
Fax: (44) 1256-817988

United States
Langenscheidt Publishers, Inc.
36–36 33rd Street 4th Floor
Long Island City, NY 11106
Fax: (1) 718 784-0640

Australia
Universal Publishers
1 Waterloo Road
Macquarie Park, NSW 2113
Fax: (61) 2 9888 9074

New Zealand
Hema Maps New Zealand Ltd (HNZ)
Unit D, 24 Ra ORA Drive
East Tamaki, Auckland
Fax: (64) 9 273 6479

Worldwide
Apa Publications GmbH & Co.
Verlag KG (Singapore branch)
38 Joo Koon Road, Singapore 628990
Tel: (65) 6865-1600. Fax: (65) 6861-6438

Printing

Insight Print Services (Pte) Ltd
38 Joo Koon Road, Singapore 628990
Tel: (65) 6865-1600. Fax: (65) 6861-6438

©2006 Apa Publications GmbH & Co.
Verlag KG (Singapore branch)
All Rights Reserved

First Edition 1991
Fourth Edition 2006

ABOUT THIS BOOK

The first Insight Guide pioneered the use of creative full-color photography in travel guides in 1970. Since then, we have expanded our range to cater for our readers' need not only for reliable information about their chosen destination but also for a real understanding of it. When the internet can supply inexhaustible (but not always reliable) facts, our books marry text and pictures to provide those much more elusive qualities: knowledge and discernment.

How to use this book

Insight City Guide: Los Angeles is carefully structured:

◆ The Best of Los Angeles at the front of the book helps to prioritize what you want to see. Unique experiences, the best shopping, best celeb spotting and family attractions are listed, along with money-saving tips.

◆ To understand LA, you need to know something of its past. The city's history and culture are described in authoritative essays written by specialists who have lived here for years.

◆ The main Places section details all the attractions worth seeing. The main places of interest are coordinated by number with the maps.

◆ A list of recommended restaurants is printed at the end of each chapter. Some of these are also described and plotted on the pull-out restaurant map that accompanies the guide.

◆ Photographs throughout the book are chosen not only to illustrate geography and buildings, but also to convey the moods of the city and the life of its people.

◆ The Travel Tips section includes all the practical information you will need

for your stay, divided into four key sections: transportation, accommodations, activities (including nightlife, shopping and sports), and an A–Z of practical tips. Information may be located quickly by using the Index printed on the back cover flap.

◆ A detailed street atlas is included at the back of the book, complete with a full index.

The contributors

This new edition was project edited by **Martha Ellen Zenfell**, and builds on other, previous editions. For these we would like to thank **Sarah Hudson** and **Mix Ryan**, **John Wilcock** and **Nancy Gottesman**.

Like many non-Californians, Zenfell had mixed experiences in Los Angeles. Early visits, when carless and friendless, were spent mostly in

tears. And yes, just like in the movies, she *did* get pulled over by the police for walking, not driving. Subsequent trips could not have been more different. Guided by locals who knew and loved the city, she was determined, in this edition, to make sense of it for other people, too.

In this she was aided by the tireless efforts of **Laura Martone**, a travel, ecology and video writer, and Insight's chief correspondent in the City of Angels. Martone turned LA's teeming, sprawling mass into a series of user-friendly neighborhoods, many of which can be covered on foot.

The images are the work of California-based **Catherine Karnow**, with the capable assistance of **David Dunai** and **Sara Remington**. The team didn't stop working from dawn to dusk in order to capture the great photographs reproduced here. Karnow even flew back from the East Coast for a frantic weekend of filling in the visual gaps.

Other contributors, past and present, include **Merrill Shindler**, **Tania Martinez-Lemke**, **Stanley Young**, **William M. Mason**. **Duane Byrge**, **Michael Tennesen**, **Barbara Horngren**, **Judith Blocker** and **Michael Webb**. At Insight's office in London, there were endless discussions with cartogaphers **Zoe Goodwin** and **James Macdonald** as to how best to document LA without turning the guide into just a book of maps. We hope we have succeeded. **Mary Pickles** processed the text with the flair and speed required for the project. The manuscript was proofread and indexed by **Penny Phenix**.

CONTACTING THE EDITORS

We would appreciate it if readers would alert us to errors or outdated information by writing to:

Insight Guides, P.O. Box 7910, London SE1 1WE, England. Fax: (44) 20 7403-0290. insight@apaguide.co.uk

NO part of this book may be reproduced, stored in a retrieval system or transmitted in any form or means electronic, mechanical, photocopying, recording or otherwise, without prior written permission of *Apa Publications*. Brief text quotations with use of photographs are exempted for book review purposes only. Information has been obtained from sources believed to be reliable, but its accuracy and completeness, and the opinions based thereon, are not guaranteed.

www.insightguides.com
In North America:
www.insighttravelguides.com

Travel Tips

THE BEST OF LOS ANGELES

Setting priorities, saving money, unique attractions...
here, at a glance, are our top recommendations,
plus some tips and tricks even Angelenos
won't always know

ONLY IN LOS ANGELES

- **Grauman's Chinese Theatre** This 1920s-era movie palace has a forecourt of famous hand- and footprints. *See pages 104, 107.*
- **Hollywood Bowl** Music lovers come to this amphitheater for classical music and jazz concerts. *See page 113.*
- **Hollywood Sign** View this from several locations. *See pages 103, 185.*
- **Hollywood Museum** The old Max Factor building contains costumes, props and sets. *See page 106.*

- **Kodak Theatre** Oscar's home is open to the public for tours. *See page 107.*
- **La Brea Tar Pits** Since the 1900s, these bubbling pools of asphalt have yielded prehistoric fossils. *See page 94.*
- **The Troubadour** For over 40 years, this West Hollywood nightclub has hosted music legends, from Elton John to the Eagles. *See page 122.*
- **Walt Disney Concert Hall** Architect Frank Gehry's metallic creation is the home of the Los Angeles Philharmonic. *See page 78.*
- **Watts Towers** Built in South LA using discarded tile, pottery and glass, these towering sculptures demonstrate that one man's trash is another man's treasure. *See page 89.*

LEFT:
the Walt Disney Concert Hall.

BEST FESTIVALS AND EVENTS

For more festivals see Travel Tips, page 227.
- **Halloween Costume Carnaval** America's largest Halloween street party lures outrageous folks to talent, dancing and costume contests, and it's all free! *See page 126.*
- **Hollywood Christmas Parade** Around Thanksgiving, this 75-year-old Hollywood Boulevard event delights onlookers with celebrities, equestrians, bands, classic cars and Santa Claus. *See page 106.*
- **LA County Fair** For three weeks in September, Pomona's Fairplex hosts a celebration of livestock,

live music, folk arts, all-American vittles and carnival rides. *See page 227.*
- **Los Angeles Film Festival** One of the most significant film festivals in North America happens here every June. *See page 125.*
- **Oktoberfest** From September to October, SoCal's oldest German festival takes place in Torrance with oom-pa-pa bands and milking contests. *See page 197.*
- **Rose Parade** Flower-covered floats and marching bands strut through Pasadena to celebrate the Rose Bowl football game. *See page 186.*

BEST CELEBRITY HAUNTS

- **The Beverly Hills Hotel** For over 90 years, the Pink Palace has been a getaway for celebs, including Howard Hughes and Halle Berry. *See page 136.*
- **Canter's Deli and Bakery** Open 24 hours, this long-standing deli has lured the likes of Marilyn Monroe and John Travolta. *See page 98.*
- **Crunch Gym** Stars like Jennifer Aniston and Will Smith have trained in this West Hollywood gym. *See page 125.*
- **The Ivy** A hot hangout for celebrities, especially at lunchtime. The Ivy's hosted stars like Jennifer Lopez and Demi Moore. *See page 139.*
- **Morton's** Spielberg and Streisand have been spotted here, but the stars really come out for the *Vanity Fair* party on Oscar night. *See page 128.*
- **Musso & Franks Grill** Faulkner and Hemingway are gone, but this old-fashioned restaurant is still popular with Brad Pitt and Charlize Theron. *See page 114.*
- **Regent Beverly Wilshire** Facing Rodeo Drive, this glamorous hotel seduces the stars. *See page 132.*
- **Spago** Wolfgang Puck's eatery has fine food and famous patrons, from Tom Cruise to Liza Minnelli. *See page 139.*
- **Sunset Strip** Hotspots like the Skybar and the Viper Room entice starlets and musicians. *See page 124.*

BEST SHOPPING

- **The Avenues of Art & Design** One of the West Coast's premier destinations for art galleries and interior design showrooms, this stylish area is also home to the landmark Pacific Design Center. *See page 122.*
- **Beverly Center** This behemoth mall has fine stores and eateries, plus Los Angeles' only California Welcome Center. *See page 124.*
- **Hollywood & Highland Center** Hollywood owes its recent revival to this mall, which has upscale boutiques, a bowling alley, several eateries and, of course, the Kodak Theatre. *See page 106.*
- **Montana Avenue** Santa Monica's answer to Rodeo Drive, this tree-lined street is home to many high-end shops. *See page 156.*
- **Original Farmers Market** Adjacent to an outdoor mall called the Grove, the produce and food stalls have been a landmark for 70 years. *See page 96.*
- **Paseo Colorado** Pasadena's gleaming white outdoor mall lures fine diners, movie lovers and fashionistas of all types. *See page 187.*
- **Rodeo Drive** Famous around the world, this three-block stretch houses top names in fashion, from Prada to Gucci. Dress up, act cool and wear shades. *See page 133.*
- **Third Street Promenade** Just a few blocks from the ocean and next to Santa Monica Place, this outdoor mall has bookstores, eclectic shops and plenty of cafés. *See page 153.*
- **Universal CityWalk** Next to Universal Studios, CityWalk has a blues club, a microbrewery, a bowling alley, a movie theater and several stores, bars and restaurants. *See pages 190–1*

BEST FOR FAMILIES

These attractions are popular with children, though not all will suit every age group.

- **Aquarium of the Pacific** This Long Beach destination tantalizes with touchable sharks, nectar-loving lorikeets, drifting sea jellies and a huge coral reef exhibit. *See page 200.*
- **Disneyland** Mickey Mouse isn't the only attraction; families flock here for Space Mountain, the Fantasmic! nighttime show and the California Adventure rides. *See page 206.*
- **El Capitan Theatre** There's Disney film premieres at this Hollywood movie palace. *See page 107.*
- **Exposition Park** Visit the IMAX theater at the California Science Center and the insect zoo at the Natural History Museum. *See page 87.*
- **Griffith Park** With picnic grounds, hiking trails, a merry-go-round, a children's zoo, a train collection and a Wild West museum, this enormous urban park keeps families busy all day. *See pages 169, 184.*
- **Knott's Berry Farm** America's first theme park delights with Ghost Town gunfights, legendary coasters, refreshing water rides, Camp Snoopy musicals and fried chicken dinners. *See page 209.*

- **Petersen Automotive Museum** The useful Children's Discovery Center teaches the basic functions of the automobile through hands-on exhibits. *See page 93.*
- **Six Flags Magic Mountain** World-class roller coasters attract older kids, though little ones will finds plenty of thrilling rides, too. *See page 211.*
- **Universal Studios** Attractions based on *Back to the Future*, *Jurassic Park* and *Shrek* are winners for kids – and adults, too. *See pages 190–1.*

BELOW: the Getty Center is free, but you must book and pay to park on the grounds.

LOS ANGELES FOR FREE

- **Cathedral of Our Lady of the Angels** Visitors can admire tapestries and stained-glass windows, enjoy organ concerts and join free guided tours of the church. *See page 78.*
- **El Pueblo de Los Angeles** History buffs will enjoy tours of this Mexican marketplace, enclosed by adobes and buildings honoring the founding of LA. *See page 73.*
- **Getty Center** This clifftop complex draws art, architecture and garden enthusiasts who can explore the beautiful setting free of charge. *See pages 148–9.*
- **Hollywood Forever Cemetery** This tranquil park lures movie fans to wander around the graves of stars, from Valentino to DeMille. *See page 111.*

- **Hollywood Walk of Fame** Running along Hollywood and Vine are over 2,000 star-shaped plaques emblazoned with celebrities' names. *See page 102.*
- **Jazz concerts at LACMA** Jazz lovers enjoy free Friday night concerts in the art museum's Los Angeles Times Central Court. *See page 93.*
- **Museums** Many of the city's museums are free, including USC's Fisher Gallery (*see page 86*); UCLA's Fowler Museum of Cultural History (*see page 142*); the Nethercutt Collection; and the LA Maritime Museum (*see page 199*).
- **Santa Monica Pier** 100 years' old, this famous pier has free activities like juggling acts, film screenings and summer concerts. *See page 155.*

BEST TOURS

- **LA Conservancy Tours** Docents lead Downtown walking tours, covering historic sites like Union Station, the Biltmore Hotel and Broadway's theaters. *See page 79.*
- **NBC Studio Tour** TV enthusiasts enjoy a 70-minute walk through a working studio, including the prop warehouse, wardrobe department and *Tonight Show* set. *See page 184.*

- **Paramount Studios** The only major studio still in Hollywood offers guided behind-the-scenes tours. *See page 111.*
- ***The Queen Mary*** Anyone interested in World War II history and ghostly legends will look forward to a stroll through this magnificent ship. *See page 200.*
- **Universal VIP Experience** Visitors receive all-day admission to the Universal Studios theme park as well as access to working sound stages, legendary movie sets, a prop warehouse and the VIP lounge. *See pages 190–1.*
- **Warner Bros VIP Studio Tour** Small groups are guided through the backlot of famous TV and film sets, and then invited to explore Warner's museum filled with memorable props and creative costumes. *See page 184.*

LEFT: Bugs is just one of the characters you'll come across on the Warner Bros studio tour; Harry Potter is another.

BEST BEACHES

- **Cabrillo Beach** Cabrillo has wind surfing, scuba diving, whale-watching, a good aquarium and views of Catalina. *See page 198.*
- **Huntington Beach** Ever wonder where "Surf City USA" is? You just found it. *See page 202.*
- **Malibu Beach** Popular with surfers, this beach offers wetlands, flower gardens, tide pools and terrific bird-watching spots. *See page 174.*
- **Manhattan Beach** Volleyball enthusiasts appreciate the oceanside courts, as well as the sculpted men and women who play tournaments here. *See page 195.*
- **Point Vicente** At the tip of the Palos Verdes Peninsula, this is an ideal place to watch passing whales. *See page 197.*
- **Santa Monica Beach** The soft white sand on either side of Santa Monica Pier is a wonderful place to enjoy Pacific sunsets. *See page 156.*
- **Venice Beach** Besides activities on the sand and in the sea, there's terrific people-watching opportunities here, from hippie artists to muscle-bound men. *See page 158.*

MONEY-SAVING TIPS

Museum Admission Many LA museums are free on certain days of the month, such as MOCA on Thursday evenings, the Natural History Museum on first Tuesdays, the Skirball Cultural Center on Thursdays and the Pacific Asia Museum on fourth Fridays. Less expensive combination tickets are available for entry into the Southwest Museum and Museum of the American West; the Guinness World of Records Museum and the Hollywood Wax Museum; and *The Queen Mary* and the Aquarium of the Pacific.

Concert Tickets If you don't mind the back rows, you can attend Hollywood Bowl concerts inexpensively. The Music Center also offers cheap tickets: same-day senior and student discounts for the LA Opera, HOT TIX! for Center Theatre Group shows, and choral bench seats at the fabulous Walt Disney Concert Hall. Visit www.musiccenter.org

Theme Parks Admission Combo tickets are available for Knott's Berry Farm/Knott's Soak City, and Six Flags/Hurricane Harbor. Universal Studios tickets are cheaper online.

Transit Passes A Metro Day Pass allows you to ride any Metro bus or rail line all day for one price. A weekly pass saves even more money. Visit www.mta.net

CityPass The Hollywood CityPass saves on admission to two museums and three tours, and the Southern California CityPass saves on five theme parks. Visit www.citypass.net

Shopping Discounts Privileged Visitor Cards pamper out-of-towners with discounts and gifts. Visit www.santamonicaplace.com

LA CONFIDENTIAL

Los Angeles is a place where people come to start a new life, to make themselves over, to find fame. It's no wonder the city's best-known product is illusion

nlike most major cities, Los Angeles is a place with no clearly defined focal point, no spot that all would agree is the center. So finding your own center – of LA in general or of Hollywood in particular – can offer an interesting subtext to any exploration, even a personal, confidential one. What makes this odyssey especially captivating is the wide variety of sets and settings with which to construct one's scenario. Only a city where the best-known product is illusion could offer so many different backdrops to those anxious to play make-believe.

Downtown Los Angeles is like a carnival with little bits of everything: futuristic architecture, 1920s and '30s theaters, exuberant Grand Central Market, and the adobe street where the city began in 1781. North and west of Downtown are scores of movie settings: beautiful Spanish patios, architecture that inspired Walt Disney, the Witch's House, glittering Rodeo Drive, the canals of Venice, Santa Monica Pier, astonishing homes and awesome views from the hills.

Movie settings

Is Hollywood's center the Hollywood sign? The fact that it is virtually inaccessible is telling in itself. Maybe the places where the early stars lived, worked, played and died are your vision of what Los Angeles is all about? If so, you'll want to inspect Musso & Franks, watering hole to Humphrey Bogart and Charlie Chaplin; take in a tour of stars' homes, or wander around the serene Hollywood Forever Cemetery.

For people in a high-profile world, the center of things might be the Beverly Hills Hotel, in whose $1,000-a-night bungalows some of them stay while the $10 million house they bought is being torn down to make room for the new $15 million home they plan to put in its place.

For some visitors and many more residents, the "center" is not a single place but, in the words of the old Irish proverb, "where you are sitting." In Los Angeles, this will no doubt be in an automobile, the best and sometimes only way to get to the center of things. ❏

PRECEDING PAGES: in Los Angeles, everybody is a star; wedding day in the Cathedral of Our Lady of the Angels, LA's lavish place of worship Downtown.
LEFT: LA provides different backdrops for people who want to play make-believe.

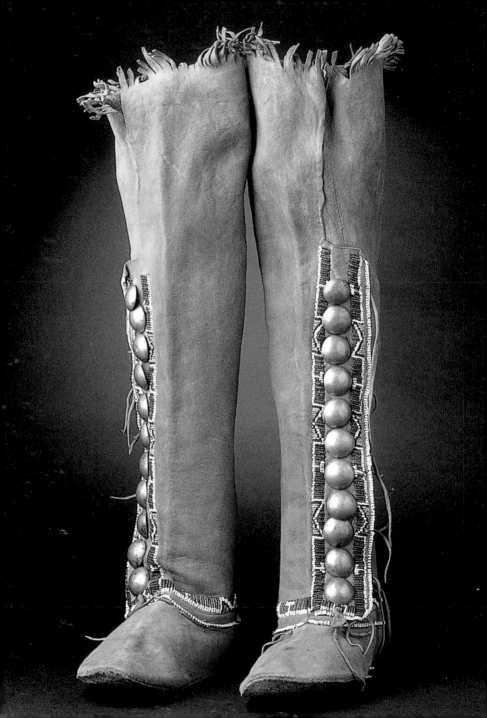

THE MAKING OF LOS ANGELES

In little more than a century, the fastest-growing city in the West became the cradle of a culture that was soon to be exported all over the world

California, as yet unnamed, was a peaceful place when the white man arrived. The land and sea provided all that was needed for nourishment, and for years Indians had lived along its sunny shores following the cycle of the seasons. Historians estimate that there were as many as 200,000 indigenous peoples, divided into a variety of tribes and nations. The Indians of California spoke many distinct languages, and each tribe had its individual customs and practices.

Finding little to exploit or acquire, the Spanish all but ignored this wild frontier for more than two centuries after 16th-century New World explorers Vizcaino and Cabrillo had first claimed the territory. At best, the land was considered little more than a place to find harbor in which to shelter and replenish the supplies of the treasure-laden galleons on the seven-month journey between the Orient and Europe. This rich cargo of silks, spices, sandalwood and mercury would be worth as much as $8 million today.

It was only when the Dutch, English and French began to show interest that the Spanish Crown grew concerned. Further impetus for the Spanish colonization of California was the Russians' advance farther and farther south from Alaskan bases in their quest for the lucrative pelts of sea otters. These could be acquired for just a few cents and then resold to Chinese buyers for more than $100.

The missionaries

From the king of Spain came the order to develop Alta California, establishing ports, outposts and missions. The Spanish had a well-tested technique for implanting their influence: priests, usually accompanied by just a handful of foot soldiers, served as the colonial vanguard, founding missions, converting Indians and, through education, changing the locals into surrogate Spaniards.

The Jesuits had been in Baja California since 1697, turning that peninsula into virtually their own dominion; but in 1767, seeking to diminish their growing political power, the Spanish Crown replaced them with Francis-

---

LEFT: Apache boots, a display from LA's Southwest Museum of the American Indian.
RIGHT: a mission depicted on a Downtown mural.

cans (or the Greyfriars, as they were known, for the habits they wore). Aware of the need for a strong-willed and determined man to be in charge of the new missions in Alta California, the Spanish viceroy chose Majorcan-born, 56-year-old Junípero Serra.

Junípero Serra arrived on July 1, 1769, with General Gaspar de Portolá, to found the Mission San Diego de Alcala just north of Mexico. One month later, Portolá and some of his men came across a friendly group of Indians with whom they exchanged trinkets. Portolá called the stream where they met El Río de Nuestra Señora la Reina de los Angeles de Porciùncula. But the city that would bear the

same name – Los Angeles – was not founded for another 12 years. Portolá continued on his way north, following the Indians' well-worn path along which the missions were later founded. This trail came to be known as "El Camino Real," or the Royal Road. In today's language, it is more or less the highway known as California State Route 1.

Each mission used Indian converts to set up large-scale "industries" – operations for making olive oil, citrus fruit growing, cattle raising (for the hides, not the meat), and soap and tallow manufacture. San Gabriel Arcangel, founded in 1771, at the edge of an inhospitable desert some 8 miles (13 km) from the present-

day downtown of Los Angeles, turned out to be one of the most agriculturally productive in the chain, and by 1811 was reaping the largest wheat crop recorded by any of the missions.

In the fall of 1781, six weeks before the British surrendered at Yorktown, Felipe de Neve, then governor of Spanish California, founded the new *pueblo* – or settlement – of Los Angeles. The settlers (or *vecinos pobladores*), most of them African, Indian and Hispanic in origin, named the colony El Pueblo de Nuestra Señora de la Reina de los Angeles del Río Porciùncula – something of an extended name for a small village that would become the center of Los Angeles. Within three years the founding fathers had started construction on a church to serve as the centerpiece of the town's plaza.

By 1790, with its population recorded as 139 residents, Los Angeles presented a pleasing sight. Aside from a few fields cleared for planting between the town and the river, the countryside was pretty much as it had looked when General Portolá had passed through 30 years previously. The terrain was what geographers call savanna country, grassland interspersed with groves of California live oak, willow and sycamore trees beside the river and streams with marshland south of town. The Los Angeles River had been selected as a promising townsite because, unlike the desert washes, it did not dry up in summer. Here, as elsewhere, the settlers learned how fickle Californian winters can be: the placid river flooded in 1818, forcing the relocation of the town's first square.

Following a 1786 law, the governor became empowered to give land grants, grazing rights and 2,000 head of cattle to the settlers, and these the early founders were awarded huge *ranchos* to develop. Many of them went to individuals whose names survive in the modern city. Los Feliz, Las Virgenes, the Verdugos, Sepulveda – now better known as freeway off-ramps or "surface streets" – were once huge haciendas.

From Mexican to American

In 1821 Mexico declared itself a republic, an act that would lead to the secularization of the missions the following decade. All Spanish-born priests were ordered out of California and 8 million acres (3.2 million hectares) of mission land was broken up into 800 privately owned ranches, then handed out like party favors by the newly installed Mexican governors. About 25 families settled on the common land of the two nearest missions to Los Angeles, San Gabriel and San Fernando. In the course of time these areas became, in effect, the city's first suburbs.

Although also eligible for land title, converted Indians were mostly swindled out of their rights by unscrupulous new Mexican *rancheros*. Many mission Indians simply went to work on the ranchos, unable to return to the way of life they had previously left. At the height of the mission era (1805–10), 20,000 Indians were tied to the system as unpaid laborers, and some were literally worked to death. Many missions had stocks, irons and whipping posts, which were in constant use.

The missions completely disrupted the Indians' way of life by destroying their traditional hunting skills and the complicated network of tribal relationships that served as the fabric of their culture. While the Franciscans may have arrived with the purest of hearts and the highest of ideals, their intrusion into California served to set off a cultural and physical genocide of the indigenous peoples.

In 1846 a succession of disagreements along the Rio Grande prompted a war between the United States and Mexico, the ultimate prize being possession of Texas. The *Californios* put up a good resistance, considering the size of the forces sent against them. At the Battle of San Pascual later that year, the Angelenos defeated the American column led by Stephen W. Kearney, although they were evidently outnumbered in the early part of the engagement.

But this was the high-watermark of the attempt to drive the *Yanquis* (Yankees) from California. A relief column from San Diego reached San Pascual, and by January 1847 the American flag was to be found flying over Los Angeles. The Mexican forces capitulated a few days later at Cahuenga Pass. The Treaty of Guadalupe was signed in 1848 and fixed the present borders.

The Gold Rush

Los Angeles quickly became Americanized. By 1850 the city was accorded the status of county seat, a mayor replaced the *alcalde*, and the first Protestant church was founded.

But Los Angeles was still just a small and dusty agricultural hamlet with a meager population of 1,500. An 1849 US government report states: "The town consists of an old adobe church and about a hundred adobe houses scattered about a dusty plaza and along three or four broad streets leading thereto." This was all to change within a few months with the discovery of gold at Sutter's Mill and the Gold Rush of 1849.

THE MISSIONS

In 1769, Franciscan missionaries left their Baja California settlement, and, led by Father Junípero Serra, established 21 missions across California during the next 54 years. Each mission lies roughly a day's horseback journey apart in a line (the "string of pearls") that stretches between San Diego and Sonoma, 600 miles (966 km) to the north. Most of these missions have now been restored, and form a unique look at California's past. Each of the timber and adobe missions has some architectural or historical distinction, although all feature the thick walls, small windows and elegant bell towers usually associated with Mexican churches.

LEFT: Indian pictograph, LA's Southwest Museum.
RIGHT: detail from San Gabriel Mission.

Gold has played a large part in LA history – not only the metal, which of course brought adventurers from all over the world to the goldfields in the north and had its obvious spillover effect on the city to the south, but also the "liquid" gold of the oil discoveries that peppered the whole region with oil derricks and pretty much shaped the automobile-obsessed California culture of today. (Stretching the metaphor only slightly, historians also talk of the "golden" oranges, a bountiful crop that did so much to familiarize out-of-staters with "the golden state" of 19th century California. Commercial orange crops date to the 1840s, when the earliest groves were planted near to

where Union Station stands today, in downtown Los Angeles.)

Although many Angelenos ventured into the gold country up north, the real wealth lay in selling food to the gold miners themselves. Their numbers had reached 100,000 by 1852 and food was at a premium, with potatoes going for 40¢ a pound. The wildly inflated prices finally created a market for the beef that had once been so much less valuable than the hide. Cattle prices, jumping tenfold in a matter of months, reached $40–$50 per steer. Enterprising rancheros employed a single trail boss and four or five *vaqueros* to drive large herds 400 miles (640 km) along the rugged trail

north. New money flowed into Los Angeles and, although the Gold Rush produced the city's first population boom, most of the newcomers were the human jetsam of the mining fields. Los Angeles quickly turned into a lawless western town where street killings, shootouts and lynchings became commonplace. In 1855, the mayor quit his position to take part in a lynching, after which he was immediately re-elected.

Vigilante law

The boom was soon over, however, and Los Angeles, like the rest of the state, fell into a severe economic depression: banks failed, and merchants went bankrupt. But the city had grown sixfold in a decade, and racial tension was high between Mexicans and whites.

Latinos suffered with the onset of the depression of the 1850s. Vigilantes drove 10,000 Mexican miners from the southern mines, aided by a cadre of eager lawyers and a handful of greedy Anglo merchants. The merchants, who had advanced credit at exorbitant interest rates, foreclosed on many of the ranchos, ensuring the impoverishment of the Mexican majority. All Spanish land grants were reviewed, and each case had to be heard five times, ensuring that legal fees were suitably exorbitant.

Enter the Chinese

Between 1851 and 1860 the Chinese population increased enormously. Many were laborers imported to help build the transcontinental railroad up north, and others were drawn by the search for gold. But, after the gold ran out and the railroads had been completed, many moved down to Los Angeles where they became merchants or laborers on the local water-irrigation ditches. On October 23, 1871, touched off by the murder of a white policeman, a mob invaded Chinatown, shooting and lynching at random. By day's end, more than two dozen Chinese had been murdered, constituting one of the bloodiest incidents in the history of the state.

In so many other ways, the city's fast-growing Asian population had already made an indelible mark on this evolving polyglot society. It is impossible to visualize how the railroads could have been completed or the vast market gardens of southern California could have evolved without their contribution. Japanese and Chinese market gardens in particular benefited the city; enlarged irrigation systems between 1860 and 1880 not only helped supply the local demand for fresh vegetables but also produced a surplus of food ready to ship to the populous north.

As a result of these and other factors, Los Angeles and its environs became a major agricultural region. Oranges, in particular, started to become the region's major crop, and within a decade the fruit was being shipped north. But it was the invention of the refrigerated rail car that made oranges a viable crop for shipping farther afield.

Orange production peaked in the 1940s. Thereafter, the demand for land for housing development – ironically much of the demand had been created by people attracted to the state by publicity about the oranges – gradually sent real-estate prices too high for growers to afford. Most of the beautiful orange-crate labels, lithographed with acid-etched granite plates, date from 1885 to the 1950s, and were intended for the gaze of the distributor rather than the consumer. Today some of these crate labels are worth as much as $2,000.

With the realization that its growth would be limited unless it improved communications with the rest of the continent, and spurred on by the example of San Francisco, LA became determined to connect with the rail system, and the Southern Pacific Railroad was persuaded to extend a track to Los Angeles. As predicted, a boom followed. The region's agriculture was by now its economic mainstay, with grapes and wine becoming primary products. The Southern Pacific reached Los Angeles in 1876; by 1877 New Yorkers were enjoying California grapes.

Waves of new settlers, including European immigrants, flooded the city: 100,000 on the Southern Pacific railroad in one year. The *Santa Fe* was bringing in three to four trainloads a day. Land prices jumped tenfold as speculators preyed on the wide-eyed newcomers, drawn by idyllic pictures of boundless fruit groves against gloriously clear skies.

LEFT: California became a US state in 1850.
RIGHT: Pio Pico, the last Mexican governor of California.

Hollywood is born

Subdividers had barely stepped off the Southern Pacific before they were establishing new towns. One of these entrepreneurs, Horace Wilcox, planned a community around his 120-acre (48-hectare) orchard at the edge of the mountains.

Chamber of Commerce publicists like to pretend that Hollywood began with the movies, but the word first appeared in print when Wilcox lettered it on the gate of his farm in 1887. Legend has it he would have preferred the name "Figwood" himself, figs being the major produce of the orchard spreading around what is now the junction of Hollywood

and Cahuenga boulevards, but Wilcox acceded to the choice of his young second wife, Daeida, who had acquired the name from a stranger she met on a train. Topeka-born Wilcox, a paraplegic who relied on crutches, subdivided his property, sold lots, unsuccessfully tried to grow holly, planted pepper trees, and dreamed of establishing a serene, temperance community like that of his native Kansas.

"And then we came," mused Cecil B. DeMille many years later, "and Wilcox saw his dream disappear the minute the first camera crews came in. Show people! What a disaster!"

The major factor in the visitors' interest in Los Angeles was climate. Having confirmed that, as the posters claimed, Southern California was a "Semi-Tropical Paradise," many of those who came on brief visits decided to stay. By the end of the 1880s, the wooden sidewalks were crowded with people, night and day; hotel rooms were double-booked; and the subsequent building boom brought another wave of bricklayers, carpenters, painters and other craftsmen. Tent cities sprang up on the fringes of town. But the boom was to last only another couple of years.

After the difficult adjustment between 1888 and 1890, Los Angeles' population stabilized

at 50,000, and the city embarked on a much-needed public works program. The new cadre of City Fathers, under the inimitable Harrison Gray Otis, later founder of the *Los Angeles Times*, were determined to make Los Angeles succeed. Boosterism was in the air: streets were paved, public buildings were constructed and many parks were initiated.

The discovery of oil, which eventually ushered in the automobile age and turned Wilshire Boulevard – for more than a century it had been the La Brea Trail – into a major highway, was not taken seriously until the final years of the 19th century. Former gold prospector Edward L. Doheny and his partner Charles

Canfield put up $400 for a vacant lot near Westlake. Using a pick and shovel, then a wooden drill, they sank a pit 160 ft (49 meters) before reaching a black liquid much like the substance that seeped out of the La Brea tar pits, the kind of heavy oil that "took a week to ooze downstairs."

Using a hand pump, the two men brought up seven barrels a day. Doheny was worth around $100 million when he died in 1935.

Enter the automobile

As derricks shot up throughout the city (2,300 in a five-year period) the black ooze suffered from overproduction and the price fell to 15¢ a barrel. The automobile had yet to arrive.

At about this time Arthur Freemont Gilmore arrived in Los Angeles from Illinois, and bought 256 acres (104 hectares) of what had once been Rancho La Brea. Finding the land ideal for grazing his cows, he sank a well to find water and instead struck oil. By the time his son Earl graduated from Stanford in 1909, the automobile had arrived and Earl stationed himself at the corner of Wilshire Boulevard and La Brea with a red-and-yellow painted farm wagon holding a large tank full of gasoline. "Fill 'er up, Earl," yelled the drivers of the new-fangled cars as they stopped to wipe their dusty windscreens. They paid 50¢ for 5 gallons. Danger was in the air, however. In 1907 Echo Park Lake, north of downtown Los Angeles, became so polluted due to oil production in the area that it caught fire and burned for three days.

With the coming of the railroad, the discovery of oil, the automobile and the acquisition of a reliable flow of water, Los Angeles tripled in population between 1900 and 1910, from 102,000 to more than 320,000, and nearly doubled in area. Neighboring communities, such as the little town of Hollywood, were annexed. The city also annexed a long strip of territory that snaked south to the new port of San Pedro. This was a small fishing village that had miraculously won out as the city's harbor. A party celebrating the new port's location at San Pedro was held in 1899, where 20,000 cheering participants ate barbecued beef and 5 tons of clams. Los Angeles continued to swallow up separate cities to the south and the west until, by 1920, the city's population had increased to nearly 600,000.

The crucial catalyst that made Los Angeles' extraordinarily rapid growth possible was water. Rain is infrequent and unpredictable in Southern California, and the burgeoning population quickly outstripped the region's rivers and meager supply of ground water. Under the leadership of William Mulholland (*see page 189*), the city greedily sucked water from other parts of the state. The farmers of the fertile Owens Valley saw their water rights stolen and the area turned into a wasteland as the water was drained away by the 233-mile (375-km), gravity-fed California aqueduct, a $24.5-million public

lack of it, remains a perennial problem in sunny Southern California.

Excellent transportation

Despite its size, getting around Los Angeles in the early part of the 20th century was not a problem. In 1905 it took just 38 minutes to reach Venice Beach from the city center. LA had one of the nation's best public transportation systems when the famous Red Car Line blanketed the region, spurring further decentralization as the communities sprang up along its tracks.

But gradually, automobiles strangled the transit system, slowing it down and drawing away passengers. By raising fares to make up

works spectacular approved by Los Angeles voters in 1907.

The addition of a parallel conduit to the aqueduct (in 1941 at a cost of $200 million) and of supplemental water from Parker Dam on the Colorado River 206 miles (332 km) away, in addition to other sources, brings today's total consumption to well over 500 million gallons (1,893 million litres) a day, a supply that is threatened by drought, environmental degradation, agricultural waste, and competing users in Arizona, Colorado and Mexico. Water, or the

for declining revenues, the systems drove away even more passengers. In the 1950s, the designers of Southern California's freeway system were using many of the trolleys' routes to the communities that had sprung up along the lines; today's regional governments are spending billions of dollars re-establishing light railway services, in most cases on the original rights-of-way.

During World War I, Los Angeles expanded rapidly and annexed land in all directions, including the now well-watered San Fernando Valley. Most of the beach communities resisted for a time, fearing that LA's "blue laws," which banned liquor sales on Sunday, would ruin

LEFT: orange-crate label depicting California cowboy.
ABOVE: Los Angeles' Temple Block in 1871.

their best business day of the week. But, finally, they too were absorbed into what was becoming, geographically at least, a mega-city.

Hollywood was one of these towns soon to fall within the grasp of the Los Angeles City Council. At the beginning of the 20th century it was a sedate country-club town, the perfect manifestation of Horace and Daeida Wilcox's dream. After the town's first formal elections in 1904 drunkenness was prohibited, the sale of liquor was forbidden, and a speed limit of 12 mph (19 km/h) was rigidly enforced. "No dogs or actors," proclaimed a sign at the Hollywood Hotel, before the movie folk transformed this quiet community forever.

The Nestor Film Company arrived in 1911 and shot *The Law of the Range* in the Blondeau Tavern – available, as it happened, by virtue of the Prohibition ordinances which had been passed at Daeida Wilcox's urging.

Two years later Cecil B. DeMille, Jesse Lasky, Samuel Goldwyn and Arthur Friend arrived and shot *The Squaw Man*, the first full-length feature movie made in Hollywood. Within 18 months, Lasky's studio occupied an entire city block.

In the early days it wasn't easy for film people to settle in good neighborhoods. "They thought we were tramps," recalled screenwriter Anita Loos. "They saw themselves as

being invaded and supplanted as elegant ladies and gentlemen, so they ganged up on us."

By 1910 the city had five fiercely competitive newspapers and five years later there were already 15,000 automobiles. As yet, there was still no major industry in the area – except for real estate. Once in California, prospective buyers – many of them suffering from ill-health and here for the rejuvenating climate – received free bus trips and free lunches to entice them to visit planned subdivisions where they might become customers.

The real estate rush

A couple of miles south of Hollywood one enterprising young realtor, A.W. Ross, had purchased 18 acres (7.3 hectares) of land on the south side of Wilshire Boulevard for $54,000. He set up his office in a white, one-story building at the corner of Ogden Drive and began to sell off lots for $100 per foot of frontage. It was hard going at first, but within just a few years retailers who had turned down corner sites for $6,000 were pleading with Ross to accept $600,000 for the same parcels of land.

Some of the suburban developments began with a bang, some with barely a whimper, but an early fanfare was no guarantee of eventual success. Tobacco heir Abbott Kinney reconstituted Venice as a sort of American residential theme park built on what had been marshes and wetlands south of Santa Monica *(see page 161)*. He was determined to inject a high level of culture into his ersatz Venice, but after a $16,000 loss on his first season of operation, Kinney eventually went bankrupt and Venice fell on half a century of hard times. In the 1950s, Orson Welles used the then-decrepit Venice as a backdrop for *A Touch of Evil*. Most of Los Angeles agreed: the seedy area had become an enclave of beatniks and artists. Though tidier now, Venice retains a hint of its earlier attitude of nonconformity.

By contrast, Beverly Hills was sedate. When the area was named in 1907, a single house went up quietly at Crescent Drive and Lomitas. The four original streets – Park Way, Carmelita, Elevado and Lomitas – still traverse the community east to west, but the four original north–south drives – Rodeo, Canon, Crescent and Beverly – have been supplanted with others. Residential lots along Sunset cost around $1,000 at the time, with a 10 percent discount for cash and an additional 10 percent discount if the property was improved (i.e. built on) within six months. Only six homes were built north of Santa Monica Boulevard in the first three years.

By 1923, however, Beverly Hills had become the movie colony's bedroom and the celebrity residents were able to wage and win a campaign to preserve their exclusivity by foiling an annexation attempt by Los Angeles. Long before the advent of the Miracle Mile in the late 1920s, Wilshire Boulevard had been a prestige address: the venerable Ambassador Hotel (where Robert Kennedy was assassi-

another oil boom as wells were sunk at Huntington Beach, Signal Hill and Santa Fe Springs and Venice, even with its canals and gondolas. Eventually a forest of derricks stretched from the mountains to the sea. Once again, confidence men and investors rushed to take advantage of the bonaza by selling shares in non-existent drilling companies to plenty of unwitting victims.

Diverse mix

Apart from oil, there was still little hard industry in Southern California, only agriculture. Los Angeles became famous as one of the most productive fertile regions in the US, and

nated and which multi-millionaire Donald Trump later bought) was erected on pastures where oil baron Arthur Gilmore had once grazed his cattle. Another tycoon, Edwin Tobias Earl, who invented the refrigerated railway car, built a large mansion with some of the money he made by selling his business in 1900. Earl, who later founded the *Los Angeles Express*, saw his rival become his neighbor when Colonel Harrison Gray Otis of the *Los Angeles Times* bought a corner lot on Wilshire at Parkview.

During the 1920s, Los Angeles experienced

LEFT: oil wells at First and Temple streets.
ABOVE: the first map of Hollywood.

agriculture would remain paramount right up until the beginning of World War II.

Despite being hampered by a 1913 law that prohibited "aliens" from owning land, Japanese truck farmers aroused the jealousy of their neighbors by becoming increasingly productive. (Their industriousness was ill rewarded after Pearl Harbor, when President Roosevelt's Executive Order 9006 sent 112,000 of them, the majority American-born, to internment camps; at the end of the war, their property was sold for taxes and "fees.") Chinese produce brokers, along with Italians, Armenians, Slavs and Anglos, began to create an ethnic agricultural mix that survives in the city today. ❑

FROM MOVIES TO THE MODERN AGE

The first local movie was made on a Downtown rooftop. Now the city – despite difficult social problems – has become the world center of filmmaking and the place many wannabes want to be

Aviation, which would become a major Southern California industry, got an early start in 1883 when the country's first glider took off near San Diego. Many of the most famous names in aviation made their fortunes in Southern California: Glenn Martin, who assembled his first plane in an abandoned church in Santa Ana and flew the first seaplane to Santa Catalina, the Lockheed brothers, who started operations in Santa Barbara in 1916; and Donald W. Douglas, who fabricated his first transport in a shack behind a Santa Monica barbershop four years later.

World's largest airplane

Following in this pioneering tradition was the eccentric Howard Hughes, whose wooden *Spruce Goose*, the world's largest cargo plane, made its only flight in Los Angeles Harbor in the late 1940s. A major tourist attraction, the giant plane was long berthed in Long Beach next to the *Queen Mary*, which is living out its genteel days as a floating hotel.

Besides oranges, oil and aviation, Los Angeles became synonymous with the emerging film industry. The first California movie was made on a downtown rooftop and movie-making spread east and south before the studios settled temporarily on what is now Glendale Boulevard. Many early Westerns were shot in the hills of Griffith Park, and in some of the surviving one-reelers, such as those featuring the Keystone Kops and Laurel and Hardy, the topology

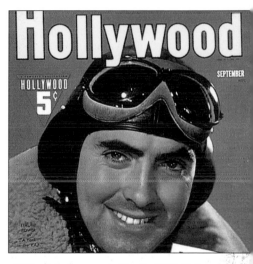

LEFT: California welcomed aviation pioneers.
RIGHT: Hollywood hunk gets in on the aviation act.

of Silverlake is recognizable. By 1915, Hollywood procured its reputation as the home of film studios and film production. Four years later it was turning out 80 percent of the world's feature films.

D.W. Griffith, the film-directing titan, had been a stage actor before he started directing in 1907. He arrived in Los Angeles in 1908, with Mack Sennett and a 16-year-old Mary Pickford among his retinue, around the time that the first of what would be over 10,000 nickel peep shows began opening in store fronts around the country. Before *Birth of a Nation* and *Intolerance* – the epic motion pictures that made his reputation – Griffith directed 142 one-reelers for

Biograph, gradually developing the technique – long shot/medium shot/close-up sequence – that is the foundation of filmmaking. Little credit has been given to his chief cameraman Billy Bitzer, who crawled along the ground under fire to film the battle scenes in *Birth of a Nation* and ascended in a balloon for the overhead shots in *Intolerance*.

By the end of 1919, Cecil B. deMille, Charlie Chaplin and W.C. Fields were already living in splendid homes on a street now grandly called deMille Drive. But they had all been preceded in the neighborhood by Mack Sennett, at whose Glendale Boulevard studio the Keystone Company had ground out 140 one-reelers in the year

before World War I, making stars out of Ben Turpin, Fatty Arbuckle, Gloria Swanson and the famous Keystone Kops.

Hollywood Babylon

Here, Mabel Normand tossed the first custard pie and Chaplin developed the tramp character who was eventually to earn him $10,000 a week. Hollywood soon turned into a new and chaotic Babylon. "It was a world," wrote one observer, "in which everybody was caught with their pants down." Over the years, many of Hollywood's citizens were caught in just such compromising positions. Even in the early days Hollywood produced scandals as well as

movies: Olive Thomas, a heroin addict and suicide, 1920; Roscoe "Fatty" Arbuckle, ruined after an accusation of rape – he was later acquitted – which ended a starlet's life in 1921; William Desmond Taylor, mysteriously murdered in 1922; Wallace Reid, a fatal victim of morphine addiction; Charlie Chaplin, satyr; romantic lover Rudolph Valentino, tagged as a homosexual; Eric von Stroheim, orgiast; Marie Provost, killed by her own dogs; Mary Astor, self-confessed adulterer; Cheryl Crane, Lana Turner's daughter, killer; and countless other drunks, drug addicts and suicides right to the present day.

The first round of Hollywood scandals prompted Adolph Zukor, William Fox, Sam Goldwyn and the other moguls to look for a censor to protect filmdom's image. They settled on Will Hays, who had been Republican Party chairman in 1920. The next year, Hays had to deal with the murder of Paramount director William Desmond Taylor, who was shot in his Westlake apartment. Among the suspects were Mabel Normand, Mary Miles Minter, and Minter's mother, each of whom had been Taylor's lover. After *Birth of a Nation* star Wallace Reid's death at 33 the following year, Hays insisted on morality clauses in future contracts and the censoring of scripts.

Hollywood wasn't big enough for the movie industry – it spilled over into Carl Laemmle's Universal City (where a producer could rent a Western town, a mansion, or a farm), Burbank, Century City and Culver City. By the mid-1920s, the movie industry employed more than 20,000 people, who between them took home $1.5 million weekly in salaries.

Los Angeles did not take the arrival of Prohibition on January 16, 1920, very seriously. Close proximity to the Mexican border and a sprawling coastline made it easy for small ships to land liquor at Malibu and other secluded beaches, and a fair amount of homemade alcohol was manufactured in the city itself. With its long tradition of pre-Prohibition unlicensed liquor parlors, known as "blind-pigs," speakeasies were not a radical step for the locals to accept. In fact, several places Downtown on Spring Street featured alcohol and gambling. They were seldom raided by police.

Tony Cornero, who became one of the biggest bootleggers along the coast, ran a lumber schooner that could handle 7,000 cases of liquor. He would load up in Vancouver with papers showing his destination as Mexico or Central America. As one of the industry's top wholesalers, he would park off the coast. His distributors, buying "over the rail," would evade customs with the 1920s' equivalent of high-speed cigarette boats. Distributors, police, customs agents and hijackers competed with each other for the cargoes, so everyone was armed to the teeth. Sometimes a load would be hijacked several times on its journey between the schooner and the speakeasy.

By 1920, The *New York Times* reported that California was wide open to the whims of gangsters and racketeers: "Alcohol is cheap and plentiful; hijacking is a favorite outdoor sport; gang murders are becoming episodical; and the police, fettered by political interference, espionage and other harassments, seem to be helpless." Fifty federal agents policed 198,000 sq. miles (513,000 sq. km) of Southern California landscape, with a population of 2.3 million. They were also expected to patrol hundreds of miles of coastline and 500 miles (800 km) along the Mexican border.

They were meant to discover alcohol in ships whose interiors had been covered with carpeting to absorb odors, and in subterranean passages of canyons where it was hidden. In addition, they had to regulate wineries where the legal sacramental wines were made, and to visit the hundreds of bogus congregations that sprang up to buy the blessed vintages (one grew to 1,200 members in a single year).

Los Angeles became known as a great town for conventions. According to The *New York Times*, "At no time since Prohibition went into effect has there been any difficulty here about securing whatever in the liquor line that may be desired by anybody." California's image as a land of plenty served as a magnet throughout the 1930s for the troubled Dust Bowl farmers of Oklahoma, Arkansas, Missouri and northern Texas. By 1940, 365,000 "Okies" had limped westward in caravans of overloaded automobiles. Three generations of a family would eat, sleep and live for months in a car or a garage.

The California boom that began in 1940 was fueled by wars: hot (World War II), lukewarm (Korea and Vietnam), and Cold (Russia). The taxes on the $100 billion defense that poured into the state between 1940 and 1970 resulted in a system of highways, schools, housing, agriculture, and social welfare that was second to none, contributing to an increase in population of over 39 million during the same 30 years. In 1941, contracts between the federal government and the California Institute of Technology alone totaled $83 million. Even with 750,000 Californians in uniform, the number of wage earners in the state increased by nearly a million.

A great many of the war dollars raining down

from Washington landed on Henry J. Kaiser, who built warships in such numbers that he was dubbed "Sir Launchalot." When they got up to speed, the Lockheed and North American factories were producing planes at twice the rate Roosevelt had called for in 1940.

Racism and riots

Despite wartime propaganda and post-war romanticizing, the home market was not all Rosie the Riveter. There was rationing of gasoline, tires, sugar and meat, which created a raging black market. Prejudice against women and blacks was rampant in the unions, industry and the military; in LA, rioting soldiers and sailors

LEFT: the 1992 Rodney King trial sparked the worst racial violence in the state's history.
RIGHT: LA continues to be rocked by earthquakes.

attacked Mexican-American "zoot-suiters." Moral precepts were endangered by social and economic disruption.

After the war, soldiers returning from the Pacific and workers who had been brought in to staff the war factories stayed on, creating pressure for housing that resulted in another land boom. Schools and libraries, post offices and police stations, freeways and airports were constructed to service the hundreds of square miles of housing developments that sprang up to take care of them. The $1.75 billion Feather River project brought more much-needed water into the Southern California region.

With the explosion in population came prob-

lems: more water shortages, declining services, environmental crises and racial strife. The black population exploded tenfold after 1940, and blacks were plagued by discriminatory housing and employment restrictions.

On a sweltering summer evening in 1965, the Watts ghetto in south-central Los Angeles erupted in widespread rioting. By the time the National Guard restored order six days later, $40-million worth of damage had been caused by vandalism, looting and fire, 4,000 people had been arrested and 34 were dead.

Later in the 1960s, busing to achieve integration drove a further wedge between the black and white communities. At UCLA, two members of the Black Panthers were killed during demonstrations over the future of the Black Studies program. Three years later, in his controversial book *The Last Days of the Late, Great State of California*, Curt Gentry would quote one disenchanted black: "Everywhere they say, 'Go to California! California's the great pot of gold at the end of the rainbow!' Well now we're here in California and there ain't no place else to go and the only pot I see's the kind they peddle at Sixth and Avalon."

In 1963, California became the most populous state in the Union, and Southern California continued to be the most populous region in the state. The city of Los Angeles now has 3.8 million residents; the population of Los Angeles County is almost 10 million.

This may be too many people. From 1910 to the 1950s, Southern California led the nation in agricultural production. But water shortages, environmental degradation and over-develop-

12 FASCINATING FACTS ABOUT LOS ANGELES

1. Plácido Domingo is the general director of the LA Opera.

2. See's Candies, the high-end confectioners, started in a small kitchen on Western Avenue in 1921.

3. The county coastline from Malibu to Long Beach is 72 miles (116km) long, and has a beach attendance of 53.8 million annually.

4. *LA International Airport* was recorded by country singer Susan Raye and became one of the biggest cross-over hits of the 1970s.

5. Although LA itself is the biggest, there are 87 other incorporated cities in the county. Vernon (population: 95) is the smallest.

6. The city has the largest street system in the US, requiring 1,500 workers and $75 million per year to maintain.

7. There are 1,500 murals located around the area.

8. Ry Cooder's *Chavez Ravine*, recorded in 2005, tells the story of the 1950s bulldozing of land occupied by an east LA Latino community; Dodger Stadium is now on the site.

9. Downtown LA is the top filming location, with City Hall (*Mildred Pierce*; *War of the Worlds*; TV's *Dragnet*) one of the top locations. The Westin Bonadventure hotel (*True Lies*) is also famous.

10. There are 200 certified plastic surgeons and 3,000 licensed psychologists in LA County.

11. All palm trees are not alike: 25 different varieties line the streets. The most common is the Mexican Fan Palm.

12. Almost 100 faults in the Los Angeles area are capable of an earthquake with a magnitude of 6.0 or greater.

ment have cut into the agricultural business. Thirty-one thousand acres (12,550 hectares) of orange groves alone fell before the bulldozers between 1950 and 1965. Severe controls on air pollutants are expected to cost billions over the next decade. In 1990, Los Angeles was forced to impose water rationing for the first time.

Minority populations

The sad truth is that, although it has a growing class of super-rich entertainment moguls and merchants involved in foreign trade, Los Angeles is no longer the land of milk and honey. Despite the fact that it is the capital city of the Pacific Rim, with a burgeoning financial center

after a substantial part of the black community exploded in 1992. The trouble flared following the beating of a black motorist, Rodney King, by officers of the Los Angeles Police Department, after he had been stopped for speeding. When the officers were acquitted, 38 people died in riots. Three years later the black and white communities were polarized again over O.J. Simpson, the black football star who was tried and acquitted of the murder of his wife.

In 1994, an earthquake measuring 6.7 on the Richter scale killed 57 people and injured 9,000. The epicenter was Northridge in the San Fernado Valley, and it was only because the quake occurred at 4 o'clock in the morning that fatali-

and the country's busiest port, the needs of its residents are going unaddressed. As its minority populations, especially Latins and Asians, increase, the city presides over a crumbling infrastructure of overburdened roads, schools, hospitals and social services.

Los Angelenos, already claiming, with a sense of irony, that their "seasons" consisted of floods, fires and earthquakes, added a fourth – "riots" –

ties were not more widespread. And water shortages continue to be a problem, joined, post-millennium, by another – power shortages. Air conditioning, tech communities and the lack of a cohesive solar energy policy has made the scarcity of power an increasing concern.

Nevertheless, the dream lives on. And new buildings like the Walt Disney Concert Hall, the Cathedral of Our Lady of the Angels, the fabulous treasures in the Getty Center and Getty Villas, and, at long last, a public transportation system that is finally making inroads into the sprawling mass of suburbs means that people will continue to be seduced by the "City of Dreams" for generations to come. ❏

LEFT: the murder trial of O.J. Simpson became a TV drama watched by millions.
ABOVE: LA's auto users are guarded by an angel etched into a window of the Cathedral of Our Lady of the Angels, the city's lavish Downtown church.

Decisive Dates

Circa **9000 BC** The first nomads reach what is now modern-day California.

Pre-1700s Indians inhabit the Los Angeles region, including the Gabrieleno, Chumash, Cahuilla and Tataviam tribes.

1771 San Gabriel Mission is founded.

1781 Don Felipe de Neve, the Mexican Governor of California, founds Los Angeles. A Franciscan monk, Junípero Serra, dedicates the town, naming it after St Francis of Assisi's first church, St Mary of the Angels – El Pueblo de Nuestra Señora de la Reina de Los Angeles.

1790 The community's first census reports 70 families living in a total of 30 adobe dwellings.

1840s The first orange groves are planted.

1842 The first California gold is discovered by Francisco Lopez in Placerita Canyon.

1847 Mexican General Andres Pico surrenders California to US General John Fremont at the Cahuenga Pass.

1848 The Treaty of Guadalupe is signed, fixing present US/Mexico borders.

1849 Gold is discovered at Sutter's Fort in the Sierra foothills – the Gold Rush begins.

1850 The borders of Los Angeles County are mapped out. The population is 1,500. California becomes the 31st state in the Union.

1850s Under successive treaties with the Federal government, Indian tribes sign away 90 percent of their 7½ million acres.

1851–60 The Chinese population grows, coming to California for the railroad and the gold.

1852 Some 100,000 miners pass through Los Angeles – it becomes a lawless western town.

Late 1850s The Gold Rush ends – and economic depression sets in.

1857 The Fort Tejon earthquake occurs (estimated 8.0 on today's Richter scale).

1860–80 Enlarged irrigation systems are constructed to keep LA supplied with water.

1867 Gas lamps illuminate the city's streets.

1871 The Chinese Massacre – in response to the murder of a white policeman, mass shooting and lynching leaves more than 24 dead.

1874 The first navel orange trees are planted at Riverside.

1876 The Southern Pacific Railway arrives. Waves of immigrants follow.

1882 The first Los Angeles phone book is issued – three pages in total.

1887 Harvey Wilcox files to form a subdivision of his ranch; wife Daieda names it Hollywood.

1890 Orange County is divided from LA County. The population of Los Angeles is 50,000.

1893 Edward Doheny and C.A. Canfield strike oil near the site of today's MacArthur Park.

1904 Hollywood passes legislation to prohibit drunkenness and enforce a speed limit of 12 mph (19 km/h).

1905 Abbott Kinney opens his Venetian-style resort near Santa Monica.

1907 Oil derricks proliferate in LA – Echo Lake is so polluted it catches fire for three days. The first house in Beverly Hills is built.

1908 Ex-Chicago filmmaker William Selig completes *The Count of Monte Cristo*, Southern California's first commercial movie.

1910 LA annexes the town of Hollywood.

1911–20 The Martin, Lockheed, and Douglas aviation companies begin production.

1911 Hollywood's first movie, *The Law of the Range,* is filmed in a former tavern at Sunset and Gower. The *Los Angeles Times* building is destroyed by a bomb.

1913 William Mulholland opens his new aqueduct, bringing water from the Owens Valley.

1920 Prohibition hits the US, but proximity to Mexico and offshore bootleggers keeps up spirits in Los Angeles.

1921 Hollywood's first national scandal hits, as Roscoe "Fatty" Arbuckle is accused of rape and murder. He is acquitted, but his movie career is over.

1923 Beverly Hills becomes a movie colony.

1926 Warner Studios adds sound to its feature *Don Juan* and the following year gives Al Jolson dialogue in *The Jazz Singer*.

1927 The first Academy of Motion Pictures awards – the Oscars – are presented at the Hollywood Roosevelt hotel.

1928 The St Francis Dam in San Fransquito Canyon bursts, sending a 180-ft (55-meter) wall of water from Santa Clarita to Oxnard, killing 400 people. Los Angeles City Hall is dedicated.

1931 The Los Angeles International Airport (LAX) is opened.

1932 The Olympic Games are staged in what is then the world's largest stadium, the Coliseum in Los Angeles.

1933 The Long Beach Earthquake (estimated 6.3 on Richter scale) kills 120 in Los Angeles.

1939 Union Station, the last of the great railroad terminals, opens.

1943 Zoot Suit Riots as sailors and Latinos clash in coastal beach communities; Downtown LA becomes a battlezone for several nights.

1950–65 31,000 acres (12,500 hectares) of orange groves fall to housing development.

1952 The Alien Land Act denying land ownership to Asians is declared unconstitutional.

1955 Disneyland opens.

1959 A citizen group saves Watts Towers from the wrecking ball.

1963 California's population becomes the largest of all US states, with the Los Angeles County population hitting 9 million. The Beach Boys form in the South Bay.

1965 Civil unrest erupts as the Watts Riots, lasting five days, kill 34 people.

1968 Presidential candidate Robert F. Kennedy is assassinated at the Ambassador Hotel.

1971 An earthquake measuring 6.6 in the San Fernando Valley claims the lives of 64 people.

1974 The oil tycoon J. Paul Getty donates his Malibu home as a museum.

1980 The former Hollywood actor and California state governor Ronald Reagan is elected as the 39th US President.

1987 The Whittier Earthquake causes structural damage throughout Downtown, East Los Angeles and Hollywood.

1988 Los Angeles Dodgers win World Series.

1990 Water rationing is imposed in the city for the first time.

1992 The acquittal of several Los Angeles police officers, charged with beating Rodney King, a black motorist, triggers riots that leave 38 people dead.

1994 An earthquake measuring 6.7 in the San Fernando Valley kills 57 people in the LA area.

1995–97 The football star O.J. Simpson is accused (and eventually acquitted in criminal court, found guilty in civil court) of murdering

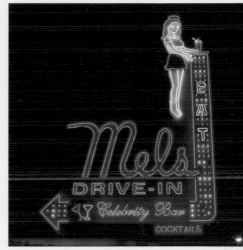

his wife and her male friend. His trial rivets TV viewers around the world.

1998 The Getty Center opens, giving Los Angeles the cultural lead over San Francisco.

2000 LA celebrates the new millennium with renovations and attractions under construction.

2002 The Academy Awards return to Hollywood in its new permanent home, the Kodak Theatre.

2003 The Walt Disney Concert Hall opens, 16 years after funds were first allocated.

2005 The Metro Orange Line opens, connecting with the North Hollywood Red Line.

2006 The Getty Villa and the Griffith Observatory reopen their doors after major refurbishments lasting many years. ❑

LEFT: LA's Sophia Greek Orthodox church.
RIGHT: Los Angeles is a neon nirvana.

THERE'S NO BUSINESS BUT SHOW BUSINESS

Everyone in Tinseltown is seeing stars: in their eyes, beneath their feet, on billboards, in kosher delis and car-lots. Most are busy being stars, too

The unofficial motto of the University of Southern California School of Cinema and Television is "Reality Ends Here." That inscription, hung above the entrance of the school famous for launching such diverse luminaries as director George Lucas; architect Frank Gehry and actor John Wayne, was enough to attract eager, young neophytes from all over the country with dizzying notions of fame, fortune and multi-picture deals swirling in their starstruck heads.

All-American myth

Los Angeles County could post the same warning, "Reality Ends Here," at the county line. Once you step across the border, no matter how well screwed on your head may be, this place is likely to be infectious if you're at all smitten by the entertainment bug. The All-American myth, that any young man or woman can pull themselves up by the bootstraps and become a success, seems to take on stellar qualities in the land of the lotus. All types of people – chefs, accountants, dog trainers, caterers – seek that five-pointed distinction that comes from being a star. And all with varying degrees of seriousness and success.

Even those new enough to Hollywood to be applying for a driver's license will sense the pervasiveness of this particular mania. The Department of Motor Vehicles in Hollywood, its

walls bedecked with autographed pictures of famous license plates, prides itself on its photographic savvy. While a driver's license may not count for much on the vanity scale, ownership of a small business can enable you to become a star in your own right. If you look in the Los Angeles phone book, for example, under "Star" or "Celebrity" you'll find: Star Camera, Star Deli and Donut Show, Star Kosher Meat Market, Celebrity Hot Dog, Celebrity Look-A-Likes, Celebrity Dry Cleaners, etc., etc., etc.

There are, of course, stars created from merely appearing in TV commercials. Local yokel car dealers have achieved a level of loony notoriety all to themselves. Cal Worthington, a

PRECEDING PAGES: longboard surfing contest winners.
LEFT: Angelyne, a quintessential LA star, famously featured on Sunset Strip billboards.
RIGHT: license to thrill.

resident of Long Beach, regularly appeared on nighttime television with his dog Spot, who was always a different animal, but never a dog. A garrulous fellow named Ralph Williams, another car dealer celeb, was long a source of jest in talk-show host Johnny Carson's late-night monologues.

"When you go out to even the most obscure mom-and-pop grocery store to ask if you can use the store to shoot a TV or movie location, they're likely to pull out a contract agreement from under the till," notes the *Hollywood Reporter*'s Robert Osborne. "The movie business itself is a caste system. It's important what car you drive, what you wear, what seat you get

at the restaurant Spago, if you're trying to put together a multi-million dollar deal. That kind of thing is very important and taken seriously. If you're going to get a 'go' on that picture, those kinds of perceptions are very important, and it carries over into the way people think out here."

Indeed, if "reality ends here," what or who is the barometer of this reality? Why do otherwise normal people get caught up in this? Because this is effectively a one-product town: the Entertainment Industry is simply referred to locally as "the industry." The most important man in this town stands at a mere 13½ inches (34 cm) tall, and is bald. He owns not a stitch of Armani, in fact he doesn't wear clothes at all.

But despite his slack of stature, most people are in awe of him. That is because he is Oscar *(see opposite)*, the gold statuette awarded annually by the Academy of Motion Picture Arts and Sciences for great "artistic" achievement.

Starry eyed

In this town where status and recognition often substitute for actual power, and where images are created, cultivated and carved into the public's mind, it's hard not to be star-conscious. Even the generally staid *Los Angeles Times* has a real estate section with a column entitled "Hot Property," accompanied by a color photograph of the hottest star who has sold his or her home or bought a new one, invariably to tear down and replace with an even more opulent and bigger one. And at least once a month, the *Los Angeles Times*' Calendar section will carry a story about some star's health-food philosophy, beef with Hollywood, or about something similarly abstruse and esoteric.

Somehow, time hasn't changed the Hollywood image of neon, pink Cadillacs, red lipstick, white tuxedos, roaring lions and laconic heroes riding into the sunset. Reality, however, is that such a Hollywood exists only on the billboards of Sunset Boulevard. In this famed street's teeming mid-section – the 7000 to 9000 blocks, called "the Strip" – the Boulevard is awash in movie ads: a manic Jack Nicholson smile; a toothpaste commercial Tom Cruise; or a recumbent pink-spandexed Angelyne.

Who's that? Angelyne *(see her on page 36)* is a self-promoting, busty, Jayne Mansfield type who takes out billboards extolling her availability. "Call Angelyne" is the admonition, and people do, even though there is little to indicate that Angelyne performs any role other than to occupy and adorn a large hunk of space in the Sunset Strip sky. Angelyne is Hollywood personified, and her billboards have appeared in more than 25 movies, including the Oscar-nominated *Get Shorty* (1995).

Stars are not just in the phone book and on billboards, but also underfoot. Hollywood's Walk of Fame, on Hollywood Boulevard and Vine Street, is renowned. While it's easy to find stars for Orson Welles, Humphrey Bogart and cowboy singer Gene Autry (he's on the Walk five times), others are noticeably absent. Don't expect to step on Dustin Hoffman, for instance.

Like so many other awards, recognition here is largely self-anointed. Stars are not selected so much as endorsed – once, that is, their publicists have made appropriate overtures to a special committee headed by Hollywood's "honorary mayor," Johnny Grant.

Meeting once a year to consider applications for the Walk of Fame, which anyone can submit, around 12 stars are awarded annually. The committee considers as part of the acceptance process professional accomplishment and longevity, sometimes even community service. In return, the honoree, if still alive, must agree to show up at the star-installation ceremony and his or her office to contribute a "sponsorship"

says Therese L. Wells, a former publicist for the Chamber of Commerce's Walk of Fame. "It sometimes seems the smaller the star, the bigger the push," notes Wells. "There is actually one star on the boulevard, Maurice Diller, who seems unknown to everybody. There's some speculation that it was a mistake and the inscription actually should read Mauritz Stiller, the Russian-Swedish director who brought Greta Garbo to Hollywood and who died there in 1928. But because of the misspelling nobody knows for sure.

"There are other stars, the Max Factor star, for instance, where the honor reflects more cooperation with the Chamber of Commerce

fee in the region of $15,000. One who heeded the New Testament message "Ask and ye shall receive" and later found his star shining brightly on the Walk of Fame was evangelist Billy Graham. He did ask quite a number of times, though. "There was a constant push from Billy Graham's people. They were relentless. Eventually, he got his star and it was justified [in that] that he was a TV personality of sorts,"

LEFT: there are around 200 autographs and star prints in the forecourt of Grauman's Chinese Theatre. Groucho Marx left an imprint of his cigar.
ABOVE: Halle Berry's Oscar in 2002 for *Monster's Ball* was an historic win for black performers.

OSCAR

A gold-plated bronze figure standing on a reel of film holds a sword upright: this prestigious statuette has been awarded since 1928 for what the Academy of Motion Picture Arts and Sciences judge the year's best achievements in film, for everybody from actors and directors to scriptwriters, costume designers, technical and effects artists. Why the name Oscar? Until 1931 the statuette had no name, until an obscure Academy librarian, Margaret Herrick (who eventually became its executive director), gave it the nickname because of its resemblance to her Uncle Oscar. The nickname stuck after it was reported in an article in a local newspaper.

than stardom," Wells added. "It's true that Max Factor makeup was instrumental in movies and that a lot of stars used it, but it's also true that the Max Factor company has been very active with the Hollywood Chamber of Commerce and its activities."

Hollywood's famous walk has spawned other, lesser walks of fame in the region, like the Avenue of Athletes (Silverlake), the Walk of Western Stars (Newhall), the Rock Walk (Hollywood) and the Orange County Walk of Stars (Anaheim). But out-of-town visitors who arrive expecting to see the glamorous Hollywood of Fred Astaire and Cary Grant movies are in for a rude surprise. Apart from the

recently refurbished area around Highland, most of Hollywood Boulevard is not exactly a black-tie area or even – after dark, at least – a good place to stroll with the family.

Hollywood has a heart

Despite the somewhat phony self-promotion, there *is* a real heart that beats beneath modern Hollywood's mean streets where, according to legend, everybody is only too willing to step on everybody else. "The movie industry is loaded with honest, down-to-earth people who make it all work, but you don't hear about them," the *Reporter's* Robert Osborne says. "Many of the [actors] who have endured seem to have a place

somewhere else, another residence in the mountains somewhere, like Clint Eastwood or Robert Redford.

"The ones who stay close get caught up in it too much and lose their creative bearings." Lucille Ball said that she and Desi avoided the party scene, and that they never told their jokes to industry people. They invented a mythical guy in Nebraska and aimed their jokes directly at him. These were the people they were trying to entertain, not the Beverly Hills cocktail crowd. Today's corporate/conglomerate/multinational movie and TV industry is vastly different from the old studio days. So different, in fact, that you will often hear it said that "the real" Hollywood no longer exists.

Legend-makers to lawyers

The biggest changes have occurred at the top of the executive ladder, where such immigrant empire builders as Louis B. Mayer and Jack Warner have been succeeded by a generation of lawyers, MBAs and power-agents. Walk into a studio with Tom Cruise's name on a contract and a copy of your local phone book as the script and you're talking "bankable project." Admittedly the current moneyman may suggest a car chase or two, a big gun shootout and some "tasteful" sex, but generally speaking they will not interfere very much with the "integrity" of your cherished project.

"Right now, it's only a notion. But I think I can get money to make it into a concept and later turn it into an idea," ran a line of Beverly Hills party talk in Woody Allen's 1977 hit, *Annie Hall,* which won the Oscar for best picture the following year.

Now, in these structured times, there is little of the kind of analysis that Columbia boss Harry Cohn was talking about 70 years ago when he said his butt itched – which meant that for him, the movie he was viewing wasn't working. Today's lawyers seem to have less sensitive asses, and instead twitch to graphs and demographics to select their projects.

The studios themselves have hopscotched all over the place, with new owners and new premises coming and going faster than a director can yell "Cut." For instance, Columbia Studios started out in Hollywood, moved to Burbank and then spent time in Culver City at the once-renowned MGM lot, overseen from across the street by MGM/UA's huge glass office complex, which looks like a modern European train station. MGM, in the mid-1990s, had no less than three owners in two years, one of them being the state bank of France.

Naturally, the wonderful world of showbiz is not totally populated by stars, even if stardom might be everyone's aspiration, including those who support the dreams: the legion of photocopiers, résumé typists, answering service operators, website designers, messengers, script readers and gofers of every variety. There are divorce lawyers, nutritionists and entertainment lawyers (law students call it "punk law"), as well as publicists, personal managers, personal

ing to write a script about it. And if they don't make it to the podium of the Kodak Theatre to accept an Oscar or land a walk-on part in a soap opera, they find some other way to pull a spotlight onto their thespian or terpsichorean skills. One former entertainer offered his services as a Shakespeare impersonator, showing up with a rose, a hand-penned sonnet and the fragrant gift of romance in a routine imaginatively entitled the Bard-O-Gram.

But even for those strip-a-grammers, muscle pumpers and pilates queens, just how easy is it to get that first break? "It's extremely difficult," says James Ulmer, who has spent considerable time covering the local labor scene

trainers, swamis and psychics. Many of these people, if not directly looking for a break, know how to take advantage of opportunities that might in time present themselves.

Always "on"

Waiters, waitresses and that guy who comes to deliver balloons for your office party are always "on." Sometimes it seems that half the local populace is auditioning and the other half is try-

for the *Hollywood Reporter*. "Just off the top of my head, I'd say they've got about a 1-in-50 chance of actually getting a speaking part, and a 1-in-15 chance of getting a walk-on. And I'm talking only about the talented, qualified people. It's the old Catch-22 situation, you can't get a union card without a part and you can't get a part without a union card."

Still, young hopefuls never fail to keep up-to-date with the industry production charts in the trade papers and their online counterparts – the *Hollywood Reporter*, *Daily Variety* – to see what movies are being shot and when and where. Interest extends to the general public, too. For years Jack Weinberg, a former attor-

LEFT: shopping for costumes in one of LA's many stores that cater to the trade.
ABOVE: female impersonators are among the performers most dedicated to glamour.

ney, ran a service that listed the shows that were shooting on the streets on any given day.

"Let's face it," Weinberg said, "everybody who comes out here, no matter how sophisticated they are, wants to see stars. When Queen Elizabeth visited they didn't give her a dinner at the Jet Propulsion Lab; they held it at 20th Century-Fox."

A similar list of productions used to be handed out daily by the city's Film & Video Permit Office on Hollywood Boulevard, but since 9/11 and fears of terrorism, circulation has been restricted to members of the movie industry. Nevertheless, many movie and TV studios still offer tours. (*see Travel Tips, page 231*).

The Polo Lounge at the Beverly Hills Hotel remains the all-round favorite haunt for star gazing visitors. It epitomizes both the old Hollywood and the current incarnation where power breakfasts of oat bran, yogurt and wheat toast cater to today's fitness-crazed entertainment types. Other popular hangouts for celebrities include the Farmers Market at 3rd and Fairfax, and the restaurants Spago and the Ivy.

Oh, there's lots to do here in the Big Orange, affectionately nicknamed to chime with New York's Big Apple monicker. And as innocent as you might be on arrival, if you hang around long enough, you may well find yourself "taking a meeting," or "doing lunch," or discussing

Star-gazing

Restaurants are still the most likely places to see the stars who might well make unscheduled public appearances. Movieland's equivalent of New York's erstwhile Algonquin Round Table is Musso & Franks Grill on Hollywood Boulevard *(see page 114)*. It's an old-style gathering place with wooden booths, white tablecloths, formal and brusque waiters and a no-nonsense menu that has barely changed since the restaurant opened in 1919. Ernest Hemingway, William Faulkner, Scott Fitzgerald and Nathanael West all sought solace here, sipping martinis and grousing about how they were treated by philistine producers.

the "big grossers." You'll know which films have great "b.o." (that's "box office" to you and me) and – the keenest test of all – you'll even understand the headlines in *Daily Variety*. "Stix nix hix pix." If that makes sense to you, you're in with a chance, babe.

So, once you're truly up to snuff, there's just one last thing to establish your arrival for posterity: put 15,000 bucks aside and have your people call Johnny Grant's people, so we can all step over your very own star, on Vine Street's Walk of Fame. ❑

ABOVE: the camera loves you, darling: filming in Venice for the Playboy Channel.

Movie Locations

Scores of movies have been made, not only in Los Angeles but starring the city itself. *Hollywood Hotel* (1937), *Hollywood Canteen* (1944), *Sunset Boulevard* (1950) *LA Story* (1991) and *LA Confidential* (1998) are some obvious examples. Others include: *Singin' in the Rain* (1952), *Rebel Without A Cause* (1955), *Gidget* (1959), *The Long Goodbye* (1973), *Beverly Hills Cop* (1984), *Die Hard* (1989), *The Player* (1992), *Short Cuts* (1993), *Mulholland Drive* (1996) and *City of Angels* (1998).

Los Angeles Plays Itself could be the ultimate self-referential Tinseltown movie, but this award-winning 2004 documentary (sharing the title, apparently, with a gay porn classic) was made by Canadian enthusiast Thom Andersen. For cineastes like Thom, LA landmarks are as familar as home. Here are just some easy-to-spot locations:

Fabulous Baker Boys: the baby grand piano Michelle Pfeiffer caressed and crooned on top of was in the Cinegrill nightclub at the Hollywood Roosevelt Hotel; other shoots here include *Internal Affairs* with Richard Gere, *Beverly Hills Cop II* with Eddie Murphy, and the TV show *Moonlighting* starring Bruce Willis and Cybill Shepherd.

Grease: John Travolta and Olivia Newton John frolicked at Rydell High, otherwise known as Venice High School.

Halloween: The Midwest setting of this screamer is actually Orange Grove Avenue in Hollywood, just north of Sunset. Jamie Lee Curtis was babysitting at No. 1530, her best friend was murdered at No. 1537.

Annie Hall: The final goodbye scene between Woody Allen and Diane Keaton was filmed at The Source, 8301 Sunset Boulevard, which still catered to the stars as The Cajun Bistro.

Back to the Future: Doc Brown's house is the Pasadena landmark, the Gamble House.

Indecent Proposal: the Huntington Library in San Marino plays Robert Redford's estate.

The Sting, *Ruthless People* and *Funny Girl* were all filmed in part on Santa Monica Pier.

RIGHT: French film poster for Rudolph Valentino's *The Sheik*, released in 1921.

Grand Canyon: Steve Martin lived in the Frank Lloyd Wright-designed Ennis House on Glendower Road in Los Feliz, as did Harrison Ford as Deckard in *Blade Runner*. *Blade Runner* also featured the Bradbury Building, at 304 South Broadway, as did *Chinatown*.

Nightmare on Elm Street: Freddie Krueger sliced up all those dreaming teenagers at the two-story white house at 1428 Genessee, just south of Sunset in Hollywood.

The Millennium Biltmore Hotel has been in many movies, including *Vertigo*, *The Sting*, *Ghostbusters*, *The Poseidon Adventure*, *Chinatown*, *Bugsy* and *A Star is Born*.

Lethal Weapon and *Mighty Joe Young* both

JESSE L. LASKY
présente une production
DE GEORGE MELFORD
LE CHEIK

rampaged on Hollywood Boulevard.

The Graduate and *Secrets of the Lost Temple* were filmed at USC's Doheny Library.

Rocky: many of the fight scenes were staged at the Olympic Auditorium in downtown LA.

Father of the Bride: Diane Keaton and Steve Martin's home in the movie was on South El Molino in Pasadena.

"Of all the movies in all the world..." *Casablanca*: The final runway scene in which Humphrey Bogart says goodbye to Ingrid Bergman was actually filmed at Van Nuys Airport, near Hangar 6. The faux streets of Paris are on the Warner Brothers tour remember "We'll always have Paris..." ❏

AUTOMANIA

More than 23 million car trips are made here every weekday, and the coming of age in California is marked by the arrival of a driver's license. This is the state, after all, that brought us the drive-in McDonald's and the drive-in church

I n his 1946 book *Southern California Country*, Carey McWilliams captured a telling local perspective: "Driving. Driving everywhere, over great distances with scarcely any thought to the enormous mileages they were logging. A car was the absolutely essential piece of social overhead capital. With it you could get a job, meet a girl, hang around with the boys, go to a drive-in, see football games away from home, take in the beach parties at Laguna or Corona del Mar, or go to the Palladium ballroom in Hollywood. To have a car meant being somebody; to have to borrow a car meant knowing somebody; to have no car at all, owned or borrowed, was to be left out. Way out."

Hit the highways

A Californian's coming of age heralds the ability to obtain a car, or at least a driver's license, without which one could feel like a second-class citizen. The driver not only gains mobility, but a kind of nobility, too – an exalted state from which the scurrying world around can be viewed with a sort of bemused tolerance.

"It's freedom," explained Skip Weshner, a newly transplanted New Yorker back in the 1960s. "The ability to just hop into your car and drive, drive as fast and as far as you like… the radio playing your favorite songs… the interesting architecture and funny billboards, glimpses of the sea…" That was a few decades ago and the cloud then seen dimly on the horizon has sadly now become an enveloping fog,

or smog, and the freedom constrained by other vehicles on every side. There are 6 million registered cars in Los Angeles County. Two-thirds of the urban space is taken up by roads, and traffic pollution is becoming the state's biggest environmental problem, pumping 18,000 tons of carbon dioxide into the atmosphere every year as well as strangling the freeways and producing oil spills, smog and contamination.

Forty percent of the respondents to a poll by the *Los Angeles Times* said they believed that cars had ruined the city and yet more than eight out of 10 hadn't ridden a bus for at least a year. Fewer than one out of three said they would make frequent use of mass transportation, even

LEFT: the Petersen Automotive Museum.
RIGHT: the Ventura Freeway is the busiest in the US.

though it is more available than previously. "Sometimes it staggers my imagination that people are still so crazy about their cars," says Nissan executive Gerald P. Hirshberg. "You watch them crawling along the freeway; they could walk faster. Then you look at their cars; clean, gleaming, polished objects of love. It's hard to think of Californians without them."

LA's ports employ 200,000 people to unload a million cars each year, with the Southern California region accounting for about one-seventh of the country's car and truck sales. Even in 1930, the region had more cars per capita than anywhere else in the world. The benefit that the city derives today from getting 10 percent of its

taxable income in one way or another from the automobile industry is counter-balanced by the frustration of trying to find more space for cars and yet simultaneously reduce pollution.

The regional Air Quality Management District talks of banning drive-through services, from banks to burger stands – this in the state where the drive-in restaurant inspired Ray Kroc to innovate the McDonald's chain, and Robert Schuller's Crystal Cathedral in Garden Grove has an outdoor screen for drive-in worshippers.

But it's also the place where, as far back as 1940, orange growers began to notice that a thick, brown haze was beginning to badly affect their crops. And yet it continues.

Sometimes drivers seem to enjoy sitting still in their cars as much as driving them; the average travel speed during rush hour is 17 miles per hour. The 1949 Ford was advertised as "a living room on wheels." In an article comparing the lifestyles of New York and Los Angeles, Joseph Giovannini wrote: "The car extends the privacy of the single family home into the streets … generally the windows are up, the doors locked, the music on, the mind set."

Homelessness, as familiar a phenomenon here as anywhere, takes on a special twist, where hundreds of people actually live in their cars. In some parts of LA, especially at the beach and in the streets bordering Griffith Park, it became enough of a problem to bring a ban on overnight parking for everyone but residents.

Design statement

Southern California is the section of the country most favored by car makers to set up their design clinics, of which there are at least 10. "This is the place where trends start," said John Schinella, head designer at General Motors' Advanced Concept Center in Thousand Oaks. "We're here to pick up on them before somebody else does." A few drivers, not content with distinctive models, express their identity by having their cars "customized," a trend that has been popular in California ever since cowboy star Tom Mix had a saddle mounted on the hood of his 1920s automobile.

Some of today's drivers have covered their cars with carpets, running shoes or even grass, but topping a Cadillac hood with a miniature candelabra (for Liberace) and gold-plating Elvis Presley's limousine was the specialty of North Hollywood's George Barris. Barris called himself the "King of the Kustomizers."

Not everybody is affluent enough to make a gold-plated statement or to meet the cost of a Lotus, Ferrari, Porsche, Lamborghini or some other exotic European model. But almost every driver can afford a few bucks for a personal license plate, and this is a state where almost one million drivers have done so. Ranging from the suggestiveness of BUSH DR (owned by a tree surgeon) to the obscurity of EZ4U2LV, the requests pour in at the rate of several hundred a day, keeping a special staff at California's Department of Motor Vehicles busy sifting out the unacceptable ones.

"You wouldn't believe the number of variations on the four-letter word," said one official, admitting ruefully that, despite the help of multilingual interpreters, mirrors, medical dictionaries and a copy of the California Penal Code ("in case they stick the code number for some particularly heinous crime on the back of their Chevy"), the occasional naughty slips through. One such example was 4NIK8 which the DMV later recalled. They also called back COKE DLR – until the recipient sent in a photo of the plate attached to his Coca Cola truck.

"There's an irresistible challenge in trying to condense an entire statement into six or seven characters, perhaps akin to that felt by writers

usually because the officer doesn't show up. Hundreds of others battle with meter maids ("parking control officers") on the street, after failing to get away with such ruses as putting an old ticket on the windshield, jamming the meter, or leaving the emergency flashers on.

In Newport Beach, which debated whether to equip its officers with cans of Mace, one meter maid spotted a disgruntled miscreant dropping a smoke bomb in the back of her car. Another was so abused that she acquired an ulcer and quit the job on her doctor's orders. "It's not worth being outside and getting beaten up," she said. "People think we [issue tickets] on purpose just because we don't like them."

in rigid poetic forms, such as haiku or sonnets," wrote University of Arizona professors Margaret Fleming and Duane Roen.

License plates are made by inmates at Folsom Prison, who occasionally enclose their own statement ("Help" or "You Bum") with the package. The most-requested plate is for PEACE, and probably the most regretted one is NOPLATE, whose owner became the recipient of parking tickets for every vehicle that was unidentified. Of the thousands of drivers who contest their parking tickets in court, about one-third win –

Valet parking became big business relatively recently, and at virtually all major restaurants and hotels it is mandatory. Tips range from zero to $50 (half up front; half handed over when the driver gets back his car fast and unharmed). Car valets tend to be young because they're usually expected to *run* to retrieve the car, and about half the customers want their vehicles to be parked "upfront" and will pay extra for this privilege. Good valets know all the legends about people who have "lost" their tickets and drive off with somebody else's Porsche or how some drivers will protest a dent that wasn't there before. Bad valets are likely to search the cars for drugs or money, make copies of the house

LEFT: Corvettes by Hollywood High School.
ABOVE: the "stack," one block from Sunset Boulevard.

keys or just treat the vehicle as if it were their own, changing the radio dial or using the stereo to play their personal iPods.

Pet peeves

Slow drivers and those who turn without signaling registered highest on the list of pet peeves of motorists polled by the *Los Angeles Times*, with about one-third declaring that what worried them most was encountering "bad drivers." Some of these complaints originate out of simple, stark fear, a syndrome widely known as freeway phobia. But for many there is no other choice. Forced out of town by escalating housing costs, these unfortuates face daily commutes

of 100 miles (160 km) or more each way.

Around 767,000 commuters say that, even without congestion, accidents or bad weather, their drive to work takes between 45 and 90 minutes. During this trip they munch on snacks, listen to the radio or books on CDs, or simply get exasperated. Doctors say long journeys are bad for the health, raising blood pressure and causing memory loss; employers note increasing stress among workers.

Motorists embraced the freeways because of the ease and speed with which they could cover great distances without having to stop for lights, but the rippling gridlock resulting from even a minor accident sometimes brings paralysis to

the system. A 2002 survey reported that Southern California drivers spend an average of 40–60 hours each year stuck in traffic congestion, costing drivers an estimated $700–$1,000 a year in wasted time and gasoline.

Aware that every minute a stalled car is on a freeway causes at least four minutes of lingering congestion, some authorities have experimented with coordinating helicopter surveillance with tow-truck routes. But the real problem – the 55 percent increase in traffic in the past decades as against a tiny percent of new roads – would take at least $8 billion to cure, according to some studies. Meanwhile, with pollution reaching "unacceptable" levels on 200 days each year, drivers increasingly sit in their cars and fume, along with the engine.

A local book, *LA Shortcuts: A Guidebook for Drivers Who Hate to Wait* by Brian Roberts and Richard Schwadel, investigated the behavior of aggressive drivers. They wrote that "shortcut sharks instinctively know that to move is to live; to stop and lose momentum is to suffocate and die." Indicating alleys, driveways, parking lots and gas stations, the authors declare: "If it's wide enough, drive it" and amplify their credo with such commandments as: "The shortest distance between two points is never a straight line," and the dictatorial admonition: "Accept no uprisings. Passengers are merely baggage and have no vote."

Psychologist Ange Lobue calls it "a metaphor for the powerlessness we experience in our daily lives… we begin to feel the delay threatens our survival. The threat becomes overwhelming and in an attempt to avoid these feelings (of helplessness) we become more aggressive, tailgating the driver in front (who), insulted by our 'territoriality,' responds with an abrupt lane-change and a passive-aggressive slowing or abrupt braking. This can be followed by an exchange of insults escalating to more dangerous manoeuvers." Occasionally this boils over into murder, as in the speight of freeway shootings that occurred one hot, sticky summer. The incidents prompted a bumper sticker reading: IF I CUT YOU OFF DON'T SHOOT.

Perhaps unconfident that they are making sufficient statement with the car itself, quite a few owners augment the display with bumper stickers to entertain or provoke their fellow drivers, with such typical Californianisms as

SORRY IF MY KARMA COLLIDES WITH YOUR DOGMA or I BRAKE FOR HALLUCINATIONS.

In a 1970 experiment, researchers asked 15 drivers with no recent traffic violations to put Black Panther bumper stickers on their cars and found that within weeks this group of drivers had collected more than 33 citations from the local police. More happily productive were the brightly colored and numbered stickers handed out by dating services – Freeway Singles Club, Tail Dating or Drive Me Wild – which enabled members to contact each other via a central office. Roadway Romeos are commonplace, as Art Seidenbaum noted when writing about this widespread flirting and concluded that: "only in

ing, passing on shoulders, abrupt lane changes and possessing a free-floating hostility (honking the horn, cursing, pounding the steering wheel, obscene gestures); and Type B, whom Martin Brenner defines as "freeway wimps" who "rarely get angry, seeing it as pointless. They don't respond to provocations from other motorists; they drive with a smile on their faces and don't fight traffic."

LA's streets see an average of 61,000 collisions a year, with 93,000 people injured. In California as a whole, a traffic accident is reported every minute, with someone killed every two hours and nine minutes. Driver fatigue and alcohol are reasons why the worst accidents occur

a culture created by car can love blossom between the lanes."

Sadly, more drivers prefer to fight than flirt. "In our cars we assume we are in charge. Our feelings of dominance and authority are increased, but they are also made vulnerable" wrote Peter Marsh and Peter Collett in *Driving Passion: The Psychology of the Car.* Speeding away at the lights is "a kind of gauntlet throwing" they say. "It presents a challenge to other drivers." Some psychologists classify drivers: Type A, a need to do more in less time, tailgat-

at night, with Friday the worst day, and the major cause of pile-ups is the habit of drivers following each other's cars too closely.

Highway officers are accustomed to watching men driving while shaving, reading newspapers or using car phones, women putting on makeup, reading maps or doing crossword puzzles, and both engaged in sexual activity at excessive speeds.

"The practice of making love on the highways is becoming alarmingly prevalent. In many cases it is flagrantly open," the city's Board of Supervisors was informed by Captain Cannon of the LA motorcycle squad. His report was filed in 1921.   ❑

LEFT: posh car and a pooch at the Petersen.
ABOVE: size doesn't matter...

MADE ON MUSCLE BEACH

It's not only Hollywood stars who watch their physiques, and believe that the world is watching with them. From European strongmen to going for the burn to championing a former body-builder as governor, getting physical is something Southern Californians love

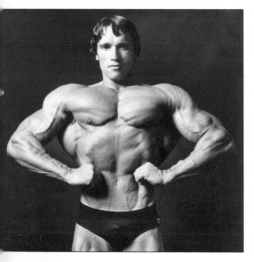

like Samson, Ulysses, Tarzan, Atlas and Hercules, who had inspired dreams of strength – but these dreams were pursued in weightlifting contests and circus sideshows. Now they are a universal obsession.

Many experts point to Eugene Sandow as spearheading the fitness revolution. Billed as "The World's Strongest Man," Sandow arrived from Europe as more than an ordinary sideshow – what set him apart was the aesthetic quality of his physique. Men and women alike considered Sandow so perfect a combination of muscular development and attractiveness that his embodiment of brawn shifted the focus from extraordinary strength to the aesthetics of muscularity. Sales of barbells and dumbbells pumped with vigor.

Contests were held to compare the physical measurements of competitors, and so began the bodybuilding industry. In 1899, this interest was boosted by a new magazine called *Physical Culture*, which sold for 5¢ and was an instant success. It was published by fitness guru Bernarr Macfadden from New York. Having developed a superb physique through a vegetarian diet and daily workouts, Macfadden was interviewed in *Time* and *Newsweek*, and at the mere sight of a press camera would strip to his underwear to flex his muscles.

Some people thought Macfadden was too eccentric, but arriving in LA, he became just one of a number of self-proclaimed health experts. Like Otto Carque (1867–1936), considered the grand old man of LA food and health gurus, he prescribed exercise, fresh air

For decades, people have come to LA for the land, the movies, the weather – and muscles. With the arrival of the railroads and, later, the telephone, word spread of the health benefits of life in the sun. Refugees from bitter East Coast winters came hoping this solar elixir would encourage good health and good fortune, in addition to relief from arthritis, colds and shoveling snow.

Historical health

In the 1890s, fitness was more about staying alive and illness-free than about working out, and diets often meant putting on weight, rather than taking it off. Muscles were for legends and nude sun bathing as the cure for nearly every ailment Similarly Arnold Ehret, who advocated a diet of only grape juice, believing it gave "supernatural strength," and held that a healthy, fasting individual could receive electrical "love vibrations" through their hair.

"This is my good side…"

Motion pictures created a new kind of celebrity. A famous actor played to maybe tens of thousands of people over a long Broadway run, while a middling movie star became instantly known to millions. But the camera has no pity; a close-up showed flaws nobody would ever see in a stage actor.

By the late 1920s, it was possible to buy fig coffee, grain-free uncooked pies, alkaline bread, and even bubbling oxygenated tooth powder. Health-food gurus like Paul C. Bragg numbered many entertainers among his followers, but these experts also drew devotees from another new way of life and entertainment.

To begin with, it really wasn't about muscles; it was about fitness and fun. Muscle Beach, Santa Monica, was just a patch of sand south of the pier. But once the tumbling platform and gymnastics equipment took their place in the sun, it became the birthplace for the modern fitness movement. Muscle Beach attracted the best bodies of the day: Jack

So while the many Midwestern retirees who fled to LA seeking health thought in terms of comfort and warmth, for actors health was a matter of career survival – once you lost your looks, you were on the scrap heap. Hollywood's feverish quest for beauty and youth had begun, and so had a symbiotic relationship – stars flocked to the newest and greatest health fads in an effort to retain their youth, while health and fitness gurus touted celebrity endorsements to promote their latest products.

LEFT: Arnold Schwarzenegger in the run-up to his career as governor – the 1977 film *Pumping Iron*.
ABOVE: working it out with equal weight.

LaLanne, John Grimek (a protegé of Bernarr Macfadden's and the first "Mr America"), Charles Atlas and Joe Gold. All would go on to fitness fame, fortune, or both.

The focus of attention at the original Muscle Beach through the 1930s, '40s and '50s, was acrobats – strong men and women who built human towers and threw themselves and each other around. It grew to include athletes, circus performers, wrestlers, college gymnasts and movie stunt people. On weekends the crowd of spectators numbered 10,000, watching acts like Paula Boelsems, who taught an elephant how to water-ski; George Eiferman, who played a trumpet with one hand while lifting weights with the other; and Abbye "Pudgy" Stockton, a dainty acrobat who became the first great female weightlifter.

Movie stars like Clark Gable and Tyrone Power came to watch. Mae West found her chorus boys here, and Jayne Mansfield met her husband at Muscle Beach (and so did Jane Russell). It was only a matter of time before the athletes began posing on a path to movie stardom. The first was Steve Reeves, discovered by Cecil B. deMille, who starred in many films as Hercules. "He was the most beautiful human to ever walk the sand of Muscle Beach," recalls Harold Zinkin, author of *Remembering Muscle Beach* and the first "Mr

California." But by the late 1950s, Santa Monica was tiring of the act. The owners of the pier allegedly complained that the free shows were drawing paying customers away, while others found the whole idea offensive.

After five weightlifters were found partying with under-age girls, the city claimed Muscle Beach had become a magnet for "perverts and narcissistic parasites," and the place was bulldozed. Use of the name Muscle Beach was forbidden, as were weightlifting and any events not approved by the city recreation department.

In the 1960s, echoes of Muscle Beach took shape about 2 miles (3 km) south at "The Pen," an outdoor weight park on Venice Beach. Exclusively for use by weightlifters, this new hangout became the providence of champion bodybuilders like Frank Zane and Dave Draper. In 1965, Joe Gold opened what has since become "the mecca" of bodybuilding – Gold's Gym. It was from here that Arnold Schwarzenegger and Lou *(Incredible Hulk)* Ferrigno crunched onto the screen in the 1977 movie, *Pumping Iron*.

Going for the burn

LA fads become national trends and in the 1980s, the Beverly Hills-based *Jane Fonda Workout* grew into an aerobic entertainment-industry networking event. Fonda started the craze in the capital of body-worship, and the *Workout* hit on the tidal wave of VCRs that was breaking across the world, although not everyone who bought the tape did it to follow the exercise program.

FOR THOSE WHO WOULD RATHER WATCH

The toughest spectator sport to watch is a Lakers game, as tickets are so hard to get. The easiest is volleyball; all you need is a beach chair. *For more information, see Travel Tips.*

NBA Basketball
LOS ANGELES LAKERS – Late Oct to mid-April, then playoffs. Home: Staples Center, Downtown. www.nba.com/lakers

Major League Baseball
LOS ANGELES DODGERS – April to Oct, then play-offs. Home: Dodger Stadium, Downtown. www.dodgers.com

NHL Hockey
LOS ANGELES KINGS – Oct to early April, then playoffs. Home: Staples Center, Downtown. www.lakings.com

Major League Soccer
LA GALAXY – April to Oct. Home: The Home Depot Center, Carson. www.lagalaxy.com

NCAA College Athletics
The University of Southern California and the University of California at Los Angeles both field strong teams. For USC: www.usctrojans.com; for UCLA: www.uclabruins.com

Volleyball
Tournaments on summer weekends. www.volleyball.org

Golf
The LA (Nissan) Open is mid-Feb at the Riviera Country Club. www.pgatour.com

The 1990s were fast and furious: a riot that left the city in flames, an earthquake that left many unsettled, and a sizzling economy that put more money in most pockets, but with less time to enjoy it. Is it any wonder that Spinning – basically a stationary bike race – and Tae-Bo, a combination of TaeKwonDo and boxing, became so popular? High intensity, they burned off a lot of stress, in addition to calories, in a short amount of time. In 1999, the Tae-Bo workout tape was No. 2 on the Billboard video sales charts, beating most Hollywood films of that year. Billy Blanks, the master behind TaeBo and a devout Christian, tried to encourage a calming effect from these fierce workouts, telling his devotees

Health gurus and celebrities continue to nourish each other – the herbal tea bar Elixir, on Melrose, became popular with stars like Susan Sarandon, Kevin Bacon and Julia Roberts, who seemed to need a fix to fend off everything from flu to stress. According to the people at Robert's American Gourmet, the *Seinfeld* gang kept up their energy with Power Puffs, a cheese-puff impostor loaded with ginseng and bee pollen. Actor Woody Harrelson invested in a Sunset Boulevard oxygen bar, where for a price you could breathe the pure thing – and even order it flavored. Juice and oxygen bars spread quickly across the country, but of course they started here.

to change their life through "will – strength – belief – perseverance."

Angelenos are always trying to work on their spiritual side as well, often through meditation or yoga, which is more popular than ever. A healthier diet has become popular, too. According to a study in the *Los Angeles Times*, Californians are drinking less alcohol – a 79-million gallon decline over the past decade. Perhaps they're replacing it with nutrition – some of the fastest-growing franchises are purveyors of juice and smoothies.

LEFT: volleyball's Hermosa Open is a big tournament.
ABOVE: surfer moms get fit.

Health here and now

The sun still shines on the health and fitness scene, and though the environment may not be as pristine, LA muscles continue to flex. Perhaps it's because life has become so fast-paced that residents are turning more than ever to gyms, bikes, surfboards, in-line skates, pilates, vitamins, additives, laxatives and herbal tonics. The challenge to remain stress-free, and, even more important, to *look* stress-free, has become a catalyst for creative innovations. New products are being hatched in minds, labs and gyms all over the city right now – because muscles, like oranges, are a valuable California cash crop. ❑

CALIFORNIA DREAMIN': THE INVENTIVE CITY

Creativity, from the movies to Mattel, blossoms and thrives under the California sun

Los Angeles, the city where the flower is the Bird-of-Paradise, is all about dreams – wild, extravagant dreams. And dreams are what great businesses are made of. Howard Hughes made aviation history here time and again, most spectacularly with the immense eight-engined H-4 Hercules flying boat known as the *Spruce Goose*. More practically, the McDonnell Douglas corporation pioneered the DC-3 Dakota and built 10,655 of these aircraft in Santa Monica and Long Beach.

Sunshine commerce

LA sunshine has incubated many an idea and entrepreneur – the city's warmth created a natural spawning ground for the health and fitness revolutions; the movie industry fled its East Coast roots and sprouted in the year-round sunny locations of LA; and tech pioneers found the mild weather ideal for empire-building.

Not everything invented in LA was weather driven (like the Zamboni ice-rink machine), but many products, if not actually invented here, were at least exploited here, and shared in LA's innovation.

Fads. Trends. Celebrity. The friction of these intangibles often heats up into a hot product – some catch fire around the world, and some go down in flames. Here are a few that started out as California dreams, but are still burning brightly.

ABOVE: In 1969, the University of California at Los Angeles (UCLA) was the first node on the ARPANET, the early computer network which, in the 1980s, evolved into the Internet.

ABOVE: Rollerblades inventor Scott Olson of Minnesota says, "When I first started selling rollerblades, the sport shops laughed me out of their stores, but packing up and moving to California made it more mainstream."

LEFT: The bikini was introduced by French designer Louis Reard in 1946, but was banned in much of Europe. It was mainly through the 1960s Hollywood "Beach Party" movies that the bikini became publicly acceptable.

BARBIE, WOMAN OF THE WORLD

Barbie has risen to international stardom since her LA charm-school days. She even has her own Hall of Fame. Her "management," the Mattel toy company, likes to point out that "in every second of every day, two Barbie dolls are sold somewhere in the world." Some models are traded for thousands of dollars apiece.

It all started when a partner in Mattel, Ruth Handler, watching her daughter Barbara play with dolls, imagined them in grown-up roles. Ruth wanted a doll to inspire little girls to think what they might be when they grew up. A 1994 Barbie biography claims that Handler found her prototype in Lilli, a comic-strip character and iconic doll much prized by truck-drivers in Germany. The other Mattel executives (all-male) said that Barbie was too expensive to produce, but she debuted nevertheless at the 1959 New York Toy Fair. Some found the doll's black-and-white swimsuit "scary, sleazy," though "spellbinding." Other buyers liked her "fresh face, with fashions to fit a girl's daydreams."

Whatever the case, Barbie hardly ever shows up in the tabloids, and had a respectable steady boyfriend for 43 years, until on February 12th 2004, she and Ken decided to "spend time apart."

RIGHT: Food fads find fame here first! After California cuisine came smoothies, wheat-grass cocktails, herbal tea baths, the oxygen bar and the Pritikin diet.

LEFT: Aviation's deep connections with Los Angeles were confirmed when the Space Shuttle construction contract was awarded by NASA to Rockwell International.

ANGELS IN THE ARCHITECTURE

With influences from the movies, sports cars, art and the beach, Californian architecture has come of age, scooping the industry's most prestigious award, the Pritzker Prize, in 2005

When Noel Coward delivered his aphorism about there being something delightfully real about what is phony in Hollywood "and something so phony about what is real," he could just as well have been talking about the architecture. Southern California may or may not have invented the style that promotes a donut-shaped drive-in, a music company's headquarters like a giant stack of records or a sign in the shape of an enormous guitar, but those kinds of iconic style-edifices are certainly at home here.

And who could fail to be as convincingly lifted from the black-and-white world as Judy Garland was spirited from Topeka, Kansas, to the magical, if not entirely real, Land of Oz?

Serious attention

"For a couple of generations during the Golden Age of the movies, LA was everybody's Hometown… The LA movie lot with corner drugstore, Main Street and Andy Hardy's neighborhood, as well as the more dangerous hideaways of Raymond Chandler's Hollywood were almost as familiar as our own backyards," wrote the late Charles Moore and his co-authors in *The City Observed: Los Angeles*, arguably the most perceptive architectural guide to Lotusland. The inevitable downside to this fantasy, has been that LA's architecture has sometimes, like so many other products, not been taken as seriously as it may deserve.

LEFT: the soaring curves of the Getty Center.
RIGHT: the Capitol Records building is shaped to resemble a stack of records.

This shifted when, at the glitzy presentation of *Progressive Architecture*'s design awards, it became clear to the *Los Angeles Times* that, "the baton of the profession which had been so firmly grasped by the post-modernists of the East Coast, had passed to the West."

Those offbeat buildings in Santa Monica and Venice, the daring houses perched precariously on Hollywood hillsides and Frank Gehry's designs for museums and cultural centers, "added up to a national phenomenon that challenged the notion that New York's sovereignty in architecture was God-given and forever," the newspaper concluded breathlessly. Santa Monica architect Craig Hodgetts explained: "New

York made a fatal turn and stepped off the trajectory. Their post-modernist architecture was about the history of architecture. It didn't draw on contemporary life so it severed itself from a source of vitality." The LA avant garde drew its inspiration from movies, sports cars, Nintendo and commonplace streetside vernacular. They used cheap and unexpected materials, including corrugated fiberglass, concrete blocks, bathroom tiles, asphalt shingles. Intellectual property – "how ordinary things are put together," is what Hodgetts believes imparts value these days. "Los Angeles is, after all, about making a piece of celluloid valuable."

The movie industry has certainly played its

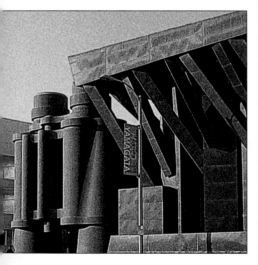

part. Hodgetts himself had worked as an art director in films, and production designer Anton Furst came off the *Batman* set to design the Planet Hollywood restaurant chain.

Dream street

Some of the projects have been tagged "site-specific urban sculptures," one of the largest being Universal CityWalk *(see page 190)* which induced, said a *Times* writer, "the feeling of being in a kind of archetypal LA dream street in which all the urban grime is edited out." Its creator, architect Jon Jerde, whose Horton Plaza in San Diego draws millions of visitors a year, called it "a movie set of quintessential LA. Its

theme is a kind of lively, stylish trash that's very Angeleno." Jerde believes architecture's prime task is to create a public space in which people can experience "a sense of common identity."

Few places do this better than Disneyland and *The City Observed* devotes 20 pages to it. "What may come as a surprise is how richly Disneyland offers us insight into many layers of reality… this incredibly energetic collection of environmental experiences offers enough lessons for a whole architectural education in all the things that matter – community and reality, private memory and inhabitation, as well as some technical lessons in propinquity and choreography." The corporation's recent extravaganza – Disney's California Adventure – only reinforces these "layers of reality."

Largely because of his work on the Guggenhem Museum in Bilbao, Spain, Canadian-born, LA-based Frank Gehry is one of the names most familiar to a lay public who would be unlikely to recognize an architect even if he answered the door of a building they admired. Now old enough to retire, Gehry studied at USC but may have been influenced by his California contemporaries in Venice, artists such as Ed Moses, Larry Bell, Robert Irwin and Tony Berlant, who in the turbulent 1960s were busy ripping apart and rearranging their studios into what amounted to walk-in sculptures.

Some of Gehry's local works – the Spiller Residence (39 Horizon Avenue), a trio of artist studios (326 Indiana Avenue), the binocular-shaped building commissioned by the Chiat/ Day advertising agency (340 Main Street) – are in the Venice and Santa Monica areas. Gehry's reputation became further enhanced by the completion of the Walt Disney Concert Hall *(see pages 63 and 78–9)*, 16 years in the making, and a project that has spearheaded a cultural revival in downtown LA.

Architectural writer Leon Whiteson described Gehry's early work as, "High-art populism of cheap materials artfully used… made a virtue out of trash," and the architect himself has said: "I am interested in finishing work but I am interested in the work's not appearing finished… I prefer the sketch quality, the tentative, the messiness if you will, the appearance of 'in progress' rather than the presumption of total resolution and finality… If you try to understand my work on the basis of frugal order, structural integrity and formalized definitions of beauty you are apt to be totally confused."

Another example of this local "found-object" style is the Simon Rodia-designed Watts Towers *(see page 89)*. Its soaring, lacy metal towers are covered with plaster and hand-gathered seashells, ceramics and glass.

Frank Gehry influence

Gehry has been an influence on younger architects "to have confidence in their own ideas," says Richard Koshalek, a committee member who hired him to design the Disney Concert Hall. "Their new community of buildings is like a community of individuals...we heard time

impact on the development and redirectioning of progressive design," and Frank Lloyd Wright and his colleagues, Richard Neutra and Rudolph Schindler. Initially following Wright's lead, both of these men soon developed styles of their own.

Mood and light

Wright designed more than 1,000 buildings in his career but built only four homes in LA, the most notable being Hollyhock House *(see page 168)*, and the endangered Ennis House *(see pages 168–9)*. Both were constructed of precast, patterned concrete blocks joined by steel rods and combine outdoors and indoors appealingly. The Ennis House has been used

and time again how architects everywhere were influenced by them... that the major influence in their work was coming from California."

Like many in his profession over the past half century, Gehry fell under the spell of such legendary figures as Louis Kahn (1901–74), architect of Southern California's Salk Institute in La Jolla, whose work according to *Contemporary Architects* "had an absolutely monumental

as a setting in films, notably *Blade Runner*.

Schindler, who worked as Wright's project supervisor before setting up on his own, often experimented with inexpensive new building materials. He became renowned for skilful combinations of climate, light and mood. Like his mentor, he was captivated by combining indoors and outdoors.

Between 1925 and 1930 Schindler shared one of his semi-outdoor houses with fellow-Austrian Richard Neutra, a former colleague of Wright's at Taliesen. Schindler and Neutra got along well in this West Hollywood home *(see page 122)*, but apparently not so their wives. One of the houses Neutra built – for film direc-

LEFT: Frank Gehry's binocular-shaped building was commissioned by advertising agency Chiat/Day.
ABOVE: architect Richard Neutra's Lovell "Health House" (overlooked by the Griffith Observatory) featured in the movie *LA Confidential.*

tor Josef von Sternberg – was bought by writer Ayn Rand but demolished in 1936 by a developer. Neutra claimed that he was the model for Howard Roark's sex appeal in Rand's monumental novel *The Fountainhead*. True or not, he garnered great acclaim in the 1930s and '40s for his designs for private houses, and made the cover of *Time*. The delicate steel-framed "Health House" he designed for syndicated health columnist Dr Phillip Lovell on Dundee Drive in Griffith Park was called by Charles Moore "one of the great monuments of modern architecture." Fourteen of Neutra's other buildings still stand in Silverlake.

Neutra had corresponded with writer Upton

Sinclair, supported his controversial bid for governor and shared his vision of low-cost housing, which he himself had acquired from architect Irving Gill (1870–1936). He was a practical visionary with a great interest in designing for people living closely in harmony. One ambitious project was called Amity Village. Most of it had been demolished by the 1980s, but residents recalled it as the most pleasant environment they had lived in.

In an article for *Sunset* magazine describing the plans, Neutra quoted a fictitious future householder praising the design. "Practically, we don't live on a street at all but in a park… [the] ingenious arrangement gives us the illusion of unlimited space." (One foreign visitor to LA wisecracked about Neutra's urge for combining open space with interiors: "Being in a Neutra building gives one a tremendous urge to go indoors.") Neutra died in April, 1970 at the age of 78.

Art Deco

By the first decade of the 20th century, when Los Angeles was growing into a major city, its downtown area started to take shape, largely as a concept in the minds of people like Charles Mulford Robinson, an influential member of the City Beautiful Movement. The main entertainment and commercial street was Broadway, with Pershing Square the symbolic city center. Farmers & Merchants' Bank (1900), a beaux arts building by Dodd & Richards, remains from those times. Other Downtown landmarks include the early movie theaters *(see pages 79–80)*. Befitting a town like LA, it's not surprising that it was entertainment complexes that were in the architectural vanguard. Splendid movie shrines were rising like beacons on Hollywood Boulevard: the Egyptian Theatre, a 1,700-seat replica of a palace in Thebes, and Grauman's Chinese Theatre *(see pages 104, 107)* were both created by Meyer & Holler, who also designed the neo-Gothic Security Pacific Building at the corner of Highland.

Downtown's earlier heyday produced such buildings as the Biltmore Hotel (Schultze & Weaver, 1923) with its impressive 350-ft (110-meter) galleria, as well as the Fine Arts Building in Spanish Renaissance Revival style, a 3000-sq. ft (280-sq. meter) cathedral-like space lit by 15 chandeliers, massive bronze doors, carved oak elevators and tall bronze-and-glass showcases exhibiting artists' works.

Other landmarks include the former *Los Angeles Herald Examiner* building at 1111 Broadway, designed by William Randolph Hearst's favorite architect, Julia Morgan. Morgan's *tour de force* was, of course, Hearst's magnificent "castle" at San Simeon, on the coast between Los Angeles and San Francisco. For years the *Herald Examiner* building lay empty, but in 2005 funds and an "adaptive use" policy were approved that will preserve the building's most important architectural elements.

Startlingly renovated in 1983 by Ratkovich & Bowers, the Fine Arts Building was originally the work in 1927 of Walker & Eisen who the following year designed another landmark, the Oviatt Building on S. Olive, its lobby decorated with tons of Lalique glass and whose penthouse had a pool with a sandy beach. The building at 818 7th Street (Curlett & Bellman, 1917) in Italian Renaissance Revival style opposite the Fine Arts Building was reputed to have been modeled after the Strozzi Palace in Florence.

Historic materials

Adobe was LA's first building material after the Spaniards arrived, and most structures have held up well. Of the many which are still preserved, the most famous is the Avila Adobe (1818) on

uted "horizontal lines, rounded corners, projecting wings and generally a sleek, machine-look that expressed efficiency and modernity," swept the US in the 1930s, influencing the aerodynamic trains of Norman Bel Geddes and Raymond Loewy.

Excellent examples of it have survived, like the ex-department store Bullocks, designed by John & Donald Parkinson in 1928 of buff terracotta, green copper and glass; the ship-like Coca-Cola building (Robert Derrah, 1937) at 1334 Central Avenue; and the Hotel Shangri La in Santa Monica. Derrah also built the Crossroads of the World *(see page 62)* at 6671 Sunset Boulevard, which opened in October 1936

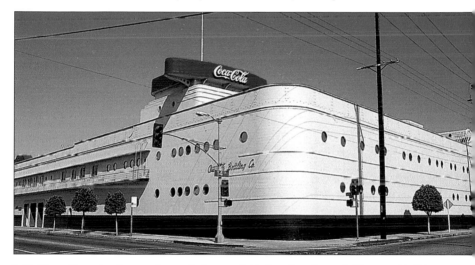

LA's Olvera Street, but there are dozen of other fine examples in the Los Angeles vicinity.

The romantic, so-called "Spanish style" of architecture so popular in Southern California (and which, one writer wittily suggested, "recalls an imaginary past in an altogether synthetic manner") has actually taken several forms: Mission; Colonial Revival; 17th-century baroque, and the Art Deco-inspired Streamline Moderne and Zigzag Moderne. Streamline Moderne, to which Sam Hall Kaplan has attrib-

as LA's first shopping mall. The central building is patterned after a ship on a world cruise, flanked by small stores – now offices – representing such architectural styles as Spanish Colonial, Tudor and French Provincial. It has a central 55-ft (17-meter) tower topped by a revolving globe.

Some structures combine styles, as for example, Union Station (John & Donald Parkinson, 1934–39 *(see pages 76–7)*, which is a mixture of Spanish Colonial Revival with Streamline Moderne touches. The Parkinson brothers, with Albert C Martin, were also responsible for LA's 28-story City Hall (1926–28, *see page 77)*. The Mission Revival style was "born of boosterism

LEFT: Donut Hole, La Puente, in the San Gabriel Valley.
ABOVE: the Streamline Moderne Coca-Cola building was designed in 1937.

not Catholicism," wrote John McKinney in his fascinating book, *The Boutiqueing of California's Coast.* "So widespread is the Mission look that visitors often jump to the conclusion that coastal towns like Carlsbad, Oxnard and Palos Verdes, given their presiding architectural bias, are mission towns founded by the Spanish padres. Their Mission motif, however, is an afterthought façade."

Santa Barbara's distinctive Spanish Colonial Revival style is a direct consequence of the 1925 earthquake's aftermath, when the architect George Washington Smith worked hard to maintain a fairly uniform style throughout the town. A particular favorite in the previous

decade had been the Mediterranean-style apartment courts with red tile roofs, fountains and the lavish use of hand-painted tiles. The husband and wife team of Arthur and Nina Zwebell excelled in this sort of style in the 1920s – a lush kind of Spanish architecture, seen in the Villa Andalucia on N. Havenhurst, and the Villa Primavera on N. Harper. In similar style is Villa D'Este on N. Laurel built by the Davis brothers in 1928, all in West Hollywood.

Genuine article

The genuine article can be admired at 1406 N. Havenhurst: Mi Casa, a two-story apartment building with balconies and twin patios imported *in toto* from Ronda, Spain, in 1926 and then reassembled.

When in the period between World War I and World War II a native Southern California style began to appear, it was ironically based on variations of such Mediterranean precedents as Italian villas and Andalusian farmhouses.

Whitley Heights was a project of H. J. Whitley, who sent his architect to Italy to study hilltop villages so that his community could be designed in a similar style. It was a popular enclave for showbiz personalities immediately before the development of Beverly Hills. Chateau Marmont, a combination of Norman and Moorish styles, was designed in 1927 by architect Arnold A. Weitzman, who had been sent to France to absorb European grandeur.

When a panel of well-known and local architects discussed "LA Architecture Comes of Age," the moderator described Los Angeles as "the most heterogeneous city in the world," and

THE ARCHITECT WHO DEFIES GRAVITY

Perhaps the most prestigious prize in the world of architecture, the Pritzker medal is presented to the year's laureate, inscribed on the reverse side with the words, "*firmness, commodity and delight.*"

Santa Monica-based Thom Mayne, the 2005 winner, has been a controversial architect since losing his first teaching job in the late 1960s. He said himself, "Architecture is an endurance sport. You put your mind to it, and stay with it for 30 years, and you're just getting started ..."

Mayne has the sculptor's love of thrilling, dynamic balance, of structures that appear precarious or gravity-defying. His projects play with the boundaries between the

interior and the exterior, intentionally blurring borders and even walls. Mayne's Caltrans District 7 Headquarters, near the Civic Center in downtown LA, changes its appearance with the light. In bright sunshine, the walls are sheer and windowless; as dusk falls, they seem to fade and the building becomes transparent. After dark the four lower floors are luminescent. "Controlled irregularity," is how Mayne likes to describe the tensions and ambiguities that are such features of his work. Pritzker juror Frank Gehry, himself the winner of the 1989 laureate, said of Mayne's work that, "He continues to explore and search for new ways to make buildings useable and exciting."

concluded that the city's architecture baffled easy definition. "It is at once sophisticated and tasteless, elitist and populist, glamorous and trashy," summarized the *Los Angeles Times*. "The buildings we see around us make up a crazy quilt of styles and mannerisms that somehow forms a whole cloth."

These are much in evidence in the work of Los Angeles' newest architectural award-winner, Thom Mayne, the winner of the 2005 Pritzer Prize *(see page 62)*. He founded his firm, Santa Monica-based Morphosis, in 1972 with an aim to "surpass the bounds of traditional forms and materials" and to go "beyond the limits of modernism and postmodernism."

Sepulveda Pass between Sunset Boulevard and the San Diego Freeway. Opened in 1997, the project had enthused Meier with its potential – breathtaking views on all sides and "the clear, golden California light, which to an Easterner like me is nothing less than intoxicating." Many of his ideas arose from the site itself – "its light, its landscape, its topography. I wanted to see the light flooding through openings on walls, casting crisp delicious shadows. I wanted to see structures set against that brilliant blue sky of Southern California. When I thought of buildings emerging out of the native chaparral, out of the rough hillside, I kept recalling the whitewashed walls of Spanish Colonial villages

Eternal adolescence

"I'd hate to say that LA has come of age or ever will," says Cesar Pelli, architect of one of the West Side's better-known landmarks, the Pacific Design Center. "The city's eternal adolescence has given our designers a rare freedom to experiment, free of the burdens of a false maturity."

Another panelist at that same discussion, Richard Meier, was responsible for one of the most expensive experiments – the highly praised Getty Center *(see pages 148–9)*, dominating a 110-acre (45-hectare) hilltop site in the

strung along a hillside or the thick-walled orderly presence of Hadrian's Villa…"

For Meier – a winner of the Pritzker Prize in 1985 – the state was new territory but its history a familiar one. "To me the architects who understood better than anyone what it was like to build in Southern California," he says, "were Richard Neutra, Frank Lloyd Wright and Rudolph Schindler. They realized that a truly Californian architecture did not necessarily consist of stucco and red tiles. To them, building in Southern California required structures that embodied qualities of light and of openness. I hope the Getty Center in some way rekindles their spirit." ❏

LEFT: Crossroads of the World, built in 1936.
ABOVE: Frank Gehry's Walt Disney Concert Hall.

PLACES

A detailed guide to Los Angeles, with the principal sites clearly cross-referenced by number to the maps

Los Angeles is such a huge, sprawling city that few of its residents could claim to know it well. Somebody who lives in Bel Air or Silverlake would rarely find a pressing need to investigate Boyle Heights or Baldwin Hills, and denizens of Hollywood – a somewhat amorphous concept anyway – rarely see the need to go anywhere else at all. Indisputably, there are native Californians who have lived here all their lives and have never been Downtown, except perhaps for a visit to the new Walt Disney Concert Hall. This is not a town that encourages neighborhood awareness – at least not of other neighborhoods.

When Los Angelenos leave the self-sufficiency of their homes, they step into their cars and travel long distances (or at least to the supermarket around the corner); walking is rarely an option they would choose. And when they do go from one place to another they seldom explore communities along the way, preferring to zoom past on the increasingly busy freeway. It is the destination that always matters, not the journey.

So it is not at all inconceivable that an adventurous visitor might end up with a more intimate knowledge of this city than many of its natives, especially anyone from a different tradition who feels there is nothing shameful about being on foot (aided, occasionally, by lengthy rides on local buses or the Metro).

And certainly there is much to see. The stores along glittering Rodeo drive; the beautiful people in the watering holes of West Hollywood; the treasures of the Getty Center and the Getty Villa. And contrary to myth, an automobile can be a luxury, not an absolute necessity. Downtown, for example, is totally unsuitable for visitors' cars: traffic is horrendous, and parking is difficult and expensive. Nor is a car needed in Beverly Hills, Hollywood, West Hollywood, Santa Monica or Venice, although it is faster to reach these places by driving than on the bus. You can, however, get to Universal Studios and Pasadena on the Metro.

Where a car is helpful, and in some cases indispensable, is for exploring the canyons and beaches beyond Hollywood: Malibu, Griffith Park, the western extremities of Sunset Boulevard and such off-the-beaten track attractions as Watts Towers, the Southwest Museum, Mulholland Drive and, of course, the coastal communities of the sunny South Bay. ❏

PRECEDING PAGES: doing what California girls do so well – riding around in their cute convertible; doing what they rarely do – nuns enjoying a day on Santa Monica Pier.
LEFT: two Hollywood icons: "Charlie Chaplin" and Grauman's Chinese Theatre.

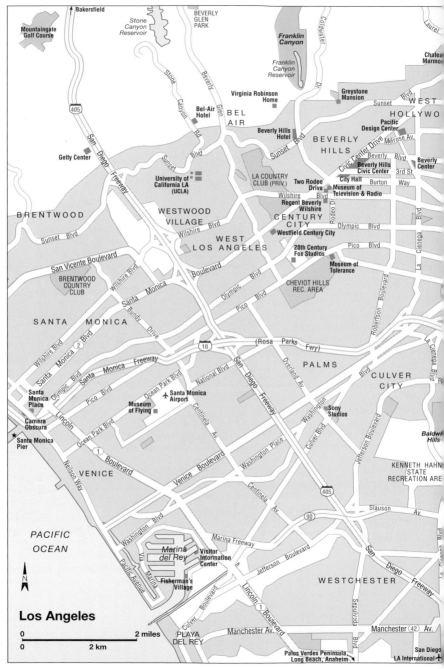

Los Angeles

| 0 | | 2 miles |
| 0 | 2 km | |

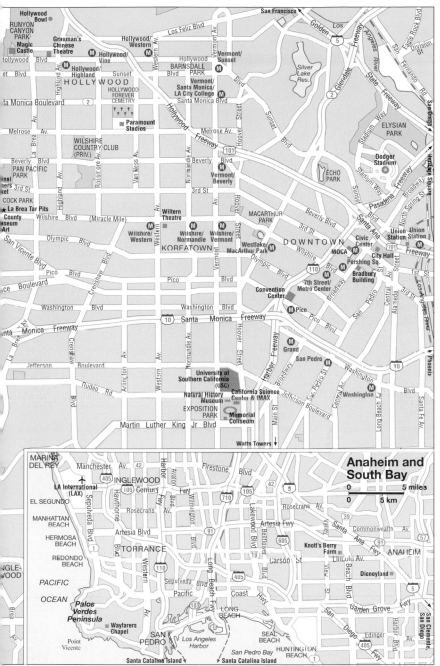

DOWNTOWN

A recent revival lures history buffs, music lovers, sports spectators and fashion plates to LA's oldest neighborhood

Acontemporary nickname for Los Angeles is "El Pueblo," and the name is based on a piece of history that began here in Downtown. Founded by governor Felipe de Neve of the Mexican state of California in 1781, El Pueblo de Nuestra Señora de la Reina de los Angeles del Río de Porciùncula was at first just a dusty plaza west of the Los Angeles River.

It was settled by 11 families, a mix of Spaniards, blacks, Indians and *mestizos*. They built adobe huts around the central square, which they then used as a meeting place and roped off with rawhide cord for Sunday bullfights and occasional horseraces. Not a trace of the original plaza remains, unfortunately; the site is marked by a parking lot.

Olvera Street

Today, the city's origins are commemorated in **Olvera Street ❶** (once Wine Street), a block-long stretch that many Latinos refer to as La Placita Olvera and which is collectively known as **El Pueblo de Los Angeles Historic Monument ❷** (tel: 213-628 1274). Open until late in the evening, it contains 27 historic buildings and a traditional Mexican-style plaza, where visitors can shop for handcrafted Mexican wares, watch as craftsmen make

jewelry and papier-mâché animals, sample cactus candy or native Mexican dishes from numerous *puestos* (stands) or dine on taquitos, tacos and enchiladas at the popular outdoor cafés. On most weekends, you will see strolling mariachis and perhaps performances by Aztec Indians and folkloric dancing. There are free walking tours given by Las Angelitas (available Tues–Sat 10am–noon). For more information, stop by the **Sepulveda House**, which serves as the visitor center.

Map on pages 74–5

LEFT:
Downtown's Westin Bonadventure Hotel.
BELOW: order great dim sum here.

Exposition Park

0   500 yds
0   500 m

55 Mount St Mary's College
56 St Vincent de Paul
57 Shrine Auditorium
58 University of Southern California
59 United University Church
60 Von KleinSmid Center
60 Doheny Memorial Library
61 Hancock Memorial Museum
62 Fisher Gallery
63 Memorial Coliseum
64 Natural History Museum
65 California Science Center & IMAX
66 African-American Museum

University Village
Jefferson Boulevard
Exposition Boulevard
ROSE GARDEN
Mercado la Ploma
EXPOSITION PARK
Memorial Coliseum
Swimming Stadium
Memorial Sports Arena
Martin Luther King Junior Boulevard

Hollywood, Universal City
Dodger Stadium
Hollywood Freeway
Pasadena Fwy
Sunset Boulevard
Temple Street
Beverly Boulevard
Beaudry Avenue

1 Cathedral of Our Lady of the Angels
Ahmanson Theatre
Department of Water and Power
18 Music Center
Dorothy Chandler Pavilion
Hall of Administration
CIVIC CENTER
14 County Courthouse
Civic Center M
State Offices
LA Times

Promenade Towers & Bunker Towers
19 Walt Disney Concert Hall
BUNKER HILL
Los Angeles World Trade Center
Union Bank Plaza 33
Westin Bonaventure Hotel 35
Wells Fargo History Museum 22
20 Museum of Contemporary Art (MOCA)
21 California Plaza
23 Angels Flight
24 Million Dollar Theater
26 Bradbury Building
27 BIDDY MASON PARK
Ronald Reagan State Building

Jonathan Club
Citibank Center 34
City National Plaza 36
38 US Bank Tower
Central Library 37
Millennium Biltmore Hotel 39
25 Grand Central Market
Subway Terminal Building
Junipero Serra State Building

Wilshire Grand 42
Visitor Information Center
43
The Standard Downtown
44 Fine Arts Building
Univ. Club
Los Angeles Conservancy
Pershing Square 40
International Jewelry Center

7th + Fig @ Ernst & Young Plaza 45
777 Tower
46 7th Street Metro Center M
Macy's Plaza
Hyatt Regency Hotel
One Wilshire Building
Oviatt Building
M Pershing Square
JEWELRY DISTRICT
Roxie Theatre
Cameo Theater
Arcade Theater

Original Pantry Cafe
First Methodist
Los Angeles Athletic Club
Jewelry Mart 41
28 Los Angeles Theatre
Palace Theatre
Pacific Coast Stock Exchange

l.a. live (under construction)
GRAND HOPE PARK
49
Fashion Institute of Design & Merchandising
State Theatre
HISTORIC CORE
29 Tower Theatre
FLOWER DISTRICT
53

47 Los Angeles Convention Center
48 Staples Center
Museum of Neon Art (MONA) 50
51
Eastern Columbia Building
30 Orpheum Theatre
LA Flower Market

Trinity Methodist
Ed Ruscha Monument
31 United Artists' Theatre
California Market Center 52
FASHION DISTRICT

Pico M
52
Mayan Theatre
Herald-Examiner Building
54 African American Firefighters Museum

30th Street
31st Place
University of Southern California
Shrine Auditorium 57
Hoover Street
Figueroa Street
Flower Street
Harbor Freeway 110
Rose Garden
Exposition Park
Pico Boulevard
Olympic Boulevard
Wilshire Blvd
6th Street
7th Street
8th
9th
Broadway
Spring Street
Main Street
Los Angeles Street

Downtown

0   500 yds

0   500 m

Child bride

On Olvera Street is the oldest house in Los Angeles, the **Avila Adobe** (constructed in 1818). Apart from being concrete-reinforced after the 1922 earthquake, the house is as it was left by Francisco Abela's widow, Encarnacion, who died here in 1855. Married at 15, she was his second wife, and the family lived in a style befitting the prosperous rancher. Opposite, the **Pelanconi Building** (*circa* 1853), the oldest brick house in the city, is now an attractive sidewalk restaurant, La Golondrina, where diners are serenaded by strolling mariachis, as at the nearby El Pasco de la Plaza.

The **Plaza Church**, built in 1818, always seems crowded, being the spiritual center of the Latino community. The church is famous for its annual Easter ceremony, to which children from miles away bring their beribboned pets to be blessed.

The **Pico House**, constructed in 1869, is the city's first three-story building and was once its finest hotel, with 82 bedrooms, 21 parlors, two interior courtyards and a French restaurant. Named after the last Mexican governor of California, Pio Pico, who lost the home after foreclosure proceedings in 1880, it shares a wall with the city's first playhouse, the **Merced Theatre**, which originally sheltered the hotel's bar and billiard saloon and was later converted into a department store.

Other notable structures include the **Hellman Building** (1900), a Chinese store and lodging house that replaced Pico's former home, and the **Garnier Building** (1890), home of the **Chinese American Museum** (tel: 213-485 8484; open Tues–Sun 10am–3pm; charge), which features art exhibits, photographic essays and personal stories that illuminate the historic journey of Chinese immigrants in America. Also on this block is the restored

Map on pages 74–5

The Original Pantry has been a landmark for nearly six decades (see page 83)

Old Plaza Firehouse, which served the area until 1897 and houses fire-fighting equipment, a horse-drawn engine and a photo of Blackie, the city's last fire horse (who passed away in 1939).

LA's Grand Central

East of Main Street, the spectacularly lavish **Union Station ④** – all black marble, mahogany, inlaid tiles and enormous leather seats – should be seen if only as a reminder of how splendid rail travel once could be. Even today, Union Station is often used as a backdrop in 1930s-era movies filmed around Downtown.

Built with a 135-ft (41-meter) high tower, arched corridors, 52-ft (16-meter) high ceilings and literally acres of space, the station opened in May 1939 and once served almost a million passengers every day. It is maintained by Amtrak, which operates trains to other parts of California every day. The city's subway system begins at Union Station with the Metro Red Line, while the Gold Line from Pasadena ends here.

Just across Alameda from Union Station is **Philippe the Original ⑤**, a funky, sawdust-on-the-floor landmark *(see page 83)*.

Chinatown

The Southern Pacific reached Los Angeles in 1876, following a trail hacked out by thousands of Chinese laborers across the Tehachapi Mountains. A decade later, when the lines of the Atchison, Topeka & Santa Fe were completed, many of the Chinese filtered down into the city, joining immigrants who had arrived during the 1840s Gold Rush. It was this sizeable colony who were evicted when the ground was cleared for Union Station in 1933, and many settled farther north.

The area called New Chinatown officially opened in 1938 between Spring and Hill streets. Here, and on Broadway north of Ord Street is LA's contemporary **Chinatown ⑥**. Chinese banks, churches, vegetable markets, stores filled with squawking poultry or captive fish, and supermarkets with barely an English label to be seen, manage to absorb seemingly endless streams of tourists without ever losing the distinctive rural ambience.

Founded in 1975, the **Chinatown Heritage & Visitors Center ⑦** (411 Bernard Street, tel: 323-222 0856) explores the history of the Chinese in Southern California and provides free self-guided tour maps.

Little Tokyo

Radiating from the intersection of San Pedro and 2nd streets, **Little Tokyo ⑧** has a more sterile appearance but is unmistakably Japanese. Most of it was rebuilt after World War II, following the return of most of the 110,000 Japanese who had been relocated to internment camps in the hysteria after Pearl Harbor. About 80,000 people – roughly one quarter of the Japanese residents in the US – live in this area.

Downtown is a good place to shop for inexpensive and whimsical souvenirs.

BELOW: off-duty at the Japanese-American festival in Little Tokyo.

The most visible landmark of Little Tokyo is the lavish **New Otani Hotel** ❾ (120 S. Los Angeles Street), topped off by the **Japanese Garden**, a rooftop oasis by the famed landscape architect Sentaru Iwaki, who modeled it after a 400-year-old garden in Tokyo. Southeast of the Otani is the **Japanese Village Plaza** ❿, a pristine mall lined with massive boulders, performance areas and the **Koyasan Buddhist Temple**. More interesting, though, is to take a walk through the gardens of the adjoining high rise and admire the attractive **Higashi Honganji Buddhist Temple**, with its distinctive overhanging tiled roof.

The major Japanese influx into the Los Angeles area was at the beginning of the 20th century when, unable to acquire or afford fertile land, they turned to making the deserts bloom, as in the now-lush Imperial Valley. A moving tribute to these impressive skills can be seen in calligraphic tiles on a wall opposite the **Japanese American Cultural & Community Center** ⓫ at San Pedro and 3rd (tel: 213-628 2725; open Mon–Fri 9am–6pm). The center has presented traditional Japanese performances and visual art displays, from Kabuki theater to 6th-century costumes, for over 20 years.

Two blocks farther north, the **Japanese American National Museum** ⓬ on 1st Street (tel: 213-625 0414; open Tues–Sun 10am–5pm, until 8pm on Thur; charge) is a stunning structure and the only museum in the country dedicated to sharing the experiences of Japanese-Americans. The museum's collections and resources are displayed through walking tours and crafts classes, as well as photographic and art exhibits.

Opposite is **MOCA at the Geffen Contemporary** ⓭ (152 N. Central Avenue, tel: 213-626 6222; open Thur–Mon 11am–5pm, until 8pm

Thur, until 6pm Sat–Sun; charge), a satellite of the Museum of Contemporary Art on Grand Avenue. Fashioned by famed local architect Frank Gehry from a former police-car garage, this building now stages MOCA's largest exhibitions.

Civic Center

The governing center of Los Angeles eventually moved from the El Pueblo area to a stretch of land south of Highway 101. By the 1930s, a group of courthouses, law libraries and office buildings, including the block-long *Los Angeles Times Building*, had formed the city's **Civic Center** ⓮ area, near to which there is a convenient stop on the Metro Red Line.

The sunken **Los Angeles Mall** ⓯ is bedecked with waterfalls and palm trees around a central area of tables and fast-food restaurants. Now somewhat shabby, the mall, which sits on the site of what was once among the world's most prolific oil wells, includes a post office and several shops. Escalators at the mall's western end lead up to **City Hall** ⓰

Map on pages 74–5

TIP

LA Artcore, a contemporary art coalition, has two Downtown-area spaces – the Union Center for the Arts (120 Judge John Aiso Street) and the Brewery Annex (650 S. Avenue 21).

BELOW: Union Station opened in 1939 and is still serviced by trains.

(200 N. Spring Street), which, when it replaced the city's second one in 1928, was the tallest building in Los Angeles. Topped by the beacon that was installed to celebrate Charles Lindbergh's flight across the Atlantic, City Hall was constructed from mortar that included sand from each California county and water from each of the state's 21 missions.

Connecting City Hall (which appeared as the *Daily Planet* building in TV's *Superman* series) with its eastern annex is a third-floor bridge. The better view, however, is from the 26th-floor balcony, offering a wide-sweeping panorama.

West of the Civic Center are several key cultural institutions, including the magnificent **Cathedral of Our Lady of the Angels** ⓱ (555 W. Temple Street, tel: 213-680 5200), with its spacious plaza, Mission-style colonnades, lush gardens and underground stained-glass windows. South of Temple is the marble-and-black-glass **Music Center** ⓲ (135 N. Grand Avenue, tel: 213-972 7211). Encompassing the Peace on Earth fountain, Ahmanson Theatre,

Cycling past one of Downtown's many outdoor sculptures.

Mark Taper Forum and Dorothy Chandler Pavilion, the center is home to several performing arts companies, including the Los Angeles Opera, Los Angeles Master Chorale and Center Theatre Group. The Philharmonic's new home is the long awaited and visually-stunning **Walt Disney Concert Hall** ⓳ (151 S. Grand Avenue, tel: 213-972 7282; www.laphil.com), a Frank Gehry-designed explosion of metallic curves, that also houses an elegant restaurant. Audio tours are available.

This entire area is in the throes of massive transformation, due for completion by 2011. The **Grand Avenue Development** is a $1.2 billion project designed by, among others, Los Angeles-based Pritzer Prize winners Frank Gehry and Thom Mayne to turn the somewhat sterile Downtown area into a place to live, dine, shop and play. Critical to the developments is a 16-acre (6.5-hectare) park that will connect City Hall with the Music Center.

Two blocks south of the Disney Concert Hall is the **Museum of Contemporary Art** (MOCA) ⓴ (tel: 213-626 6222; open Thur–Mon 11am–5pm, until 8pm Thur, until 6pm Sat–Sun; charge), a distinctive brick-red, geometric building designed by well-known Japanese architect Arata Isozaki. Currently, it houses one of America's premier collections of post-1940 American and European art, from Jackson Pollock's abstract expressionism to Andy Warhol's pop art.

Farther south is the **California Plaza** ㉑ and the colored dancing fountains of the adjacent **Water Court**. Directly opposite stands the Wells Fargo Center, with the engaging **Wells Fargo History Museum** ㉒ (tel: 213-253 7166; open Mon–Fri 9am–5pm). Exhibits like a 19th-century stagecoach, a re-created telegraph agent's office, early coins, old travelers' checks and min-

ing equipment collectively evoke the atmosphere of the Gold-Rush days. On the other side of California Plaza is **Angels Flight** , the restored 1901 funicular railway. Unfortunately, after a fatal accident in 2001, the attraction remains closed.

The Historic Core

The busiest street in Downtown, **Broadway** ②, with its jangle of fast-food counters, jewelry shops and amusement arcades, is still the nearest the neighborhood gets to a lively, bustling street scene. Broadway is intensely Latino in style, as a visit to the festive, always-crowded **Grand Central Market** ② (317 S. Broadway) will confirm. Hot chilis, cheap Mexican dishes, day-old pastries, produce sacks, fish and floral bouquets – these and hundreds of other items are stacked under a plethora of bilingual neon signs.

The Grand Central Market's owner, Ira Yellin, worked with architect Brenda Levin, who designed its stylish neon signs, to renovate both the market and the adjoining **Million Dollar Theater** ②, a paragon of el-

egance when it was opened by the showman Sid Grauman in 1918. Across the street is the wonderful **Bradbury Building** ②, a beautifully preserved showcase of wrought-iron balconies, old-fashioned hydraulic elevators and elegant stairways surrounding a skylight-illuminated atrium. Designed by novice architect George H. Wyman for a mining mogul in 1893, it was once occupied by law firms but in recent years has mostly been rented out for moviemaking, notably as Philip Marlowe's "Hollywood office" in the 1969 adaptation of Raymond Chandler's *The Little Sister* and in the dark, futuristic film *Blade Runner* (1982).

Many other Downtown sites are popular with filmmakers but, in the old days, most people came here to see movies and rowdy vaudeville shows. Between 5th and 6th streets stand two of the oldest movie palaces: the tiny **Cameo Theater**, which opened in 1910 as a nickelodeon, the type of place from which many early movie moguls made their fortunes, and the **Arcade**

Map on pages 74–5

TIP

The LA Conservancy (tel: 213-623 2489) presents films in Broadway's Orpheum Theatre every summer and offers walking tours of City Hall, Union Station, Little Tokyo and the Historic Core.

BELOW: members of the Los Angeles Philharmonic take a bow at their new home, the Walt Disney Concert Hall.

Silent movies are sometimes shown at the Orpheum, with music provided by a Wurlitzer organ.

Theater, built by Alexander Pantages, who had grown rich in Alaska producing shows popular with entertainment-starved goldminers.

Even more splendid is the **Los Angeles Theatre** ㉘ (615 S. Broadway), hurriedly completed by designer S. Charles Lee for the 1931 premiere of Charlie Chaplin's *City Lights*. The last of the great Downtown movie palaces, it once included an art gallery, a mahogany-paneled ballroom, a fountain and a children's playroom. Two blocks south, the **Tower Theatre** ㉙, the first to be designed specifically for the new talkies, was an earlier Lee creation, modeled after the lobby of the Paris Opera House.

Since it was paintakingly restored, glamorous movie and media events have returned to the lovely **Orpheum Theatre** ㉚ (842 S. Broadway). The **United Artists' Theatre** ㉛ (933 S. Broadway), commissioned in 1927 by film stars Mary Pickford and Douglas Fairbanks, Jr, was reminiscent of a European castle. Marilyn Monroe appeared at the **Mayan Theatre** ㉜

(1038 S. Hill Street) – described as "somewhere between a pre-Columbian temple and a wedding cake iced by a madman" – which opened in 1927 with Anita Loos' *Gentlemen Prefer Blondes*. Today, it is a popular nightclub, The Mayan.

Financial District

West of the historic core lies a newer part of Downtown, the **Financial District**, which contains impressive skyscrapers like the **Union Bank Plaza** ㉝ and **Citibank Center** ㉞, named for the companies that they now house.

The **Westin Bonaventure Hotel** ㉟ (404 S. Figueroa Street), with its four futuristic-looking cylindrical glass towers, is a Downtown showpiece popular with moviemakers (*True Lies*; *In the Line of Fire*). Designed by John Portman & Associates, its interior is both amusing and confusing, with mini-lounges at different levels. A glass elevator ascends to the **BonaVista Lounge** *(see page 83)*, the revolving cocktail lounge on the 34th floor, for drinks and panoramic views of the city.

Far below, from the skybridges that connect the hotel to its neighboring skyscrapers, Downtown's landmark buildings look more impressive than ever. Dotted among the waterfalls, escalators and 30-ft (9-meter) high palm trees of the adjoining **City National Plaza** ㊱ are enormous sculptures by Mark di Suvero, Robert Rauschenberg, Frank Stella, Bruce Nauman and Michael Heizer. Underneath the twin towers of the complex is a subterranean shopping center.

East of the plaza is the stylish **Los Angeles Central Library** ㊲ (630 W. 5th Street, tel: 213-228 7000), a 1926 creation of architect Bertram Goodhue. Although it was restored after the damage from a catastrophic fire in 1986, some hints of its former beaux arts grandeur can still be

gleaned from the surviving blue-tiled, pyramid-shaped tower. Just opposite stands the 73-story **US Bank Tower** ❸❽, designed by I.M. Pei & Partners. A contender for the tallest building in the West, it was nicknamed the **Library Tower** because it used the air rights of the library during construction in exchange for helping to fund the renovation of the bibliotech. Curving around the west side of the tower, the dramatic **Bunker Hill Steps** ascend the hill from 5th to Hope streets.

The **Millennium Biltmore Hotel** ❸❾ (506 S. Grand Avenue) opened with a star-studded party in 1923. The 1,000 rooms made it at the time the largest hotel in the West, with a lobby festooned with frescoes, murals and a remarkable cherub-and-cloud ceiling that evokes 14th-century Italy to this day. Featured in many films, the Biltmore has held a special place in Hollywood's history since 1927, when MGM's art director Cedric Gibbons first sketched the then-unnamed Oscar statue (*see page 39*) on his hotel napkin. A picture inside the hotel depicts attendees at the 1937 Academy Awards.

One block east along 5th Street, the 1932 statue of Beethoven, erected by musicians from the Philharmonic in garishly remodeled **Pershing Square** ❹❶, is a reminder that a century ago the plaza became an upscale alternative to the fast-declining Olvera Street neighborhood. In 2005, Pershing Square added WiFi access, so that visitors sitting in the square can work on their laptops.

At Pershing Square's southeast corner, the **Jewelry Mart** ❹❶ was once a Pantages theater, a venue that combined films with vaudeville shows. Nine years after the opening, tycoon Alexander Pantages was falsely accused of raping a 17-year old female usher, and served two years in jail before being acquitted

on appeal in 1931. Just behind the Jewelry Mart, off 7th Street, is a little-noticed alley called **St Vincent's Court**, an appealing dead-end of shops and eateries. Despite the tow-away signs, it would seem a tempting spot to park, but it also happens to be a popular place for parking enforcement officers.

A few blocks west of the Jewelry District, near the **Wilshire Grand** ❹❷ hotel, which contains four distinct restaurants and a tiki bar, is the **Los Angeles Visitor Information Center** ❹❸ (685 S. Figueroa Street, tel: 213-689 8822; open Mon–Fri 9am–5pm), a repository of information about local hotels, restaurants and activities. If you cross the street and walk half a block, you'll discover the **Fine Arts Building** ❹❹ (811 W. 7th). Erected in 1936, the building has a medieval-style lobby with 15 chandeliers and a tiled fountain, but the artists' studios were long ago converted to offices. South along Figueroa is **7th + Fig @ Ernst & Young Plaza** ❹❺, a stylish mall with a sunken courtyard among palm trees three storys high, shading

Map on pages 74–5

The Museum of Neon Art (MONA).

BELOW: soaking up the rays, surrounded by skyscrapers.

Maps on pages 74–5, 86

Soulful singer at Downtown's Grand Avenue Festival.

BELOW: dancers at the African Marketplace.

Arnie Morton's Steakhouse, and the stalwart Robinsons-May department store. Among the interesting artwork enlivening the plaza is a stooping bronze businessman. Nearby, the stepped, white tower of the **777 Tower** ④⑥ was created by Argentine-born Cesar Pelli, who was also responsible for the distinctive Pacific Design Center in West Hollywood *(see page 123).*

Sports and entertainment

Straight down Figueroa Street is another neighborhood, currently dominated by the **Los Angeles Convention Center** ④⑦ and the gleaming **Staples Center** ④⑧ sports complex. Staples Center is home to LA's beloved Lakers (basketball), with its legion of movie-star fans; the lower profile Clippers (also basketball); and the Kings (hockey). In late 2005, ground was broken adjacent to Staples Center for a $4.2 billion sports and entertainment district known as **l.a.live** ④⑨. Over the next 10 years, new businesses, including a Grammy Museum with a permanent display of music genres; a tow-

ering Hilton Hotel; and an ESPN sports studio will be constructed on the site. The first phase will be the completion of the 7,100-seat Nokia Theatre, scheduled to open in 2007.

Just east of this new development is the **Museum of Neon Art (MONA)** ⑤⓪ (501 W. Olympic Boulevard, tel: 213-489 9918; open Wed–Sat 11am–5pm, Sun noon–5pm; charge), a Downtown institution dedicated to the art of electric and kinetic media, from neon signs to glowing, kaleidoscopic sculptures. Behind the museum lies the charming **Grand Hope Park** ⑤①, whose centerpiece is a bougainvillea-lined Poet's Walk.

Five blocks east of the park, the city's expansive **Fashion District** stretches for roughly 90 blocks. The apparel shops, textile showrooms and accessory boutiques are bordered by 7th Street, San Pedro Street, Main Street and the 10 freeway. The centerpiece is the **California Market Center (CMC)** ⑤② at Main and 9th (tel: 213-630 3600), a wholesale buyer's mart that houses hundreds of clothing manufacturers and occasionally opens to the public for "super sample sales."

Northeast of the CMC is the **Los Angeles Flower District** ⑤③ (open Mon–Sat 8am–noon, open at 6am Tues, Thur, Sat; charge), two enormous white buildings at 7th and Wall streets, where hundreds of growers service gardeners, landscape artists and flower lovers. The wholesale produce market, several blocks to the east, keeps similar hours.

South of these markets is another museum of note, the **African American Firefighter Museum** ⑤④ (1401 S. Central Avenue, tel: 213-744 1730; open Sun 1–4pm, Tues and Thur 10am–2pm; free). In a formerly segregated firehouse, the 1913 structure displays an array of vintage engines, uniforms, badges, helmets and photographs. ❑

RESTAURANTS, BARS & CAFES

Restaurants

Cafe Pinot
700 W. 5th Street. Tel: 213-239 6500. Open: L and D Mon–Fri, D only Sat–Sun. $$$

Not far from the Walt Disney Concert Hall, this elegant brasserie is a preferred pre-concert destination. Romantic garden seating and dramatic skyline views complement the decor and chef Mark Gold's sophisticated take on classic California cuisine.

Ciudad
445 S. Figueroa Street. Tel: 213-486 5171. Open: L and D Mon–Fri, D only Sat–Sun. $$$

Famed culinary partners Mary Sue Milliken and Susan Feniger present traditional dishes and innovative cuisine from places as far afield as Spain, South America, Cuba and Guatemala. Latin-themed murals highlight the jazzy Downtown space and underscore such inspired creations as Peruvian *ceviche*, Argentine *empanadas* and Brazilian *moqueca*.

Clifton's Cafeteria
648 S. Broadway. Tel: 213-627 1673. Open: B, L and D daily. $

Opened in 1935 by Clifford Clinton and run by his family ever since, this cafeteria continues to live by its motto: "Dine free unless delighted."

Engine Co. No. 28
644 S. Figueroa Street. Tel: 213-624 6996. Open: L and D Mon–Fri, D only Sat–Sun. $$

This restored 1912 firehouse still retains its early 20th-century charm. The classic American cuisine, inspired by regional cooking from around the country, suits the historic landmark.

The Original Pantry Cafe
877 S. Figueroa Street. Tel: 213-972 9279. Open: 24 hours daily. $

A true Downtown landmark for nearly six decades, this 1950s-style diner is currently owned by the former mayor of Los Angeles, Richard Riordan, who upholds his motto "Never closed. Never without a customer."

Philippe the Original
1001 N. Alameda Street. Tel: 213-628 3781. Open: B, L and D daily. $

A block north of stylish Union Station lies this busy, low-key eatery, known since 1908 for its famous French dip sandwiches.

Water Grill
544 S. Grand Avenue. Tel: 213-891 0900. Open: L and D Mon–Fri, D only Sat–Sun. $$$$

Considered by many to be one of the finest seafood joints in Southern California, this sophisticated grill revises its menu often. On any given night, you might be treated to Dungeness and blue crab cake, tuna tartar with avocado or slow-steamed Alaskan halibut with artichokes and Kalamata olive purée. Reservations are strongly recommended.

Bars and Cafés

BonaVista Lounge
404 S. Figueroa Street, lures guests to the revolving top of the stylish Westin Bonaventure Hotel, where they can sip cocktails and view the city in all directions. Particularly spectacular at night.

Grand Avenue Sports Bar
506 S. Grand Avenue, is a contradiction – a lively, casual sports bar inside one of the most elegant hotels in town, the Biltmore.

The Standard Rooftop Bar
550 S. Flower Street, is retro minimalism at its most fun. Sexy patrons relax at the vivid red bar or nibble on salads and sandwiches at the 1960s-style tables on the rooftop patio.

PRICE CATEGORIES

Prices for a three-course dinner per person with half a bottle of wine:
$ = under $25
$$ = $25–40
$$$ = $40–60
$$$$ = more than $60

RIGHT: Ciudad has Latin-themed murals.

DOWNTOWN ENVIRONS

Beyond Downtown is a wealth of cultural and recreational sites, including Dodger Stadium, Heritage Square, Exposition Park and the Watts Towers – to name just a few

S ome of the oldest, most diverse ethnic cultural areas in Los Angeles are the neighborhoods and villages just outside the main Downtown area, beyond the rectangle bounded by the Santa Ana (101), Golden State (5), Santa Monica (10) and Pasadena (110) freeways.

To the south is the 125-year-old campus of the University of Southern California, and museums of art, science and culture. North of Chinatown, by the venerable home of the blue-and-white LA Dodgers baseball team, are some of LA's oldest communities. Historic adobes and Victorian homes lie east of the bone-dry Los Angeles River. In every direction are attractions worth exploring.

Around the campuses

About a half-mile southwest of I-10, at Figueroa Street and Adams Boulevard, spreads the lovely campus of **Mount St Mary's College 55**, a Catholic women's school that opened in 1962 on the historic Doheny Estate. **Chester Place**, which bisects the property, was once a private enclave of spacious Victorian mansions, including the gorgeous home of oil tycoon Edward Doheny, now offices for the college communications and alumnae relations departments. Doheny also built the nearby eye-catching dome and

ornate bell tower of **St Vincent de Paul 56** church.

Five blocks south, the Moroccan-style **Shrine Auditorium 57** dominates the corner of Royal Street and Jefferson Boulevard. A Hollywood landmark, this historic theater restaged the 1912 Democratic convention for Darryl Zanuck's 1950 flop *Wilson,* and was the setting for the ill-fated romance between Judy Garland and James Mason in the 1954 version of *A Star Is Born.* An early venue for the Oscars, the Shrine

Map on pages 74–5

LEFT:
Dodger Stadium.
BELOW:
USC's Von KleinSmid
Center (VKC).

Founded in 1929 with the help of the Academy of Motion Picture Arts and Sciences, USC's School of Cinema-Television is the oldest film school in the US. Alumni include film directors George Lucas and Ron Howard.

has also hosted the Grammys, the Emmys and other awards shows.

Across Jefferson Boulevard is the tree-shaded campus of the **University of Southern California (USC)** 58, the oldest private research university in the West. An informative 50-minute, walking tour (tel: 213-740 6605; available on the hour Mon–Fri 10am–3pm; free) is available by reservation. *The Graduate* (1967) and *Legally Blonde* (2001) were among the films shot here, and famous alumni include directors George Lucas and Ron Howard.

Virtual museum

Structures on campus of particular interest include **Bovard Tower** and the futuristic-looking **Von Klein-Smid Center (VKC)**. The Romanesque **United University Church** 59 (817 W. 34th Street), erected in 1931, serves as an inclusive house of worship, a concert venue and a much-used set for USC film students.

Two blocks down Trousdale Parkway, the **Doheny Memorial Library** 60 was USC's first free-standing library when it was dedicated to university trustee and alumnus Edward L. Doheny Jr in 1932. Across Childs Way, in the Allan Hancock Foundation Building, is the **Hancock Memorial Museum** 61 (tel: 213-740 5144; open by appointment only), with four exquisite rooms of marble, oak, stained glass and crystal, all salvaged from the Hancock mansion in 1939 as a memorial to Hancock's mother.

Just west, the **Fisher Gallery** 62 (823 Exposition Boulevard, tel: 213-740 4561; open Tues–Sat noon–5pm; free) was Los Angeles' first fine-art museum. Today, this highly unusual gallery focuses on yesterday as well as tomorrow – some of the Fisher's collections date back five centuries, but the museum also presents interactive programs as a test bed for the "virtual museum of the future."

Downtown Environs

Exposition Park

When Agricultural Park opened in 1880, it featured a racetrack that attracted the sporting crowd as well as the classier hookers from the red-light district on Alameda Street. Initially presenting camel races, the racetrack later became an auto course, where, in 1903, Barney Oldfield set a world speed record in his *No. 2 Bullet*. With USC's help, the city rehabilitated the park's reputation by forming Exposition Park in 1913. The **Memorial Coliseum** 63 hosted the Olympic Games in 1932 and again in 1984; today it dominates the park.

Exposition Park also offers a **sunken rose garden** and the **Natural History Museum** 64 (tel: 213-763 3466; open Mon–Fri 9.30am–5pm, Sat–Sun 10am–5pm; charge), which is undergoing massive renovation. The original 1913 building is being cleaned up, and a new extension is planned by 2009. Other Exposition Park highlights are the **California Science Center** 65 (tel: 213-744 7400; open daily 10am–5pm, free), which includes an IMAX Theater and an Air and Space Gallery. The

California African-American Museum 66 (tel: 213-744 7432; open Wed–Sat 10am–4pm; free) presents an eclectic collection of traditional African masks, 19th-century landscapes, vivid Haitian oil paintings and memorabilia from the singer Ella Fitzgerald's estate.

You might also enjoy the **Museum of African-American Art** (4005 Crenshaw Boulevard, tel: 323-294 7071; open Thur–Sat 11am–6pm, Sun noon–5pm; free) to the west.

Back toward Interstate 10 is one of the city's little-known landmarks, the intriguing **William Andrews Clark Memorial Library** (2520 Cimarron Street, tel: 323-731 8529). Built by the founder of the LA Philharmonic Orchestra as a memorial to his father – a Montana rancher, copper tycoon and US senator – and part of the library system for the University of California at Los Angeles (UCLA), the 1926 Italian Renaissance library has a vast collection of 16th and 17th-century volumes, as well as original editions of works by Chaucer, Shakespeare, Daniel Defoe and Oscar Wilde.

Map on pages 74–5

Billboards advertise the high-energy Latino music scene.

BELOW:
University of Southern California campus.

A museum chronicling the life of the late Ray Charles is scheduled to open in late 2007 on the South LA site of the legendary musician's recording studios.

Echo Park

Northwest of Downtown is Echo Park, one of the oldest neighborhoods in Los Angeles. Its namesake, the 33-acre (13-hectare) **Echo Park** includes swaying palm trees and the lotus-covered Echo Park Lake. It is ringed by sites like the cavernous, 5,300-seat **Angelus Temple** (1100 Glendale Boulevard), dedicated in the winter of 1923 as a backdrop for the fiery sermons of Canadian-born evangelist and pioneer religious broadcaster Aimee Semple Mcpherson.

Directly east of the park lies the city's first suburb, **Angelino Heights**, which contains a wealth of architectural landmarks, including Mission Revival homes, Craftsman bungalows, Streamline Moderne structures and turreted Queen Anne-style Victorian houses, many of which have been added to the register of National Historic Monuments.

Beyond Echo Park's eclectic mix of restaurants, shops and music clubs (like **The Echo**, 1822 Sunset Boulevard), is **Elysian Park** , the oldest park in the city and second in size

BELOW: Echo Park.

only to Griffith Park *(see page 184)*. Offering numerous hiking trails and picnic areas, the park is located just north of 56,000-seat **Dodger Stadium** (1000 Elysian Park Avenue, tel: 323-224 1448), the home ground of the Los Angeles Dodgers baseball team. Attracting an average of 2.7 million fans per season for more than four decades, the ballpark also provides commanding views of the skyscrapers of Downtown and, to the north, the hazy but lovely San Gabriel Mountains.

Celebrating the Southwest

Northeast of Downtown, near the **Mount Washington** district, old-time California is preserved with several distinctive sites. Chief among these is the hilltop Mission-style **Southwest Museum of the American Indian** (234 Museum Drive, tel: 323-221 2164; open Tues–Sun 10am–5pm; charge). With an absorbing collection of Navajo blankets, moccasins, weapons and Indian artifacts, including tightly-woven baskets meant for carrying water, the museum was founded in 1907 by Charles Fletcher Lummis, once a reporter for the *Los Angeles Times*.

The city's museum also houses exhibits about the native peoples of California, the Southwest, the Great Plains and the Pacific Northwest.

Nearby is the **Casa de Adobe** (4605 N. Figueroa Street), an authentically furnished replica of a pre-1850s Spanish-California rancho.

Not far south, Lummis built his home, **El Alisal** (200 E. Avenue 43, tel: 323-222 0546; open Fri–Sun noon–4pm), partly from granite and railroad ties, as his tribute to "primitive" styles. Among the luminaries he entertained at home was Will Rogers, who delighted guests with his rope tricks long before becoming famous. Today, El Alisal is the headquarters of the Historical Society of California and includes a museum about the life

Map on page 86

of Lummis. Nearby, in a grassy enclosure at the end of a dead-end street, is **Heritage Square** 73 (3800 Homer Street, tel: 323-225 2700), a city-sponsored restoration project that has tracked down and renovated many wonderful Victorian houses.

Way down south

Given the stories of riots and unchecked crime over the years, out-of-towners might be cautious about visiting the Latino and African-American communities south of Downtown, but there are a number of attractions that are well worth a visit – though preferably in the daytime.

Two such sites can even be appreciated without getting out of the car. The first, one of California's largest public murals, is in the industrial city of **Vernon** 74, once a wide-open community with around-the-clock gaming houses, saloons and brothels. Amid miles of drab factories, the outer walls of the **Farmer John** 75 meat-packing plant (3049 E. Vernon Avenue) distinguish themselves with a series of pastoral murals, begun in 1957 with Hollywood set decorator Les Grimes' *Hog Heaven*, depicting vivid green fields, bright red barns, several denim-clad farmers and, of course, the pigs that gave Farmer John his award-winning bacon, pork sausage and smoked ham.

Southwest of the murals is another of the city's most astonishing masterpieces: the **Watts Towers** 76, created between 1921 and 1955 by Simon Rodia, a penniless Italian tilesetter who patiently constructed the 17 lacy spires as an affectionate tribute to his adopted land, though he eventually died in poverty at the age of 86. It is now part of a state historic park (1765 E. 107th Street, tel: 213-847 4646), which includes an arts center.

Unappreciated for years, these innovative sculptures suffered repeated acts of vandalism and several demolition attempts by the city. Eventually the Watts Towers began to garner praise, and benefitted from extensive restoration before collectively becoming listed as a national historic landmark. Every September, a free, two-day musical event is held. Jazz is featured the first day and drumming the next. ❑

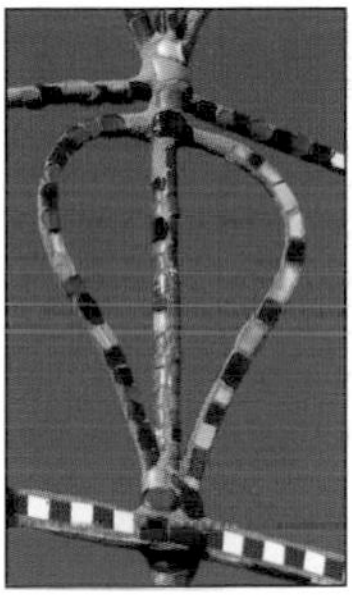

Materials used in the Watts Towers include tiles, pottery shards, broken bottles, pebbles and seashells.

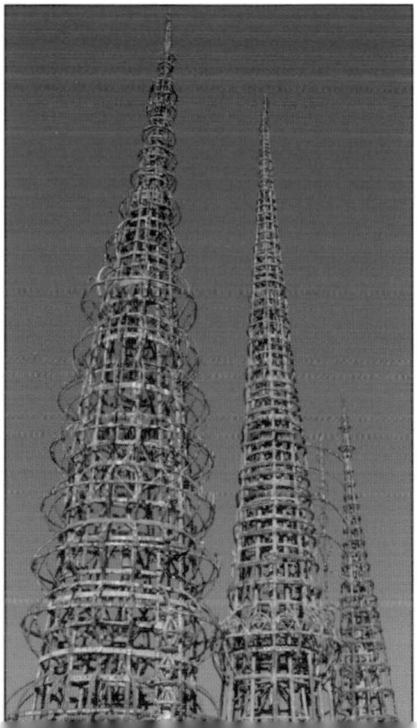

BELOW: Watts Towers.

RESTAURANTS

Chichen Itza
3655 S. Grand Avenue, No. C6. Tel: 213-741 1075. Open: B, L and D daily. $
USC students like this casual family operation in Mercado La Paloma, featuring cuisine from the Yucatan.

Pacific Dining Car
1310 W. 6th Street. Tel: 213-483 6000. Open: 24 hours daily. $$$$
When Fred and Grace Cook opened their railroad dining car in 1921, they may not have guessed how fine a restaurant it would, over the decades, become. Unusual for an elegant steakhouse, the door is open around the clock. Guests can enjoy breakfast, lunch, afternoon tea, dinner and late-night meals in a moody, old-fashioned setting.

Taix Restaurant
1911 Sunset Boulevard. Tel: 213-484 1265. Open: L and D daily. $$
For inexpensive cuisine and an extensive wine list, Echo Park residents love this bistro. Operated by the Taix family since 1927, diners can expect to be delighted by the abundant portions of French country cuisine.

Prices for a three-course dinner per person with half a bottle of wine:
$ = under $25, $$ = $25–40, $$$ = $40–60, $$$$ = more than $60

MIRACLE MILE AND BEYOND

Wilshire Boulevard's Miracle Mile beckons
shoppers and culture seekers with famous
museums, historic neighborhoods, nearby
design boutiques and art galleries

Like many major thoroughfares in Los Angeles, Wilshire Boulevard passes through several distinct neighborhoods, including Beverly Hills, but the stretch between Fairfax and La Brea avenues, otherwise known as the Miracle Mile, is probably the most well-known. Coined in the 1920s by developer A.W. Ross, this mile-long course became the world's first linear shopping district catering, with its wide store windows and large rear lots, to the emerging auto age.

Wilshire Boulevard

Long before that, however, the area was home to such historic figures as oil magnate Arthur Gilmore, Colonel Harrison Gray Otis, publisher of the *Los Angeles Times*; and Henry Gaylord Wilshire, the real-estate trailblazer whose name graces the road that he long ago envisioned.

As well as influential inhabitants, this intriguing area of Wilshire Boulevard is known for some excellent sites. Directly northeast of the Miracle Mile lies **Hancock Park ❶** *(see page 94)*, an affluent neighborhood that is home to some of the most powerful residents in LA and includes the exclusive **Wilshire Country Club**, once popular with such stars as Clark Gable and Jean Harlow. At the southeastern corner of Wilshire and West-

ern stands the **Wiltern LG**, a refurbished Art Deco movie theater built in 1931, unique for its light-green exterior and now a venue for live music and comedy shows.

Seven blocks east, the site of Robert F. Kennedy's assassination in 1968, the **Ambassador Hotel**, now scheduled for demolition, hosted Oscar ceremonies, gatherings for Hollywood's elite, and film sets, including *The Fabulous Baker Boys* (1989). At 3050 Wilshire is the former department store Bullocks, built

Map on page 92

LEFT: making music in a Miracle Mile store.
BELOW: the Miracle Mile.

in 1928 as America's first large suburban store. Upscale shoppers were enticed by its Art Deco beauty, luxurious fashions and high-teas. It now houses a law library for the Southwestern University School of Law.

But the big tourist attraction along Wilshire is the Miracle Mile itself, notably the stretch called Museum Row near Fairfax Avenue. Locals and visitors also flock to the areas north of Wilshire, where art galleries define a two-block track of La Brea Avenue, trendy design boutiques line Beverly Boulevard, whimsical shops converge on 3rd Street and Jewish delis can be found in the Fairfax District.

The Miracle Mile

Although no longer the shopping mecca that it was 80 years ago, the **Miracle Mile** is still popular with out-of-towners. Nowadays, it's cultural exhibits – not fashion displays – that draw the crowds, and most head for the blocks east of Fairfax Avenue,

Be alert! There are more than 800 highway miles in Los Angeles.

BELOW:
the third floor of the Petersen Museum has exhibits on fuel.

known collectively as **Museum Row**. Here, the biggest attractions are the Petersen Automotive Museum, the Los Angeles County Museum of Art and the Page Museum.

Begin with the **Los Angeles Museum of the Holocaust ②** (6435 Wilshire, tel: 323-651 3704; open Mon–Thur 10am–4pm, Fri 10am–2pm, Sun noon–4pm; free), located at the northwest corner of La Jolla Avenue and Wilshire. The first of its kind in America, this non-profit museum was established in 1961 by Holocaust survivors to educate younger generations.

Exhibits explore such themes as the birth of Israel, pre-Holocaust culture and Jewish ghetto life. Collections include Leskley's satiric watercolors, inspired by his internment at Terezin, a Nazi camp and ghetto in Czechoslovakia.

East on Wilshire, just shy of Fairfax, are the **ACME** art galleries (6150 Wilshire, tel: 323-857 5942), where

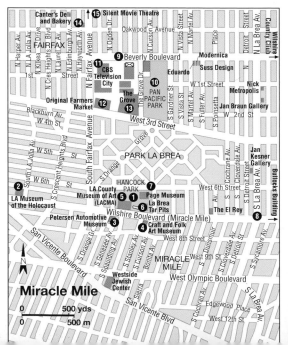

Miracle Mile

Canter's Deli and Bakery ⑭ ⑮ Silent Movie Theatre
FAIRFAX
Oakwood Avenue
⑨ Beverly Boulevard Modernica
⑪ CBS Television City ⑩ Eduardo Suss Design
Nick Metropolis
Original Farmers Market ⑫ The Grove ⑬ PAN PACIFIC PARK Jan Braun Gallery
West 3rd Street
PARK LA BREA
Jan Kesner Gallery
HANCOCK PARK ⑦
② LA Museum of the Holocaust LA County Museum of Art (LACMA) ⑤ ① Page Museum ⑥ La Brea Tar Pits West 6th Street The El Rey ⑧
Petersen Automotive Museum ③ Wilshire Boulevard (Miracle Mile) Bullocks Building
④ Craft and Folk Art Museum
West 8th Street
MIRACLE MILE West 9th Street
Westside Jewish Center West Olympic Boulevard
Edgewood Place
West 12th Street

0   500 yds
0   500 m

contemporary artists display abstract sculptures, kaleidoscopic paintings and experimental photographs. Just a block away, at the southeastern corner of Fairfax and Wilshire, stands a mighty four-story tribute to America's obsession with cars, the **Petersen Automotive Museum** ❸ (6060 Wilshire, tel: 323-930 2277; open Tues–Sun 10am–6pm; charge).

Named after Robert Petersen and his wife, Margie, who contributed over $30 million to the fulfillment of a longtime dream, the museum traces the history of the automobile.

Covering more than 300,000 sq. ft (27,900 sq. meters), the institution presents more than 150 vintage cars, trucks, motorcycles and rare automobiles. On the first floor, visitors can experience over 30 dioramas that represent the 90-year historical span of Los Angeles, the only major city virtually built by the automobile.

The second floor has rotating exhibits of concept cars, vintage motorcycles, hot rods, celebrity vehicles and automotive technology, while children will enjoy the learning center on the third floor, where they can hop on a police motorcycle, practice on a computerized driving simulator, and learn something about alternative fuels.

The Egg and the Eye

Four blocks east, the **Craft and Folk Art Museum (CAFAM)** ❹ (5814 Wilshire, tel: 323-937 4230; open Wed–Sun 11am–5pm; charge) offers a less technological experience than the Petersen. Founded as "The Egg and the Eye" in 1965 by the late Edith Wyle, a passionate promoter of handmade art, CAFAM presents exhibits and programs to honor its original mission of celebrating the traditional and contemporary arts and crafts of diverse ethnicities in LA and around the world. The CAFAM has exhibits from hand-painted kites to straw costumes and masks, and holds artistic extravaganzas, including the International Festival of Masks.

Of course, the CAFAM is virtually dwarfed by the mammoth fortress of art and design across the street – the **Los Angeles County Museum of Art (LACMA)** ❺ (5905 Wilshire, tel: 323-857 6000; open Mon, Tues, Thur

Map on page 92

Miracle Mile catered to the emerging auto age of the 1920s.

BELOW: hot wheels in a cool place: the Petersen Automotive Museum.

Tom Cruise and John Travolta are two of the stress-free stars to follow Scientology.

BELOW:
the La Brea Tar Pits.

noon–8pm, Fri noon–9pm, Sat–Sun 11am–8pm; charge, but free after 5pm), also established in 1965. Evolving from the Museum of Science, History and Art in Exposition Park *(see page 87)*, LACMA began as a three-building facility in Hancock Park and has now become the West's premier encyclopedic art institution.

Currently, the museum covers more than 700,000 sq. ft (65,100 sq. meters) and consists of six main buildings, including the Pavilion for Japanese Art and LACMA West, the adjacent 1939 Art Deco building that once belonged to the May Company and now houses an impressive Latin American art collection. In 2006, ground was broken on the Broad Contemporary Art Museum, a fantastic expansion project to a design by august Italian architect Renzo Piano.

Art lovers could get lost in LACMA and still explore only a fraction of the museum's treasures, which include ancient and contemporary art from the Roman Empire, the Islamic world, the Himalayas, Korea and Europe. In addition, there are displays of early American furniture, modern ceramics and studio glass; drawings from Paul Gaugin; and significant works of art, including Winslow Homer's *The Cotton Pickers*, Diego Rivera's *Flower Day* and Rembrandt van Rijn's *The Raising of Lazarus*. Aficionados may also appreciate the B. Gerald Cantor Sculpture Garden, a peaceful backdrop for several bronze sculptures by Auguste Rodin. But art isn't all LACMA offers – many visitors enjoy the museum's free Friday night jazz concerts or Tuesday afternoon showings of classic Hollywood movies.

Mammoths

Also in Hancock Park are the **La Brea Tar Pits ❻** *(see below)* and the **Page Museum ❼** (5801 Wilshire, tel: 323-934 7243; open Mon–Fri 9.30am–5pm, Sat–Sun 10am–5pm; charge), the fossil research center established by George C. Page, a self-made entrepreneur and philanthropist who was fascinated by the unusual La Brea asphalt deposits. Archaeology and natural history lovers can see fossilized plants, saber-toothed felines and life-size mammoth replicas near

Hancock Park and the La Brea Tar Pits

Hancock Park is the name shared by two places: a mid-Wilshire neighborhood and a recreational park along the Miracle Mile. Both were named for Major Henry Hancock, a gold prospector, who, with his brother John, helped the Rocha family prove their claim for the Rancho La Brea, a Mexican land grant covering parts of present-day Hollywood and named for the tar pits there. As payment, the Rochas eventually transferred the Rancho to the Hancocks. Later on, Henry Hancock made a fortune by drilling for oil here, and refining asphalt for San Francisco's streets. Hancock Park, the neighborhood, is part of the original Rancho La Brea. Developed in 1919 by Henry's son, it became a lavish community with long streets and grand mansions. It is currently one of the wealthiest areas in the country, mainly populated by rich white and Orthodox Jewish families.

Even better known is the Hancock Park north of Wilshire between Ogden and Curson avenues. This park includes the La Brea Tar Pits – pools of sticky, bubbling asphalt full of prehistoric remains. The pits were recorded in 1769, mapped in 1849 and excavated in the early 1900s, eventually yielding over 3 million ancient fossils, many of them housed in the adjacent Page Museum.

the bubbling goo. Every summer, visitors can watch the work in Pit 91, the lab where paleontologists and volunteers recover, clean, identify and store the bones from the dire wolves, giant sloths, bison, rodents and insects that have been preserved in the sticky tar for more than 28,000 years.

Artists' Row

To properly see the exhibits in the museums along Wilshire takes at least a few days. If there's time, though, art lovers and trend-conscious shoppers might also like to check out the art galleries and odd emporiums on **La Brea Avenue 8**.

For home accessories, the first stop should be **Liz's Antique Hardware**, halfway between Wilshire and 3rd. This formerly Chicago-based store has amassed a gargantuan inventory of vintage lighting, bath accessories, contemporary fixtures and hardware for doors, windows and furniture (*circa* 1850 to 1970).

Three blocks north, decorators can continue the quest for unusual and eye-catching home accessories at **Nick Metropolis** (100 S. La Brea), a kitschy marketplace popular with Hollywood set dressers for its eccentric collection of leopard-print couches, theater seats, ship models and tiki bars, among other vintage goods. Several nearby art galleries showcase a wide spectrum of talent.

From the **Jan Baum Gallery** (170 S. La Brea), a forum for modern art and tribal sculpture, to the **Jan Kesner Gallery** (164 N. La Brea), a 20-year-old establishment featuring fine art photography, art lovers can browse among displays of Latin American art, Chinese furniture, Asian antiquities and vintage photography.

Designers' Delight

From La Brea to Stanley Avenue, **Beverly Boulevard 9** attracts a mix of Orthodox Jews attending *shul,* and Hollywood stylists and production designers scouting for costumes and set dressings from a cornucopia of art galleries, furniture stores and vintage clothing shops.

Fashionistas can explore unusual stores like **Suss Design** (No. 7350), whose hand-knit apparel has been

Map on page 92

Jeongwol Daeboreum is a tradition that celebrates the first full moon of the New Year with special games and foods like nuts, rice and vegetables. This is one of many cultural events sponsored by the Korean Cultural Center (5505 Wilshire Boulevard).

BELOW:
Los Angeles County Museum of Art.

The Farmers Market was established in 1934; circus acts used to perform here.

popular with celebrities like Julianne Moore, and used in such TV shows as *Buffy the Vampire Slayer*. **Modernica** (No. 7366), which also has a downtown prop-rental facility, offers hip mid-century furniture, while the **Eduardo Lucero** boutique (No. 7378) enables starlets like Carmen Electra to make slinky, "look at me" announcements on the red carpet. Other emporia along this stretch include a custom letterpress shop and a vintage-steel furniture supplier.

Nearby, on the south side of Beverly, is **Pan Pacific Park ⑩**, on the site of the 1930s-era Streamline Moderne Pan Pacific auditorium. The Pan Pacific hosted hockey games, car shows, political rallies and circuses until it was burned down by arsonists in 1989. Today, the park attracts athletes, picnickers and visitors to the Holocaust monument, a memorial to the 6 million Jews killed between 1933 and 1945.

Immediately to the west is the overwhelming **CBS Television City ⑪**, built in 1952 and home of many soap operas, sitcoms and talk shows. Elvis Presley made his 1956 debut

TV appearance on *The Ed Sullivan Show* in a studio in the complex here.

Shopping on 3rd

South of CBS are two of LA's busiest shopping centers. At 3rd and Fairfax is the sprawling **Original Farmers Market ⑫** (tel: 323-933 9211; open Mon–Fri 9am–9pm, Sat 9am–8pm, Sun 10am–7pm). Founded in 1934 by Arthur Gilmore's son, Earl, for farmers and artisans to sell their wares, the market presently has produce stands, gift shops and food stalls, offering a variety of inexpensive cuisine, from Texas barbecue ribs to French crepes to seafood gumbo.

Once home to circus acts, petting zoos, parades and baseball games, the market was popularized by Hedda Hopper, a powerful gossip columnist who reported on movie stars dining here. Marked by a historic clock tower and the 1852 Gilmore family adobe, the market beckons visitors to a relaxing meal at one of several outdoor tables and to enjoy special events ranging from a summertime music series to holiday festivals.

A pedestrian walkway and a

replica of LA's famous old Red Car trolley connect the marketplace to **The Grove ⑬**, a fairly new 26-acre (10-hectare) outdoor shopping center. Here, shoppers can amble between upscale clothing stores, enjoy a meal at outdoor bistros, or watch a flick at the centralized movie theater. Parking at both the Market and the Grove is free with validation.

Farther west on 3rd Street a wealth of intriguing boutiques await travelers, bookworms, home decorators and accessorizers. Between Harper and Croft avenues, stores offer an assortment of practical and whimsical items, from luggage and cookbooks to handcrafted glass vessels and inflatable pillows.

Fairfax District

North of the Farmers Market, Fairfax Avenue was once the hub of LA's Jewish community. Today, only a few Yiddish shops and eateries remain. **Canter's Deli and Bakery ⑭** *(see page 98)* near Oakwood Avenue is probably the district's most famous landmark, a 24-hour kosher delicatessen. A music lounge rocks on

weekend nights and the dining area is a terrific place to spot celebrities. It's also one of the largest delis, selling 1,500 gallons of chicken soup and 4,000 knishes each week.

Two blocks north, on the west side of Fairfax, is a unique film institution, the **Silent Movie Theatre ⑮** (611 N. Fairfax, tel: 323-655 2520). In the 1940s, John and Dorothy Hampton opened the theater as a shrine to silent film. After four decades of collecting and restoring film classics, John closed the theater in the late 1970s. Following John's death from lung cancer, probably due to his longtime exposure to toxic chemicals, a close family friend renovated and reopened the little theater in 1991 before his own death forced its closure again. Eventually purchased by a Santa Monica-based songwriter, the theater reopened in November 1999 with the last silent feature ever made, Charlie Chaplin's *Modern Times*, and has since shown highly regarded classics, including rare finds of screen legends like Greta Garbo. Live music accompanies the silent films shown here. ❑

Map on page 92

Gilmore the Lion Cub, the supposed model for Leo the MGM lion, logged more than 30,000 air miles as the "co-pilot" for Gilmore Oil, the company that founded the Original Farmers Market.

BELOW: Bob's claims to be "the Best in LA."

RESTAURANTS, BARS & CAFES

Restaurants

Angelini Osteria
7313 Beverly Boulevard. Tel: 323-297 0070. Open: L and D Tues–Fri, D only Sat–Sun. $$$
Presented in the style of a traditional Italian meeting place, chef Gino Angelini's rustic trattoria entices savvy LA gourmets with fine Italian wines and country-style dishes like grilled quail with guanciale.

A.O.C.
8022 W. 3rd Street. Tel: 323-653 6359. Open: D daily. $$$$
After the success of Lucques, in West Hollywood, partners Suzanne Goin and Caroline Styne opened this European-style tapas and wine bar.

Warm, cream-colored walls and chocolate-hued banquettes suit the sophisticated menu of salads, fish, meats and vegetable dishes, and selections of cheeses. Reservations necessary.

Buddha's Belly
7475 Beverly Boulevard. Tel: 323-931 8588. Open: L and D daily. $$
This bright, Feng Shui-designed restaurant has Pan-Asian cuisine at affordable prices. Sit beneath Chinese lanterns and nibble Japanese eggplant, Singapore seafood noodles or green curry chicken.

Campanile
624 S. La Brea Avenue. Tel: 323-938 1447. Open: L and D Mon–Sat, Br only Sat–Sun. $$$–$$$$

Housed inside a Tuscan-style structure that once served as Charlie Chaplin's offices, this elegant establishment offers a California-Mediterranean cuisine amid numerous flowers and fountains. Chef Mark Peel presents beautiful dishes like fried zucchini flowers and cedar-smoked king salmon, while his wife, pastry queen Nancy Silverton, creates divine bread and masterful desserts that have made her next-door La Brea Bakery equally famous.

Canter's Deli and Bakery
419 N. Fairfax Avenue. Tel: 323-651 2030. Open: 24 hours daily. $$
An LA landmark since 1931, this combination delicatessen, bakery and music lounge is always open and never empty. The comfortable, noisy atmosphere welcomes tourists, native Angelenos and movie stars, and the menu has everything from spinach omelettes to éclairs. For homesick New Yorkers, there's also corned beef, matzo balls and lox.

El Coyote Café
7312 Beverly Boulevard. Tel: 323-939 2255. Open: L and D daily. $
A 75-year LA institution, this energetic Mexican eatery thrills an eclectic patronage with festive decorations and zesty

margaritas. Waitresses, in embroidered folk dresses, serve cheap, colorful creations like rib eye fajitas and cheese enchiladas.

Flora Kitchen
468 S. La Brea Avenue. Tel: 323-931 9900. Open: B, L and D daily, Br only Sun. $$
Adjacent to Rita Flora's flower shop. As you shop for the perfect bouquet, taste scones and scrambled tofu for breakfast, spinach and feta cheese pie for lunch or penne pesto pasta for dinner.

The Gumbo Pot
6333 W. 3rd Street. Tel: 323-933 0358. Open: B, L and D daily. $
Validated parking, fresh produce and assorted cuisine attract countless tourists and Angelenos, including nearby CBS employees, to LA's Original Farmers Market; this stall is one of the main attractions. New Orleans specialties include gumbo ya ya or light, powdery beignets.

Jar
8225 Beverly Boulevard. Tel: 323-655 6566. Open: D daily, Br only Sun. $$$$
A contemporary chop-house and retro lounge, this place knows how to prepare a steak you'll never forget. Tender rib eyes and prime porterhouse share the menu with braised lamb shanks and ox tails.

Blood orange sorbet and fine port are perfect accompaniments.

Joan's on Third

8350 W. 3rd Street. Tel: 323-655 2285. Open: L and D daily. $

With a menu that changes often, this café invites curious epicures, like Courteney Cox and Reese Witherspoon, to savor tarragon chicken salads, lemon bundt cakes, and French baguettes filled with apricot-glazed ham and brie. Outdoor seating is available, while the marketplace has wines, olives, imported cheeses and frozen soups.

The Little Door

8164 W. 3rd Street. Tel: 323-951 1210. Open: D daily. $$$$

Candlelight, tinted windows and a luscious courtyard enhance the picture-perfect elegance of this romantic hideaway. Celebrate with Mediterranean dishes like chilled cucumber and dill soup, grilled marinated calamari or seven-vegetable couscous.

Rosalind's Ethiopian Restaurant

1044 S. Fairfax Avenue. Tel: 323-936 2486. Open: L and D daily until 2am. $

Wicker seats and lighted canopies set the stage for an Ethiopian experience. Here, diners are encouraged to eat without cutlery, using the *Enjera* pancakes to mop up stews, including *shifenfen* (lamb), *yedoro wot* (chicken) and *awaze tibs* (beef). The menu also includes dishes from Nigeria and Ghana. Live music on weekends.

Surya

8048 W. 3rd Street. Tel: 323-653 5151. Open: L and D Tues–Fri, D only Sat–Mon. $$

Both family-friendly and upscale, this Indian restaurant sets the mood with yellow walls, soft music and aromas of curry and cloves. Even people of Indian descent flock to this address for *channa masala*, tandoori oven-cooked meats and *naan* breads.

La Terza

8384 W. 3rd Street. Tel: 323-782 8384. Open: B, L and D daily. $$$

This white-walled eatery adjacent to the Orlando Hotel offers the same menu of exquisite pastas and rustic Italian dishes that patrons of sister restaurant Angelini Osteria have come to expect. This classical, multi-tiered space is also one of the city's few restaurants with a wood-burning rotisserie and grill.

Bars and Cafés

Caffe Latte, 6254 Wilshire Boulevard, satisfies with muffins, brunch dishes, salads and pastas in an aromatic atmosphere not far from Museum Row.

El Carmen, 8138 W. 3rd Street, has the moody look of an untamed Mexican tequila bar. Open til 2am every night, this kitschy, often crowded watering hole stocks 300 kinds of tequila; the walls are plastered with black velvet paintings and mounted bull heads.

Susina Bakery & Café, 7122 Beverly Boulevard, is an elegant, light-filled café where patrons relish gourmet candies, homemade pies, fruit smoothies, salads and sandwiches.

Toast, 8221 W. 3rd Street, is a dog-friendly café where trendy locals sit beneath umbrella-shaded tables and savor breakfast sandwiches, lunchtime salads and sinful desserts.

Tom Bergin's, 840 S. Fairfax Avenue, is a late-night Irish pub that has been attracting old-timers and happy-hour yuppies for five decades.

PRICE CATEGORIES

Prices for a three-course dinner per person with half a bottle of wine:

$ = under $25
$$ = $25–40
$$$ = $40–60
$$$$ = more than $60

LEFT: Canter's has been open 24 hours since 1931.
RIGHT: Flora Kitchen: sample the scrambled tofu.

HOLLYWOOD

**Lights! Camera! Action!
Grauman's Chinese Theatre, the Walk of Fame,
Paramount Studios and the famous Hollywood
sign. After years of more cheese than charm,
new attractions make Tinseltown tempting again**

L ike the stars of the its famous industry, Hollywood hasn't been averse to a few facelifts over the last century. In the 1880s, this part of Rancho La Brea was an agricultural community known for its grain and pineapples. By the early 1900s, several years after the Wilcoxes had purchased the land to create a place called Hollywood, it had become a prosperous town, filled with gorgeous homes and schools. Although Los Angeles annexed it in 1910, Hollywood soon gained its first film studio – the Nestor Film Company, located in a defunct tavern at Sunset and Gower – and the district evolved again.

Birth of an industry

Soon, filmmakers like the legendary D.W. Griffith were drawn by the moderate climate and excellent light to make movies in the area, and Hollywood expanded to welcome the infant industry. During the 1920s and '30s, banks, restaurants, nightclubs and movie palaces grew along Hollywood Boulevard, ushering in the Golden Age of Hollywood, a time of glamorous movie stars and big-budget premieres.

By the 1960s, however, many of the stars had moved to Beverly Hills, the nightclub scene had shifted westward along the Sunset Strip and

music recording studios were replacing movie lots. Eventually, Hollywood experienced a sharp decline, and Hollywood Boulevard became a seedy place, filled with more sex shops and teenage runaways than tourist-friendly sites. In 1985, the Hollywood entertainment district was officially listed in the National Register of Historic Places, but it wasn't until 2001, when the Hollywood & Highland Center was unveiled, that Hollywood began to recapture some of its former glory.

Map on page 102

LEFT: Spiderman, a tourist and Jack.
BELOW: read all about it.

Today's Hollywood has absorbing museums, classic watering holes, kitschy shops and architectural landmarks. Its boundaries are somewhat nebulous, but most Angelenos agree that the heart of Hollywood centers on Hollywood and Sunset boulevards, between Gower Street and La Brea Avenue.

Hollywood Boulevard

Probably the shortest of LA's famous thoroughfares, Hollywood Boulevard begins at the intersection of Sunset Boulevard and Hillhurst Avenue and ends in the twisting hills above West Hollywood. There's little to see, however, until Gower Street, where the world-famous **Hollywood Walk of Fame ❶** begins, running along the boulevard to La Brea and along Vine Street from Yucca to Sunset. Initiated in 1960, the Walk of Fame currently has more than 2,100 bronze star-plaques, each commemorating

Hollywood's first movie palace, which opened in 1922. The Egyptian currently shows classic films.

someone in film, television, music recording, radio and theater. Featured along the sidewalk are many notable names, some obscure personalities and a few famous canines and animated characters, but there are also surprising omissions; Clint Eastwood and Mel Gibson have yet to garner stars, for instance. For the honor, an entertainment professional must be nominated and sponsored *(see page 38)*. To watch a dedication ceremony, contact the **Hollywood Chamber of Commerce** (tel: 323-469 8311) for upcoming events.

In these few blocks are a heady crop of entertainment venues, including the dazzling **Pantages Theatre ❷** (6233 Hollywood Boulevard, tel: 323-468 1770), where such Broadway hits as *The Producers* have played in recent years. Opened in 1930 as a movie palace, the historic theater has a varied past, having hosted many star-studded premieres like *A Star Is*

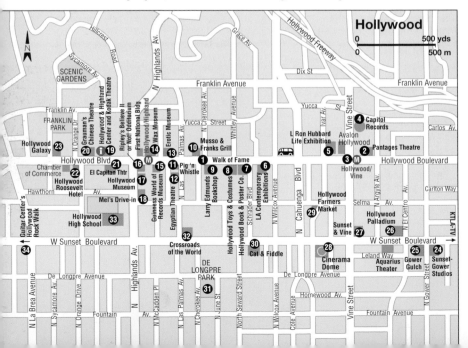

Hollywood

0 — 500 yds
0 — 500 m

Born (1954); 1950s-era Academy Awards ceremonies (including the first televised one in 1953); and every Emmy Awards presentation until 1977.

Just a block west is one of the boulevard's most famous corners, **Hollywood & Vine ❸**. Nothing remains here of the silent-movie era except the churrigucresque Hollywood Playhouse (1735 Vine Street), built in 1926 and the venue for *The Lawrence Welk Show*. In 1964, it was renamed The Palace and, since 2003, has been known as Avalon Hollywood, a high-energy dance club and concert venue.

Opposite is the plum of Vine, the cylindrical **Capitol Records ❹** building *(see photo on page 57)*, shaped as a stack of records and topped by a light that blinks out H-O-L-L-Y-W-O-O-D in Morse code. Music legends like Frank Sinatra and the Beach Boys recorded tracks in the studio, and the lobby is decorated with the gold records of artists like Pink Floyd and the Beatles. John Lennon's star on the Walk of Fame is just outside the building.

Exhibits and Souvenirs

At the northeast corner of Ivar and Hollywood is a huge shrine to the founder of Scientology, the religion which celebrities like Tom Cruise and John Travolta faithfully follow. The **L. Ron Hubbard Life Exhibition ❺** (6331 Hollywood Boulevard, tel: 323-960 3511; open daily 9.30am–10pm; free) opened in 1991 to much fanfare and offers the curious a view of some facets of Hubbard's life, from his aviation experience to his science fiction.

After a dose of modern religion, you may enjoy cultural refreshment at the **Los Angeles Contemporary Exhibitions (LACE) ❻** (No. 6522, tel: 323-957 1777; open Wed–Sun noon–6pm, Fri until 9pm; free) three blocks east. An artists' co-op, LACE showcases a wide range of modern art, from Minimalist painting to stream-of-consciousness music.

For anyone with an appetite for Hollywood memorabilia, there's a short row of intriguing shops on the south side of the street, between Schrader Boulevard and Cherokee Avenue. At the **Hollywood Book**

Map on page 102

TIP

The best places to see the HOLLYWOOD sign: Hollywood & Highland complex; the corner of Beachwood Canyon Drive and Glen Holly; the corner of Franklin Avenue and Gower; and around Hollywood Lake (this last one is difficult to reach).

BELOW:
the director of the Erotic Museum, and a bearded friend.

TIP

If you don't want to hoof it to Hollywood's famous landmarks, take a guided trolley tour. Call Hollywood Fantasy Tours (323-469 8184), Hollywood-land Tours (323-462 4116), LACityTours.com (323-960 0300) or Starline Tours (323-463 3333) for schedules and prices.

BELOW:
Grauman's Chinese Theatre opened with Cecil B. DeMille's *King of Kings* in 1927.

and **Poster Co.** ❼ (No. 6562), you'll find rare movie posters, classic headshots and feature film scripts. Next door, **Hollywood Toys & Costumes** ❽ (No. 6600) has been providing masqueraders with fancy, unusual duds since 1950. If you're looking for King Arthur's armor or Lady Godiva's long locks, this is definitely the place. Farther down, the 60-year-old **Larry Edmunds Bookshop** ❾ (No. 6644) houses an awesome collection of photographs, posters, lobby cards and books about cinema and theater and their history.

Hollywood's Golden Age

At Cherokee Avenue, the old-fashioned **Musso & Franks Grill** ❿ *(see page 114)* offers patrons a re-creation of Hollywood's Golden Age, when stars like Charlie Chaplin and Humphrey Bogart frequented the joint. In the 1930s and 40s, this Tinseltown landmark was a favorite watering hole for writers like Nathanael West and Dorothy Parker, while today's starry visitors include Tom Selleck and Al Pacino.

A key scene between George Clooney and Brad Pitt was shot here for the 2001 movie *Oceans 11*.

A block west, at 6714 Hollywood Boulevard, another landmark restaurant still stands. Opened in 1927 and built by the same architects who designed the magnificent El Capitan Theatre down the block, the stylish **Pig 'n Whistle** ⓫ *(see page 115)* featured elaborately carved wooden ceilings and an impressive organ.

Following a 50-year closure and an extensive renovation, the Pig 'n Whistle transports visitors back to the 1920s and 30s, when stars such as Shirley Temple and Spencer Tracy would be spotted reading the trades over lunch, or dining before a movie premiere at the Egyptian Theatre next door.

A replica of an Egyptian palace, with huge columns along the front entrance, the **Egyptian Theatre** ⓬ (No. 6712, tel: 323-466 3456) was the brainchild of exhibitor Sid Grauman *(see box below)*. Opened in 1922, the stupendous movie house was built by the same pair who

The Master Showman's Movie Palaces

Hollywood's red-carpeted Golden Age was largely due to the legendary exhibitor Sid Grauman. Born in Indianapolis in 1879, Grauman already owned a few theaters when he came to LA and began building noteworthy movie palaces, including Downtown's Million Dollar Theater and the Egyptian Theatre on Hollywood Boulevard. A few years later, Grauman decided to erect his dream theater. With the aid of architect Raymond Kennedy and co-owners like stars Douglas Fairbanks and Mary Pickford, the showman designed an Asian-inspired movie palace where the dramatic bronze roof and opulent pagoda-like exterior were enhanced by real temple bells and two stone Heaven Dogs. On May 18, 1927, thousands of fans crowded near the Chinese Theatre, ogling the movie stars that arrived for the world premiere of DeMille's *The King of Kings*. Grauman, who remained the theater's managing director until his death in 1950, was also responsible for the famous forecourt, which contains cement panels of celebrity handprints, footprints and signatures. Still the most prestigious venue for world premieres, the theater became an historic landmark in 1968.

designed the neo-Gothic **Hollywood First National Building** at the northeast corner of Hollywood and Highland Avenue. In the 1920s, actors dressed as Egyptian guards would march across the roof parapet, calling out the start of each performance.

Currently owned by the nonprofit American Cinematheque, the Egyptian shows classic and independent films, and movie lovers can also participate in monthly tours of the theater. In addition, every weekend (Sat–Sun 2pm and 3.30pm; charge), viewers can watch *Forever Hollywood*, a 55-minute movie narrated by Sharon Stone and designed to give tourists a behind-the-scenes look at moviemaking history.

Five museums

In the block between McCadden Place and Highland Avenue are five museums catering to a variety of interests. On the north side sits the **Erotic Museum** ⓭ (No. 6741, tel: 323-463 7684; open Sun–Thur 11am–9pm, Fri–Sat 11am–midnight; charge), which since 2004 has

investigated various visions of sex through film, fine and folk art, sculpture and multimedia.

The permanent collection features exhibits like Marilyn Monroe's nude photos and examples relating to John Holmes, America's famous male porn star and the inspiration for the character Dirk Diggler, in 1997's *Boogie Nights*. Temporary exhibits have explored items such as surgical implants and recordings of phone sex sessions.

Just a few doors west, the somewhat dated **Hollywood Wax Museum** ⓮ (No. 6767, tel: 323-462 8860; open daily 10am–midnight; charge) offers a less "educational" experience. For over 40 years, the museum has exclusively showcased wax figures of movie stars, from Katharine Hepburn to Catherine Zeta-Jones. Visitors might enjoy the museum store, which features movie souvenirs, some cheesy and some good, like *Gone with the Wind* lunchboxes, Elvis Presley clocks and personalized Walk of Fame stars.

Across the street stand two simi-

Map on page 102

The lights of Hollywood Boulevard.

BELOW: a starlet gets the red carpet treatment at the Black Movie Awards.

lar shrines to the wacky and the tacky. At the **Guinness World of Records Museum** (No. 6764, tel: 323-463 6433; open daily 10am–midnight; charge), visitors learn about the most record-breaking feats from around the globe, including displays about the world's heaviest man and the movie star who's received the most fan letters (hint: he's known for big, round black ears and even bigger amusement parks).

The neighboring **Ripley's Believe It or Not! Odditorium** (No. 6780, tel: 323-466 6335; open Sun–Thur 10am–10.30pm, Fri–Sat 10am–11.30pm; charge) celebrates the world's curiosities with grotesque glee. Exhibits range from miniature pool tables to shrunken heads and torture chambers – results of explorer Robert Ripley's extensive travels and foragings.

At the busy southeast corner of Hollywood and Highland stands the historic Art Deco-style Max Factor building, now home to the restored **Hollywood Museum** (1660 N. Highland Avenue, tel: 323-464

7776; open Thur–Sun 10am–5pm; charge). The four-story museum shows an impressive and fun collection of props, costumes, posters and memorabilia from films and television shows. Exhibits include Cary Grant's Rolls Royce and, deep in the basement, Dr Hannibal Lecter's creepy cell from *The Silence of the Lambs* (1991).

Not far from the entrance are a number of make-up rooms, each painted a different shade to enhance the coloring of the female divas who were being powdered up at the mirrors. After this fascinating but exhausting stroll through the celluloid annals, grab a burger and a shake at the adjacent **Mel's Drive-In** *(see page 114)*.

Hollywood & Highland

The most notable sight at the intersection of Hollywood and Highland – the heart of the Hollywood entertainment district – is the **Hollywood & Highland Center** (No. 6801, tel: 323-467 6412, tours available), an upscale shopping mall built above a Metro rail station and cen-

TIP

You can save money by purchasing a combo ticket for entry into the Guinness World of Records Museum (6764 Hollywood Boulevard) and the Hollywood Wax Museum (6767 Hollywood Boulevard).

BELOW: Santa arrives at the Chinese Theatre during the Hollywood Christmas parade.

tered around two theaters. The **Kodak Theatre**, modeled after a European opera house and host to numerous musicals and concerts, has been the home of the annual Academy Awards since 2002. On the western end of the complex, the magnificent **Grauman's Chinese Theatre ⑳** *(see box on page 104)* attracts throngs of tourists, all eager to investigate the refurbished exterior and the **famous forecourt**, which sports numerous impressions of movie-star palms and feet, from John Wayne's hands to Trigger's horseshoes.

The Hollywood & Highland Center has helped to restore some glitz to the formerly seedy boulevard and has also allowed the Oscars to return to the street where they began in 1929 at the Hollywood Roosevelt Hotel opposite *(see page 108)*. Many feel, however, that the new building lacks the grandeur that its status would indicate, certainly compared to the beautiful old movie palaces that surround it. Nevertheless, the tour is fun, seeing the auditorium with its cardboard cut-outs

of where certain stars sit on Oscar night, and visiting the room set aside to display row-upon-row of the diminutive, coveted statuettes.

The multi-level mall contains a number of fashion boutiques, casual eateries and unique restaurants, all centered around the Babylon Court, which is built to resemble the massive set from D.W. Griffith's *Intolerance* (1916). There's an elaborate archway through which tourists can glimpse the distant hillside with the **HOLLYWOOD sign** *(see pages 103 and 185)*. The **Visitors Information Center** (tel: 323-467 6412; open Mon–Sat 10am–10pm, Sun 10am–7pm), is good for brochures about other local activities.

Directly across the street, the **El Capitan Theatre ㉑**, one of the lavish, old-fashioned movie palaces from Hollywood's Golden Age, once hosted the world premiere of Orson Welles' Oscar-winning *Citizen Kane* (1941). Today, following an extensive restoration, the elegant El Capitan is an exclusive first-run theater for Walt Disney Pictures, presenting live stage shows and

Map on page 102

El Capitan Theatre shows first-run Disney pictures.

LEFT: Al Pacino makes his mark in front of Grauman's.
BELOW: collecting a star signature.

world movie premieres. It's also worth stepping next door to the old-fashioned ice cream parlor and Disney studio store.

At Hollywood and Orange Drive, the **Hollywood Roosevelt Hotel**  harkens back to a classic age, when co-owners Mary Pickford, Douglas Fairbanks, and Louis B. Mayer enticed the stars of stage and screen into its splendid Spanish-Colonial lobby. It was here Clark Gable and Carole Lombard honeymooned, and Marilyn Monroe posed for her first advertisement shot; where Errol Flynn supposedly created his famous gin recipe; and Shirley Temple took her first tap-dancing lesson. The hotel has been featured in recent films like *Catch Me If You Can* (2002). It was nearly demolished in the 1980s, but a $35 million renovation has been a massive success, attracting so many new Hollywood style setters that the hotel's permanent presence is assured.

Just before Hollywood Boulevard begins to fade into the suburban hills, the **Hollywood Galaxy** ❷ (No. 7021) offers two interesting

Love Me Tender: Elvis on the Walk of Fame.

attractions: a jazz club called The Knitting Factory and the less well-known **Hollywood Entertainment Museum** (tel: 323-465 7900; open Thur–Tues 11am–6pm in winter, daily 10am– 6pm in summer; charge), another shrine to Hollywood history, film, TV and radio.

More educational than the Hollywood Museum, the experience includes interactive exhibits, a six-minute multi-screen video presentation, a miniature 45-block layout of classic Hollywood and a backlot tour of the (real) former sets of *Star Trek*, *Cheers* and *The X-Files*. The touring shows are worth a look, too.

Sunset Boulevard

Made famous by the 1950 film *Sunset Boulevard*, in which an actress past her prime seduces and kills an impressionable young screenwriter, Sunset Boulevard is an equally important avenue in the evolution of Hollywood. Just west of Highway 101 is **KTLA-TV**, which in 1947 became the first commercial TV station west of the Mississippi River. Four blocks west, the 17-acre (7

hectare) **Sunset-Gower Studios** ㉔ was founded as Columbia Pictures Studios in 1921 and served the now-defunct production company for 50 years. During that time, many films and TV shows were shot here, including *On the Waterfront* (1954). Recently, the lot has rented out soundstages for TV productions like *Six Feet Under*. Tours are not available, but audiences can attend tapings of TV shows *(see Travel Tips)*.

At the southwest corner of Sunset and Gower, the Western style and the name of the **Gower Gulch** ㉕ strip mall recalls a time when the area was rife with small studios, churning out low-budget cowboy movies. Opposite, the **Hollywood Palladium** ㉖ opened in 1940 with Frank Sinatra and the Tommy Dorsey Orchestra. It is now a rock concert venue.

Two blocks west at **Sunset & Vine** ㉗, a sidewalk plaque reads, "On this corner, Hollywood was born with the filming of *The Squaw Man* in 1913" – even though the actual location was Selma and Vine. On the northwest corner is a resi-dential and retail complex called **Sunset + Vine**, of course, which attracts attention with its kaleido-scopic tower.

A market, a pub and a park

Not far away, at 6360 Sunset, another shopping center delights passersby with its eye-catching geodesic **Cinerama Dome** ㉘, a theater built in 1963 and now sur-rounded by an **ArcLight** movie multiplex, a seven-level parking garage and a health club.

North, near the intersection of Ivar and Selma avenues, the popu-lar open-air **Hollywood Farmers Market** ㉙ takes place on Sunday mornings and provides a great shop-ping opportunity for produce, baked goods, nuts, ethnic foods, clothing and jewelry.

At Schrader and Sunset, sample the beer, the jukebox and the leg-endary service at the popular **Cat & Fiddle** ㉚ English rock 'n roll pub and restaurant *(see page 114)*. Turn-ing left onto Cherokee Avenue, you'll come upon **De Longpre Park** ㉛, a peaceful patch of green-

Map on page 102

Hollywood has three Metro stops, so leave the car behind.

LEFT: buy tour maps here.
BELOW: "Johnny Depp" on the Walk of Fame.

Director Billy
Wilder's magnificent
melodrama (1950).

ery with a monument to silent film
star Rudolph Valentino.

Back on Sunset are a few more
"old Hollywood" sites, including the
whimsical **Crossroads of the World**
32, LA's first modern shopping mall
(*see page 61*); the modest **Hollywood High School 33**, with its list
of alumni including John Huston,
Lana Turner and James Garner; and
the **Guitar Center's Hollywood
RockWalk 34** (7425 Sunset, tel:
323-874 1060; open daily 10am–
6.30pm; free), which celebrates
many of rock 'n' roll's greatest stars,
from Jimi Hendrix to Johnny Cash,

with a collection of handprints, signatures and memorabilia.

Grave plots and studio lots

South of Hollywood's main tourist
district are two thoroughfares also
worth exploring – Santa Monica
Boulevard and Melrose Avenue.
Between these famous roads lie two
intriguing attractions: the Hollywood Forever Cemetery and Paramount Studios. As these sites attest,
stars of long ago often evoke as
much affection in fans as the living
screen idols who they are sometimes
able to spot in local restaurants.

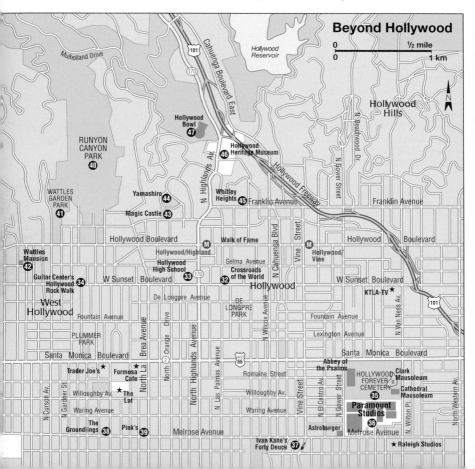

Touring cemeteries might appear to be a rather somber pastime, but the staff members at the recently refurbished **Hollywood Forever Cemetery** ㉟ (6000 Santa Monica Boulevard, tel: 323-469 1181; open daily 8am–6pm; free) are quite prepared for streams of curious visitors. The flower shop sells a map of the property, with the most notable graves marked to ease the search.

Resting luminaries like Mel Blanc, the voice behind Bugs Bunny, and Victor Fleming, the director of *Gone with the Wind* (1939), would be pleased to learn that they still entice fans. Also reposing here are actress Jayne Mansfield and actor Peter Lorre, director Cecil B. DeMille, gangster Bugsy Siegel and Daeida and Harvey Wilcox, the couple who founded Hollywood.

Romantic silent film star Rudolph Valentino, whose funeral attracted 10,000 fans, is buried in the Cathedral Mausoleum, and there is a bronze statue immortalizing punk guitarist Johnny Ramone.

Visitors are welcome to stroll amid the old buildings, ponds, gardens and palm trees, and use the touch screens that give presentations of the words, photos and video clips of the people who are buried here. Tourists should keep in mind that this is a cemetery, and not just another attraction, though; please take care to respect the deceased and also the relatives and friends who may be here to visit them.

Paramount Studios

Behind the cemetery is the expansive lot of **Paramount Studios** ㊱ (5555 Melrose Avenue, www.paramount.com), established here in 1926. Celebrated for countless classic films, from *Wings* (1928), one of the first recipients of the Academy Award for Best Picture, to later Oscar winners such as *Ordinary People* (1980), *Braveheart* (1995) and *Titanic* (1997), Paramount is also where Cecil B. DeMille produced such epics as *Cleopatra* (1934); Spock and Captain Kirk saved the universe in the *Star Trek* films; and Indiana Jones protected the Ark of the Covenant from villainous raiders. In recent years,

TIP

Paramount Studios has a guided two-hour tour that sheds light on the daily operations of this famous motion picture and TV facility. You can also attend a taping of the TV show, *Dr Phil*. Reservations required, tel: 323-956 1777.

BELOW: the Hollywood Hills.

some of America's top TV shows, such as *Frasier,* have been made on the lot. In late-2005, Paramount launched a successful bid to buy DreamWorks, the creative enterprise started by Steven Spielberg and David Geffin.

Farther west on Melrose Avenue are three more Hollywood diversions. Near Beachwood Drive, you can glimpse the sexier side of Hollywood at **Ivan Kane's Forty Deuce** ❸❼ (tel: 323-465 4242), a slinky and sassy burlesque club. Stars at the bar and starlets on the runways confer glitz on the nightspot, recently featured in a Bravo television series.

A mile and a half (2.5km) away, **The Groundlings** ❸❽ theater (7307 Melrose Avenue, tel: 323-934 4747) has been showcasing offbeat comedy for more than 25 years. Famous alumni have included Lisa Kudrow *(Friends)* and Paul Reubens, whose Pee Wee Herman character was invented here. On the way to a show, take time to stop at the legendary **Pink's** ❸❾ *(see page 115)* for a chili dog and fries.

Family-owned Pink's, in business for 65 years, serves hot dogs named after the stars that have eaten them.

BELOW:
supporting cast: Frederick's of Hollywood.

North of Hollywood

In the Hollywood Hills are several hidden and some not-so-hidden jewels, including parks, mansions and amphitheaters. Hollywood Boulevard gives access to two urban wilderness parks. At Vista Street, turn left to the 130-acre (50-hectare) **Runyon Canyon Park** ❹⓪, with wild chaparral, evergreen forests and hilltop views of the Griffith Observatory *(see page 184).*

Trails connect to the adjacent **Wattles Garden Park** ❹❶, an uncrowded canyon hideaway that can also be reached via Curson Avenue. The centerpiece is the lovely **Wattles Mansion** ❹❷, the Spanish Mission Revival home built in the early 1900s by the architects who designed the Beverly Hills Hotel and Pasadena's Rose Bowl. Tours are available through the nonprofit Hollywood Heritage (tel: 323-874 4005).

Franklin Avenue, north of the main Hollywood district, is marked by two gorgeous buildings. The whimsical 1908 **Magic Castle** ❹❸, a Victorian-style mansion located at

7001 Franklin, has been a private clubhouse for the Academy of Magical Arts for over 40 years. The moody, labyrinthine castle is only open to members, their guests and Academy students, but, if you can swing an invite, dinner and a magic show is an incredible experience.

Also stunning is the **Yamashiro** **44** *(see page 115)* farther up the hill. The 1914 teak-and-cedar replica of a mountain palace near Kyoto, Japan is set amid some of the finest Japanese gardens in California. In the late 1920s, the mansion was headquarters for the exclusive "400 Club," whose membership included Lillian Gish and Ramon Novarro. Heavily restored, the Yamashiro is now an award-winning restaurant with a peerless view of the city.

A twisting drive through **Whitley Heights** **45**, once the exclusive enclave of celebrities like Rosalind Russell and Bette Davis, will take you to the **Hollywood Heritage Museum** **46** (tel: 323-874 4005; open Sat–Sun 11am–4pm; charge) at Highland Avenue and Milner Road. This yellow building, the Lasky-DeMille Barn, has been relocated three times since its original spot at Selma and Vine, where in 1913 Hollywood's first feature-length film, *The Squaw Man*, was produced. Today, it's open to the public and features archival photographs, movie props and memorabilia of the silent-movie era.

Hollywood Bowl

Not far away, one of the world's largest natural amphitheaters, the **Hollywood Bowl** **47** (2301 N. Highland Avenue, tel: 323-850 2000) has given a summertime home to the Los Angeles Philharmonic since 1922. Angelenos flock here for nightly picnic concerts. Musicians who have graced the Bowl's stage include John Williams, Nat "King" Cole, Simon and Garfunkel and Placido Domingo.

There's also a museum (tel: 323-850 2058; open Tues–Sat 10am–4.30pm, until show time in summer; free) where visitors can enjoy archival film footage, old programs and audio clips of previous Hollywood Bowl concerts. ❏

Map on page 110

A block east of the Hollywood & Highland Center is Frederick's of Hollywood. This new location, at 6751 Hollywood Boulevard, means its legendary bra museum is reduced to just a few items, but it's still a great place for devilish dainties.

BELOW: the Hollywood Bowl is the summer home of the LA Philharmonic.

RESTAURANTS, BARS & CAFES

Restaurants

Catalina Bar & Grill
6725 Sunset Boulevard. Tel: 323-466 2210. Open: L and D Mon–Fri, D only Sat–Sun. $$$

Wynton Marsalis, Dizzy Gillespie and other jazz greats have played this club, and its new location still attracts the best. Soft spotlights, linen tablecloths and cozy booths give the joint a groovy elegance, and the eclectic menu is as delightful as the music.

The Cat & Fiddle
6530 Sunset Boulevard. Tel: 323-468 3800. Open: L and D daily until 1am. $$

For 20 years, this pub with food has continued the starry tradition of the location, where movie

wardrobes were stored in the 1920s and Katharine Hepburn and Humphrey Bogart dined in the 1940s. Patrons come for the Guinness Boddington's and dishes like bangers and mash.

Dar Maghreb Restaurant
7651 Sunset Boulevard. Tel: 323-876 7651. Open: D daily. $$$

Some Angelenos might argue that more authentic Moroccan cuisine can be found elsewhere, but this lively, lushly decorated restaurant is a favorite among tourists. Costumed servers usher diners into a Moroccan-style house, where painted tiles, cushions and feasts of lentil soup await. Reservations are recommended.

Hamburger Hamlet
6914 Hollywood Boulevard. Tel: 323-467 6106. Open: L and D daily. $$

In the shadow of Grauman's Chinese Theatre, this burger-and-cocktail joint attracts moviegoers before and after shows. Part of a local chain that began in 1950, regulars and hungry tourists enjoy a stylish atmosphere and a big menu, including lobster bisque and chicken pot pie.

Joseph's Café
1775 N. Ivar Avenue. Tel: 323-462 8697. Open: B, L and D Mon–Sat. $$

By day, this is a peaceful Greek-Mediterranean restaurant; by night, a sexy dance club. But no matter what time, this long-respected café has delightful meals.

Kung Pao Kitty
6445 Hollywood Boulevard. Tel: 323-465 0110. Open: L and D daily. $$

Near the corner of Cahuenga and Hollywood boulevards is this sassy Asian eatery, known for delicious morsels like leaping dragon pot stickers, clear noodle soup, golden Thai coconut curry, red miso flank steak and mahi mahi with pan-fried noodles.

Mel's Drive-in
1650 N. Highland Avenue. Tel: 323-465 3111. Open: B, L and D Sun–Thur until 3am, 24 hours Fri–Sat. $

In the shadow of the

Hollywood & Highland complex, this classic diner entices tourists, natives and night owls alike. Though not the original Mel's featured in *American Graffiti*, this one has the charm of those innocent days.

Miceli's
1646 N. Las Palmas Avenue. Tel: 323-466 3438. Open: L and D Mon–Fri, D only Sat–Sun. $$

Home of Italian cuisine and serenading servers, this family establishment has been in the neighborhood since 1949. Pasta connoisseurs will savor the sausage cannelloni, while pizza lovers will be equally tempted.

Musso & Franks Grill
6667 Hollywood Boulevard. Tel: 323-467 7788. Open: B, L and D Tues–Sat. $$$

Red-jacketed waiters present a traditional American menu in an elegant, old-fashioned Hollywood hangout, where writers Ernest Hemingway and Raymond Chandler dined, and modern-day luminaries still do. Since 1919, Tinseltown's oldest restaurant has served steaks, oyster stew, chicken pot pie, martinis and other classic standbys in a film-noirish setting.

Pig 'n Whistle
6714 Hollywood Boulevard. Tel: 323-463 0000. Open: L and D daily until 1.30am. $$

Like the neighboring

Egyptian Theatre, this classy pub, recently restored, harkens back to the 1920s, recapturing Hollywood's heyday with a modern-day vibe. High ceilings, cozy booths, moody lighting and canopy beds in the back room enhance menu favorites like clam chowder, pork ribs and shepherd's pie.

Pink's Hot Dogs

709 N. La Brea Avenue. Tel: 323-931 4223. Open: B, L and D daily. $

What began as a 10¢ hot-dog cart more than 65 years ago has become a landmark, as legendary as the movie stars who frequent it. The family-owned stand has hosted the likes of James Earl Jones and Henry Winkler, and the menu evokes celebrities like Martha Stewart with hot dogs named for them.

Roscoe's House of Chicken 'n Waffles

1514 N. Gower Street. Tel: 323-466 7453. Open: 24 hours daily. $

This down-to-earth restaurant offers Southern soul food at its greasiest. Saucy waitresses serve piles of crispy chicken, springy waffles and collard greens to all-day diners and late-night snackers.

The Hollywood locale was the first of this local chain and the best one to spot finger-licking celebrities.

Uzbekistan

7077 Sunset Boulevard. Tel: 323-464 3663. Open: L and D daily. $$

Warm and lively, this elaborate eatery blends Asian and Russian cultures in both decor and cuisine. Plants, murals, carpets and Moorish arches accentuate the assortment of vodkas and ethnic dishes, including beef stir-fry and chicken Kiev.

White Lotus

1743 N. Cahuenga Boulevard. Tel: 323-463 0060. Open: D Tues–Sun. $$$$

White canopies, stone lions and wooden soldiers: the alluring decor harmonizes with Euro-Asian cuisine like the Thai spicy coconut bouillabaisse. The bamboo-shaded patio and nightclub are as enticing as the food.

Yamashiro

1999 N. Sycamore Avenue. Tel: 323-466 5125. Open: D daily. $$$$

This hilltop Japanese mansion has overlooked Hollywood for the last nine decades. Through windows or from above the classic gardens, the view is incredible, espe-

cially on misty evenings. The creative Cal-Asian menu has the finest sashimi and the most potent sake; the lounge stays open until 2am.

Bars and Cafés

Beauty Bar, 1638 N. Cahuenga Boulevard, has long been a popular nightspot. The interior resembles a mid-1960s hair salon, with drying chairs and vanity tables. **Boardner's**, 1652 N. Cherokee Avenue, transports patrons to the film-noir 1940s, with its snug leather booths, dark furniture and low lighting. **The Bourgeois Pig**, 5931 Franklin Avenue. Coffee-and-tea drinkers unwind with a book, a snack or a round of pool

in a dimly lit, art-filled, bohemian setting. **Daddy's**, 1610 N. Vine Street, is a classic dark, crowded Hollywood bar – perfect for lounging. **Highland Grounds**, 742 N. Highland Avenue, is a bohemian coffeehouse just south of Hollywood, where java-drinkers listen to live acoustic music, drink spirits, and enjoy an assortment of light bar food.

PRICE CATEGORIES

Prices for a three-course dinner per person with half a bottle of wine:
$ = under $25
$$ = $25–40
$$$ = $40–60
$$$$ = more than $60

LEFT: Yamashiro has some the finest views in LA.
RIGHT: Pig 'n Whistle: old Hollywood with a modern vibe.

HOORAY FOR HOLLYWOOD

Movie magic is everywhere in Tinseltown, with a star – or at least a look-alike – around every corner

In this one-industry town if there's a buzz, a crowd, a stirring surge down the sidewalk, the hum and throng is nearly always following a movie star. Screen icons are commemorated in the stars and handprints outside Grauman's Chinese Theatre, with lookalikes often posing nearby to lend a tingling frisson to the photo-memories.

Star-spotting is a favorite pastime in all the good restaurants and bars; sellers of Beverly Hills star maps do brisk business, and everywhere you go, from hair salons to hardware stores, autographed photos of screen gems beam down with personal messages like, "thanks to Julio and the gang."

Lionized in constant, fickle rotation on huge billboards along the Sunset Strip, and then in person once a year on Oscar night, they glitter and enchant. The stars are the sparkling gravity that all life in LA orbits around, and their luminous dust sprinkles a trail of luster on candy stores, candlemakers and lunch-counters alike. From the wax-works to the Wal-Marts, there's some stardust everywhere in LA, and a fairytale waiting to begin around every street corner.

ABOVE: There are more than 2,000 stars on the Walk of Fame, but Gentlemen (still) Prefer Blondes.
BELOW: Morgan Freeman gets down and dirty in the forecourt of Grauman's Chinese Theatre, June 5, 2002.

ABOVE: The motion picture industry generates $31 billion annually.

AND THE OSCAR GOES TO...

The Academy of Motion Picture Arts and Sciences was founded in 1927, with 36 original members. Today, there are more than 6,000 members. The first Academy Award went to Emil Jannings *(left)* in 1929, Best Actor for *The Last Command* and *The Way of All Flesh*. Most nominees, and even winners, didn't attend. Only the producer of *The Jazz Singer* made a speech. Winners were known ahead of time, as the sealed-envelope was introduced in 1941.

So how does one become a member of the Academy? The same way one gets to attend the ceremony – by invitation. The Academy is divided into 14 branches reflecting the many disciplines of creative arts. Approximately 1,500 actors, 500 producers, 400 directors, 400 writers and 3,500 other industry professionals are polled for the awarding of the year's Oscars. Nominations are made by members of their own branches (directors for Best Director, actors for Best Actor, etc). The person who walks away with the Oscar is the one with the most votes cast by the entire membership.

ABOVE: Oscar winners past and present celebrate the 70th anniversary of the Academy Awards in 1998.

LEFT TOP: The tagline for *Sunset Boulevard* (Paramount, 1950) is "A Hollywood Story." The movie stars Gloria Swanson as an aging star who falls for William Holden, a young screenwriter.

LEFT BOTTOM: Darth Vader and Chewbacca get real.

WEST HOLLYWOOD

West Hollywood is edgy, exciting, creative and challenging. Its inhabitants look good and dance even better. So come on – dress up, step out, and discover what this hot LA neighborhood is all about

"**W**hy don't we walk?" Victoria Tenant asks Steve Martin in *LA Story*. "Walk?!" his eyes pop when he hears her. "A walk in LA?" The movie is both a caricature of the city and a fairly reliable primer. This is Los Angeles, and the idea of walking would be as absurd as carrying an umbrella or not having a screenplay to tout (real or imaginary, it doesn't really matter). Walking is just not something people do here. Except in West Hollywood (called "WeHo" by some – can't you just hear Steve Martin's whacky weatherman saying it?).

Sassy and classy

Parts of West Hollywood are a pedestrian's paradise. Despite the steady stream of cars on its thoroughfares and the prevalence of valet parking, even New Yorkers could feel at home on the busy sidewalks of this bold, sophisticated, eclectic neighborhood. By day, strollers meander around elegant art galleries, bohemian clothing shops and intimate cafés.

By night, young ladies and gents – many celebrities included – hop between classy bistros, slick hotel lounges and pulsing music clubs. Throughout the year, star-studded events like Elton John's and *Vanity Fair*'s Oscar-night parties, or street

affairs like the Halloween Costume Carnaval enhance West Hollywood's reputation as a daring and diverse creative enclave.

Little more than two decades old, West Hollywood is one of the youngest cities in Los Angeles County, with a sizable Russian population and a large gay community. Under 2 sq. miles (5 sq km) in size, it is an oddly shaped area, stretching west from La Brea Avenue to Doheny Drive, and roughly bounded by Sunset Boulevard on the north,

Map on page 120

LEFT: hotel with a view, the Standard.
BELOW: the Pacific Design Center.

Mogul makes a phone call while soaking up some rays.

ern end and Beverly Boulevard along the southern edge. This densely packed district divides into three distinct sections: edgy Santa Monica Boulevard, the cultured and fashionable Avenues of Art & Design, and the hip-and-happening Sunset Strip. To get the feel of the area, it's a good idea to explore all three – and take as long as you like.

The Boulevard

Santa Monica Boulevard, part of historic Route 66, begins in bohemian Silverlake *(see page 166)* northwest of downtownLos Ange-

les, and winds west all the way to the Pacific Ocean. Within the asymmetrical contours of West Hollywood, it is known simply as "the Boulevard" and, as this city's longest thoroughfare, roughly extends from just east of La Brea Avenue to Doheny Drive, which borders Beverly Hills.

Two of West Hollywood's most riotous and populous events are staged along this route: the boisterous Christopher Street West Gay, Lesbian and Transgender Pride Parade in June, and the equally vibrant West Hollywood Halloween

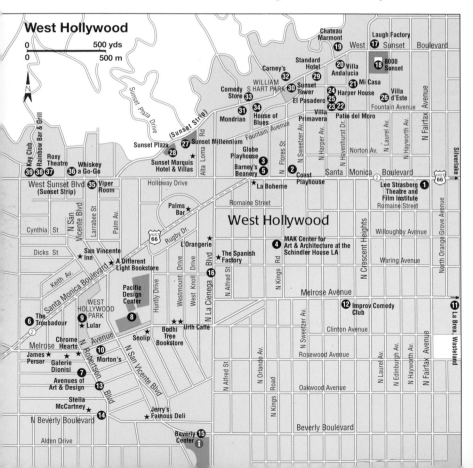

Costume Carnaval in October. But you don't have to wait for these annual bashes to see the Boulevard in its funky glory – there's excitement here every day of the week.

Industry hang-out

On the far eastern end of the Boulevard, between La Brea and **The Lot**, the independent movie studio property which has belonged to United Artists, Samuel Goldwyn and Warner Bros, is the **Formosa Café** (7156 Santa Monica Boulevard, tel: 323-850 9050; *see map on page 110*). This modest brick-red Asian watering hole featured in the films *LA Confidential* (1997) and *The Majestic* (2001), and has been a movie star haunt for over 80 years.

Hollywood history is worn on the walls here – they're almost covered with autographed headshots of famous guests, including Frank Sinatra, Paul Newman, Grace Kelly and Elvis Presley. When the Formosa's lease expired in the early 1990s, the joint was nearly demolished to make room for a studio parking lot, but the loyal patronage

and excellent pedigree convinced city fathers to register the industry hangout as an historic landmark, sparing it from extinction.

West of the old studio lot, this eight-block stretch of the Boulevard isn't too impressive, save for a couple of LA-original chain establishments; the Trader Joe's specialty market at Greenacre Avenue and the Astroburger near Vista Street.

Just past Spaulding Avenue, the unofficial "Boystown" section of West Hollywood begins. Here, you'll spy naughty adult shops, male clothing boutiques, gay-friendly eateries and outrageous late-night alternative clubs, where drag queens glitter in the throng.

In among all this fun-loving notoriety are a couple of culturally significant gems. For the past 30 years, the **Lee Strasberg Theatre & Film Institute** ❶ (7936 Santa Monica Boulevard, tel: 323-650 7777) near Fairfax Avenue has been training thespians and screen actors, including performers like Scarlett Johansson and Alec Baldwin. Visitors are invited to attend monologues, one-

Map on page 120

Numerous events take place during the Art & Design Walk in June. For more info, call 310-289 2534.

BELOW:
Chateau Marmont.

act plays and full-length dramas at the Strasberg. Young actors who graduate from the Institute might just appear on stage at one of two small theaters roughly eight blocks away, the **Coast Playhouse** ❷ (8325 Santa Monica Boulevard, tel: 323-650 8507) or the **Globe Playhouse** ❸ (1107 N. Kings Road, tel: 323-654 5623).

Farther south on Kings Road is a worthwhile detour, the **MAK Center for Art & Architecture LA at the Schindler House** ❹ (835 N. Kings Road, tel: 323-651 1510; open Wed–Sun 11am–6pm; charge). Designed by Rudolph M. Schindler *(see page 59)*, a Viennese colleague of architect Frank Lloyd Wright, the glass and concrete house was built in the early 1920s and eventually became a joint studio and residence for Schindler, his fellow architect Richard Neutra and their wives. Cleverly integrating interior and exterior spaces, the Schindler house has served as the prototype for a uniquely Californian architectural style. Exhibitions, lectures and concerts are held here.

Go-go dancing originated at the Whisky a Go Go, the first discotheque on the West Coast; the Doors perfected their sound as the club's house band in 1966. At The Troubador, Elton John played his first major concert in America.

BELOW: day spa for dogs.

Back on the lively Boulevard are a clutch of popular restaurants, hangouts and specialty stores, most of them catering to a friendly, alternative crowd. At La Cienega, the Boulevard begins its southerly slant toward the Pacific. Beyond the Gothic **La Boheme** restaurant and the stalwart **Barney's Beanery** ❺ pub and eatery *(see page 128)* are gay-friendly establishments like the **Palms**, West Hollywood's oldest lesbian bar; **A Different Light Bookstore**; the **San Vicente Inn & Resort**, and a huddle of alternative nightclubs on Robertson Boulevard.

Not far from Beverly Hills, on the north side of the Boulevard, is one of Los Angeles' legendary nightclubs: **The Troubadour** ❻ (9081 Santa Monica Boulevard, tel: 310-276 6168). For more than four decades, this landmark has weathered the music scene's shifting landscape, helping singer-songwriters, heavy metal groups and rockers to fame and fortune. Elton John, Tom Waits and the Eagles are just a few artists whose reputations grew with their performances at The Troubadour in the 1970s.

Avenues of Art & Design

South of the Boulevard is what may be the West Coast's premiere destination for artistic, decorative and culinary innovation. The trend-setting **Avenues of Art & Design** ❼ encompasses sections of Melrose Avenue and Robertson, Beverly and La Cienega boulevards. Art and fashion lovers flit between scores of art galleries, antiques shops, home furnishing stores, wine and book emporia, fashion boutiques and interior design showrooms. Every year the Avenues hold two showcase events – West Week, a springtime interior design show attracting more than 15,000 architects and design professionals, and the annual Art & Design Walk in June.

Pacific Design Center

The heart of the Avenues is the **Pacific Design Center (PDC)** ❽ (8687 Melrose Avenue, tel: 310-657 0800; open Mon–Fri 9am–5pm; free), an enormous blue-tinted glass structure designed by architect Cesar Pelli. Behind the somewhat overwhelming exterior is an expansive, well-illuminated lobby leading to 130 design showrooms, featuring products from furniture and fabrics to lighting and bathroom fixtures. Interior designers, architects, decorators and dealers scout here for the latest trends, and to attend screenings, lectures and festivals.

The **West Hollywood Convention & Visitors Bureau** (tel: 310-289 2525) is also here, as is a satellite gallery of Downtown LA's **Museum of Contemporary Art** (**MOCA**) (tel: 310-289 5223; open Tues–Sun, hours vary; free), which displays changing exhibits of modernist paintings, furniture, photography and Hollywood memorabilia.

Directly across the street from the PDC, **West Hollywood Park** ❾ is the setting for lively annual events, including Los Angeles's Gay Pride Festival in June and the West Hollywood Book Fair in October.

The PDC seems to split Melrose into two personalities. To the west, restaurants like **Morton's** ❿ *(see page 128)* and high-end showrooms like **James Perse** lure a well-heeled, exclusive clientele. With each block heading toward **La Brea** ⓫, Melrose becomes funkier and more avant-garde. There are pillows and greeting cards at **Soolip**, organic coffees and teas at **Urth Caffé**, prayer flags and metaphysical tomes at the **Bodhi Tree Bookstore** and famous but low-key diners at celebrity-owned eateries.

From La Jolla to La Brea, anyone still in an "up for it" mood can take in a show at the **Improv Comedy Club** ⓬ (8162 Melrose Avenue, tel: 323-651 2583) or visit the **Wasteland** thrift store for inexpensive and vibrant, vintage apparel.

Sought-after spas

Robertson Boulevard ⓭, which runs from Santa Monica Boulevard to 3rd Street, has sought-after spas,

Sugar and spice and all things nice.

BELOW: grooming galore of girls, boys and pets happens here.

antiques shops, clothing boutiques and accessory stores. If you're not too exhausted from strolling along Melrose, you might try on the latest girly fashions at **Curve**, sample caviar and chocolate at **Petrossian Paris**, squeeze into black leather duds at **Chrome Hearts** – one of Cher's favorite haunts – or unwind at **Lulur Spa**, where Barbra Streisand often comes for Bali-inspired facials and massages.

Beverly Boulevard ⑭ also has its share of hip boutiques and popular eateries. **Stella McCartney** sells her rock-chick clothes from a "country cottage" at 8823 Beverly Boulevard. Two blocks east, weary shoppers are rejuvenated by the enormous menu at **Jerry's Famous Deli**. The biggest fashion and dining mecca along this stretch is the behemoth **Beverly Center** ⑮, at the southwestern corner of Beverly and La Cienega boulevards. Besides more than 150 shops and eateries, the mall has LA's only **California Welcome Center** (tel: 310-854 7616), where visitors can make hotel and dinner reservations, pick up information about the city, and secure tickets to the area's attractions and museums.

Not to be outdone, **La Cienega Boulevard** ⑯,offers one-of-a-kind boutiques with fancy names like **Trashy Lingerie** and **Immortal Treasures**. Known locally as "**Restaurant Row**," La Cienega sports several standouts, including **Sona**, **The Spanish Kitchen** and **L'Orangerie** *(see page 129)*.

The Sunset Strip

Tourists often assume that the "Sunset Strip" refers to the whole length of Sunset Boulevard, which rumbles all the way from Dodger Stadium to Pacific Palisades. In reality, the **Sunset Strip** begins and ends at West Hollywood's city limits; it's the part of Sunset Boulevard stretching from Crescent Heights to the eastern edge of Beverly Hills.

Glorified in countless song lyrics and movies, the historic Strip is generally perceived as a glittering oasis, densely populated with glamorous hotels, trendy boutiques, celebrity-backed restaurants and huge, ego-

The Beverly Center and Hard Rock Café.

BELOW: the House of Blues is just one of many live-music clubs on Sunset Strip.

Long-Ago Haunts of the Sunset Strip

West Hollywood's history stretches back to the early days of Tinseltown and Route 66. During the 1920s and 30s, developers seduced the stars out to the Sunset Strip with nightclubs and classy apartment houses. Some of these legendary hangouts have been torn down, but their legacies remain. Two famous buildings formerly stood at the corner of Sunset and Crescent Heights. On the southeast corner, where the Crunch Gym now helps celebrities sweat it out, Schwab's Pharmacy was the neighborhood shop for Charlie Chaplin and F. Scott Fitzgerald. On the opposite corner, an apartment complex called the Garden of Allah was home to Ava Gardner, Humphrey Bogart and the Marx Brothers. Farther west along Sunset, the Art Deco-style Sunset Towers (now the Sunset Tower Hotel) was the temporary home of John Wayne, Howard Hughes and gangster Bugsy Siegel. The career-launching Comedy Store was formerly Ciro's, a popular nightclub where celebrities like Desi Arnaz, Mae West and Sammy Davis, Jr, appeared on stage. On the western end of the Strip, the Rainbow Bar & Grill stands on the site of the former Villa Nova restaurant, where Marilyn Monroe supposedly met her future husband, Joe DiMaggio, on a blind date.

gratifying billboards. Just east of the Strip are two establishments worth mentioning: the Laugh Factory and the 8000 Sunset mall.

Founded over 25 years ago, the **Laugh Factory** ,at 8001 Sunset (tel: 323-656 1336) has spotlighted such comedy giants as Rodney Dangerfield, Richard Pryor and Jerry Seinfeld. Across the street is **8000 Sunset** , the rather obviously-named outdoor shopping mall where famous musicians are often spotted at the **Virgin Megastore**, waiflike actresses like Renée Zellweger work out at the **Crunch Gym** and events like Outfest and the Los Angeles Film Festival take place at the art house movie theater beside the health club.

Towering over the Sunset Strip like a gleaming white castle is **Chateau Marmont** (8221 Sunset Boulevard, tel: 323-656 1010), built as luxury apartments in 1927. Privacy-seeking celebrities, such as Greta Garbo, Robert Mitchum, Natalie Wood, Robert de Niro and the unfortunate John Belushi, who died here in 1982, often prefer the

Chateau to its more glitzy, upstart neighbors. Gazing at the Chateau Marmont provides a glimpse into the architectural history of West Hollywood, especially during the 1920s. While the Marmont's exterior recalls French Gothic influences, other buildings along and just off the Strip explore a wide variety of architectural styles, including Spanish Colonial, Art Deco and Italian Renaissance Revival (as with the **Piazza del Sol** building a few blocks west).

Courtyards

In the blocks between Fountain and Sunset just west of Crescent Heights are a number of lush courtyard apartment complexes worth peeking at (unfortunately, you'll have to peer through or around some locked gates). Courtyards are associated in many people's collective memories with LA, in part because they have featured in so many movies (think *Mulholland Drive*). Like South Beach's Art Deco apartment buildings in Miami, most "courts" were built as low-rise, high-density inex-

TIP

Many restaurants, nightclubs and hotel lounges require reservations and have a dress code, so be sure to check before hitting the town.

BELOW: a typical day at work.

Divas, the decadent and the divine will have few problems here. Dress to thrill.

pensive housing for workers; in Miami, these were hotel workers, in LA, studio workers. The more elaborate were inhabited by movie stars, like the **Villa Andalusia** ❷⓪ (1471 N. Havenhurst Drive). Designed by husband-and-wife team Arthur and Nina Zwebell and built in 1926, it was once home to Cesar Romero and Clara Bow.

Across the street, the lovely balconies of the Spanish import **Mi Casa** ❷① (1406 N. Havenhurst Drive) overlook a pair of jungle-like patios. Two blocks west are two other Zwebell creations, the Arabian-influenced **Patio del Moro** ❷② (8225 Fountain Avenue) and the **Villa Primavera** ❷③ (1300 N. Harper Avenue), a vision of tiles, foliage and outdoor fireplaces. Both Katherine Hepburn and Hollywood's original "bad boy," James Dean, lived at the Primavera.

Also in the 1300-block of Harper Avenue are the **Harper House** ❷④ (1929, architect Leland Bryant) and **El Pasadero** ❷⑤ (1931, architects Jason and Irene Reese), both of which surround unusual Spanish-

style courtyards. Also intriguing is the **Villa d'Este** ❷⑥ (1355 N. Laurel Avenue), where water cascades from the mouths of lions into different pools and waterways. It was designed by F. Pierpont Davis and his brother Walter S. Davis, in 1928, who took their architectural inspiration from a Tuscan villa. Cecil B. DeMille lived here.

Back on the Sunset Strip, if shopping is your bag, then you'll find it along here. Celebrity-frequented stores line both sides of the street, including **Tower Records**, **Book Soup** and **Hustler Hollywood**. Specialty shops are common in the **Sunset Millennium** ❷⑦ (8570–8590 Sunset), while the **Sunset Plaza** ❷⑧ (8600–8700 Sunset) is one of LA's oldest shopping areas, dating from the 1920s. Today it's hot and happening, with names like Hugo Boss and Nicole Miller.

Throbbing

The Sunset Strip is most famous for its throbbing nightlife, but if you're still in your tourist clothes, you may feel a little out of place. Only the

famous or fabulously dressed are able to easily cross the red-velvet rope across the thresholds of some of these lounges and nightclubs.

Don't worry, if you can't bump elbows with the beautiful people at the **Standard Hotel** **㉙**'s slick lounge (8300 Sunset); dine with Leonardo di Caprio inside the Art Deco **Sunset Tower Hotel** **㉚** (8358 Sunset); or sip cocktails in the **Mondrian** **㉛**'s rooftop **Skybar** *(see page 129)* – you can take refuge with the good-natured crowd across the street at **Carney's** **㉜** *(see page 128)*, the 40-year-old hot-dog stand that's housed in a bright yellow railroad car.

For classic stand-up routines, there's the ever-popular **Comedy Store** **㉝** (8433 Sunset, tel: 323-656 6225), where hilarious alumni have included Robin Williams, Eddie Murphy and George Carlin.

For mainstream rock, blues or zydeco fans, the **House of Blues** **㉞** (whose investors include Dan Aykroyd and James Belushi) features star headliners, Cajun cooking and a gospel brunch on Sunday

(8430 Sunset, tel: 323-848 5100). If you're looking for a more edgy, alternative sound, check out the infamous **Viper Room** **㉟** (8852 Sunset, tel: 310-358 1881), once owned by actor Johnny Depp and often lit up by major acts like the Red Hot Chili Peppers, Counting Crows or Billy Idol.

The Whisky

At the far western end of the Sunset Strip, from San Vicente to Doheny, is another row of nightclubs. The epicenter of the 1960s rock scene, the **Whisky a Go-Go** **㊱** (8901 Sunset, tel: 310-652 4202) may well be most famous.

Since 1964, the Whisky has witnessed a multitude of key moments, including the Sunset Strip's 1966 youth riots, the Doors' stint as the club's house band, and countless 1970s-era concerts by such rock legends as Led Zeppelin, Blondie and the Kinks. Rocking vibes or eradefining history can also be felt at the nearby **Roxy Theatre** **㊲**, the **Rainbow Bar & Grill** **㊳** and the **Key Club** **㊴**. ❑

Map on page 120

The billboards and painted buildings along the Sunset Strip are second only to Times Square as the most expensive outdoor advertising vehicles in the US.

BELOW: the Sunset Strip at dusk.

RESTAURANTS, BARS & CAFES

Restaurants

Asia de Cuba

8440 Sunset Boulevard. Tel: 323-848 6000. Open: B, L and D daily. $$$

Trendy gourmets who believe that presentation is as important as the food will fall in love with this restaurant inside the Mondrian Hotel. Patrons sit on white furniture in the chic, white-walled interior or beneath bougainvillea vines on the patio. Either way, you're guaranteed peerless Asian-Latino cuisine and a terrific view of the Los Angeles skyline.

Barney's Beanery

8447 Santa Monica Boulevard. Tel: 323-654 2287. Open: B, L and D daily until 2am. $$

This friendly and casual-watering hole has been serving up burgers and beers for nearly 80 years. Today, the funky juke joint hosts pool players, artists and fun-seekers of all kinds, and the newspaper-sized menu lists an assortment of breakfast plates, fried appetizers, sandwiches, pizzas, salads and pastas. Hundreds of domestic and imported beers, too.

Carney's

8351 Sunset Boulevard. Tel: 323-654 8300. Open: L and D daily. $

Comfortably housed in a vibrant yellow 1920s-era passenger train car, this Sunset Strip landmark tempts passersby late into the night with cheap

and cheerful hot dogs, hamburgers and thick milkshakes.

Dan Tana's

9071 Santa Monica Boulevard. Tel: 310-275 9444. Open: D daily until 1am. $$$

Old-school charm throbs throughout this Rat Pack-era icon, complete with red leather booths and checkered tablecloths. A local landmark since 1964 and not far from The Troubadour nightclub, the dimly-lit restaurant is a celebrity magnet – perhaps for the unpretentious, urban atmosphere but more likely for the food, which includes traditional Italian dishes, well-prepared steaks and NY-style cheesecake.

Le Dôme

8720 Sunset Boulevard. Tel: 310-659 6919. Open: D Tues–Sat. $$$$

The name evokes images of glamorous stars and powerful executives, and following a major renovation, it promises even more. Though decidedly modern, the brick-and-cobblestone decor is reminiscent of an old Tuscan villa, and the continental cuisine includes Belgian mussels, Russian caviar, Japanese pork ribs and Hawaiian tuna, not to mention the harlequin soufflé for dessert. Reserve ahead.

Katana

8439 Sunset Boulevard.

Tel: 323-650 8585. Open: D daily. $$$

Cosmic decor melds with rustic Japanese cooking at this relative newcomer to the Sunset Strip's stellar dining roster. Textured walls, steel beams, moody lighting and revealing windows lend almost as much drama as the beautifully arranged spider rolls, noodle dishes and charcoal-grilled robata-yaki combinations.

Lucques

8474 Melrose Avenue. Tel: 323-655 6277. Open: L and D Tues–Sat, D only Sun–Mon. $$$$

Exceptional cuisine and understated ambience are the hallmarks of Lucques, where the menu is always a work-in-progress. Creative concoctions like grilled duck breast with duck confit-dandelion salad, black olives and bing cherry jam are the norm for partners Suzanne Goin and Caroline Styne. Desserts are equally bold.

Morton's

8764 Melrose Avenue. Tel: 310-276 5205. Open: L and D Mon–Fri, D only Sat. $$$$

An enduring LA landmark, this stylish hotspot still attracts Hollywood's movers and shakers for souped-up American classics like free-range lime chicken, sesame-encrusted ahi tuna and banana-walnut beignets. The red carpet *Vanity Fair* Oscar party here is a "must attend" event for A-listers and up-and-coming celebs.

O-Bar

8279 Santa Monica Boulevard. Tel: 323-822 3300. Open: D daily. $$$
In a setting of draped cabanas, flickering candles and tranquil gardens, this dramatic space is part Manhattan, part Miami Beach. Regulars may come for the stylishly festive atmosphere, but they stay for the affordable haute cuisine. Billed as "familiar with a twist," the food consists of such new classics as lobster macaroni and Mexican style meatloaf.

L'Orangerie

903 N. La Cienega Boulevard. Tel: 310-652 9770. Open: D Tues–Sat. $$$$
This intimate, long-standing French venue entices many a celebrity into its stunning dining rooms or onto the tranquil garden terrace. Sculpted plants and peaceful landscapes enhance such elegant dishes as foie gras with spiced apple chutney and candy-crusted breast of squab. The wine is also wonderful.

The Porch

8430 Sunset Boulevard. Tel: 323-848 5136. Open: L and D daily, Br only Sun. $$
Part of the Sunset Strip's barnlike House of Blues, this Southern-style restaurant specializes in Cajun and Creole favorites like Voodoo shrimp, jambalaya, seafood gumbo and white chocolate banana bread pudding. As a bonus, diners with concert tickets get first access to the music hall after dinner. Sunday's gospel brunch has uplifting tunes with an all-you-can-eat buffet.

The Spanish Kitchen

826 N. La Cienega Boulevard. Tel: 310-659 4794. Open: D daily. $$$
Vibrant murals, enormous plants and wrought-iron chandeliers transport diners to an airy hacienda south of the border. The neon sign promises "authentic Mexican" and the menu delivers. Delight in festive creations like Mexican cocoa crepes filled with sautéed lobster, leeks and manchego cheese. Good wine list.

Bars and Cafés

The Abbey Food & Bar, 692 N. Robertson Boulevard has evolved from a coffee house to a hotspot, where gay and straight patrons come for martinis and round-the-clock vittles.

Bar Marmont, 8171 Sunset Boulevard, caters to starlets and young industry types in a sexy, elegant setting beside the Chateau Marmont. Mojitos and late-night bites served with flair.

Lola's, 945 N. Fairfax Avenue, is home of the famous apple martini and known for its dainty decor, eclectic cuisine and, of course, martinis.

Real Food Daily, 414 N. La Cienega Boulevard, invites hip West Hollywood dwellers and curious epicures to explore vegan and vegetarian creations like lentil-walnut pâté and black-bean tostadas.

Skybar, Mondrian Hotel, 8440 Sunset Boulevard, offers stylishly dressed gadabouts incredible views of the city from its ivy-covered, wooden pavilion above the pool.

The Whiskey Bar, Sunset Marquis Hotel, 1200 Alta Loma Road, provides an intimate place to sip high-end cocktails with high-end people. Located just off the Sunset Strip and frequented by wealthy rock bands.

PRICE CATEGORIES

Prices for a three-course dinner per person with half a bottle of wine:
$ = under $25
$$ = $25–40
$$$ = $40–60
$$$$ = more than $60

LEFT: California cuisine with a twist.
RIGHT: Barney's Beanery has been around for 80 years.

BEVERLY HILLS

Famous for being famous, star-studded Beverly Hills has the chic boutiques, power-lunch eateries, ritzy hotels and movie-star mansions that fantasy demands

Chocolate-hued, gold-trimmed official shields around the perimeter herald the hallowed grounds of Beverly Hills. The pace shifts, from West Hollywood edge to a smooth Sunset Boulevard purr as the avenue winds between thick foliage and wrought-iron gates, and the clubs along Santa Monica Boulevard give way to a long, lovely park.

The Heart of the Hills

For new visitors, **Rodeo Drive ❶** summarizes the appeal of this wealthy enclave. Appointment-only shops, reservation-only restaurants, pampering day spas and glamorous hotels populate the Golden Triangle – the stylish heart of Beverly Hills – apt for a city where the average house costs $1 million, where every lawn is manicured and where families employ a cook, a maid, a gardener, a nanny or all of the above.

The allure of Southern Californian affluence suffuses the tree-lined boulevards. Neighborhoods are quiet, flowers are perpetually in bloom and the police are very responsive, encouraged, perhaps, by the notoriety of some residents. Beverly Hills is a place where locals are used to tourists gawking, trying to glimpse any movie-star connection.

Most of Beverly Hills is bounded by Olympic Boulevard on the south,

Doheny Drive to the east, Sunset Boulevard to the north and the Los Angeles Country Club to the west. Once home to the peaceful Tongva Indians, this water-rich area provided abundant game, vegetation and wildflowers. After European smallpox killed most of the tribe, the Mexican governor of California deeded the Rancho Rodeo de las Aguas to a Spanish soldier's widow. Subsequent droughts brought a succession of owners until Burton Green and his partners formed the Rodeo Land and

Map on page 132

LEFT: pampered pooch on a Rodeo retail experience.
BELOW: the Museum of Television & Radio.

Water Company in 1906, and renamed Beverly Hills after a Massachusetts town. The mission-style Beverly Hills Hotel *(see page 136)* became the focus of the new community, and stars like Gloria Swanson, Will Rogers and Buster Keaton built mansions nearby. Since then, Beverly Hills has become one of the world's most glamorous places to live, eat and shop, mythologized in television shows like *The Beverly Hillbillies* and *Beverly Hills 90210*.

The Golden Triangle

The heart of this tranquil town is the **Golden Triangle**, a collection of well-tended streets, exclusive shops and celebrity-graced restaurants between Wilshire Boulevard, Rexford Drive and Santa Monica Boulevard. A good first stop is the **Beverly Hills Conference & Visitors Bureau ❷** at 239 S. Beverly Drive (tel: 310-248 1015; open Mon–Fri 8.30am–5pm), for free information on attrac-

tions and activities. Here you can also arrange private four-hour walking tours of Beverly Hills with knowledgeable, docent-led "Ambassadears," or, less expensively, walk to the corner of Rodeo Drive and Dayton Way and climb aboard for a 40-minute, **Trolley Tour** of the city (tel: 310-285 2438; available Sat in off-season, Tues–Sat in summer and holiday season; charge).

A self-guided walking tour of the Golden Triangle is also a good start. Begin at the **Regent Beverly Wilshire ❸**, at Wilshire Boulevard and Rodeo Drive. From the Visitors Bureau, walk north one block and turn left onto Wilshire. The elaborate European facade and striped awnings are hard to miss. The opulent structure is the anchor of Rodeo Drive and a recognizable landmark from films like *Beverly Hills Cop* (1984) and *Pretty Woman* (1990).

Movie stars have lived here (or at least pretended to): Elvis Presley

TIP

The Beverly Hills Civic Center hosts a number of free activities, including public art walking tours (tel: 310-288 2202), a monthly speaker series (tel: 310-285 2529) and summer-time concerts (tel: 310-550 4796).

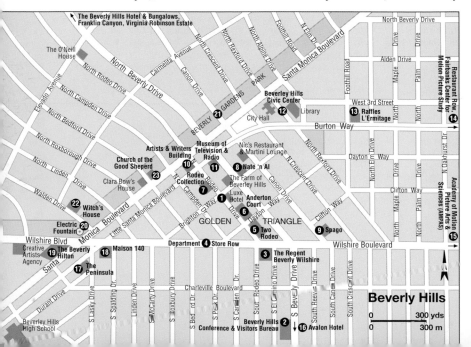

Beverly Hills

lived here in the late 1950s while making movies for Paramount Studios, and Warren Beatty stayed in the Penthouse Suite for years, entertaining actresses Julie Christie and Diane Keaton. This 1928 Beverly Hills landmark had a successful facelift some years ago, and even if you're not staying in one of the expensive rooms or suites, you can appreciate the fresh flowers, white marble and large chandelier in the small elegant lobby, or savor an early-evening cocktail or a meal.

West of the Beverly Wilshire, along the southern border of the Golden Triangle, is **Department Store Row ❹** – a stretch of famous emporia like Barneys New York, Saks Fifth Avenue, Neiman Marcus and Robinsons-May.

Rodeo Drive

Most visitors come wanting a glimpse at the world's most prestigious shopping avenue: Rodeo Drive. The reputation exceeds its size; it doesn't take long to stroll along the three-block path between Wilshire and Santa Monica boulevards, and

the street is, in fact, surprisingly sterile at first visit, with few luxurious trees to shield it from the hot sun. Nevertheless, here are branches of world-renowned purveyors like Prada, Gucci, Chanel and Cartier. As befits the attitude, "sales associates" treat customers with cool suspicion if they're judged underdressed for the occasion. Some boutiques open only by appointment. Bijan, for instance, a supremely exclusive menswear, fragrance and jewelry store, ushers only the wealthiest shoppers into its airy yellow space, where a day's receipt can easily total $100,000.

Besides individual stores, Rodeo Drive also has impressive shopping complexes. Near Wilshire is **Two Rodeo ❺**, an ostentatious $200-million structure styled after a cobblestoned European village, housing Porsche Design and Tiffany & Co, a stylish two-story display of fine jewelry and glassware. In the next block is **Anderton Court ❻** (328 N. Rodeo Drive), an eccentric, well-lit mall designed in 1952 by Frank Lloyd Wright. Farther up the street, the **Rodeo Collection ❼** (421 N.

Map on page 132

Ninety percent of Beverly Hills is zoned for residential use.

BELOW:
ladies lunch
on Rodeo Drive.

Rodeo Drive) invites shoppers to five levels of lavish design, fashion and jewelry boutiques around a sunken central courtyard.

Adjacent streets offer innumerable shopping and dining options. One block east, Beverly Drive has more casual stores like Crate&Barrel and Pottery Barn and low-key eateries like the New York-style deli **Nate'n Al** ⑧ *(see page 139)*. On the next street, Cañon Drive, are smaller boutiques and **Spago** ⑨ restaurant *(see page 139)*, a good place for celebrity spotting. After a long day of spending money and window-shopping, you might like to stop at the **Luxe Hotel**, the only hotel on Rodeo Drive, for a sumptuous meal at the lovely Café Rodeo, or a cocktail at the bar.

There's more to the Golden Triangle than just shopping, however. At the northwest corner of Rodeo Drive and Little Santa Monica Boulevard, is the **Artists & Writers Building** ⑩. This four-story Spanish Colonial edifice was built in 1924, and was home to creative tenants like writer Ray Bradbury and director Billy Wilder. One block east is the

The waters of wealth.

BELOW: Spago: the most famous restaurant in LA.

Museum of Television & Radio ⑪ (465 N. Beverly Drive, tel: 310-786 1000; open Wed–Sun noon–5pm; donation suggested), a gleaming white building with a bright, airy lobby designed by Richard Meier *(see page 63)*, the architect behind the Getty Center.

Like its sister branch in New York, the museum has an enormous library of radio and television programs (perfect for one of LA's rare rainy afternoons), holds afternoon screenings and presents seminars with performers, critics, writers and producers. Children also enjoy the special screenings and radio workshops offered on weekends, and fans of television trivia appreciate the gift shop, with unique postcards, cassettes, books and posters.

Spanish renaissance

Two streets east of the Museum of Television & Radio are several impressive structures. First is the swooping, space-age canopy of the 1960s-era **Union 76 gas station** at Little Santa Monica Boulevard.

Across the street is the eight-story tower of the magnificent tiled dome and gilded cupola of the Spanish Renaissance-style **City Hall**. The **Beverly Hills Civic Center** ⑫ is the cluster of buildings embracing both sides of Rexford Drive. Vivid flowers and palm trees grace the front of the stately City Hall building, designed by William Gage in 1932. Heavily renovated and expanded in the 1980s, this is where local officials enforce ordinances requiring, among other things, permits for garage sales, lawn maintainence and the prompt removal of holiday decorations.

The rest of the Civic Center, inspired by the architecture of City Hall and completed in 1990, contains the city's police and fire departments and the fine **Public Library**. Exhibits about the city's history, and events like lectures and storytelling concerts

are held here. Visitors are also invited to peruse the public sculpture and paintings featured throughout City Hall, the library and the Civic Center. Every Sunday morning, just east on Civic Center Drive, produce farmers and specialty vendors converge for the Beverly Hills Farmers' Market.

Past the **Raffles L'Ermitage** 🔞 hotel on Burton Way is the stretch of La Cienega Boulevard between Wilshire and Melrose known as **Restaurant Row** 🔞, where eclectic cuisine ranges from Indian to Italian.

Oscar's home

West on Wilshire is the impressive, seven-story screening facility for the **Academy of Motion Picture Arts and Sciences (AMPAS)** 🔞 (8949 Wilshire Boulevard). Opened in 1975, this is the headquarters of the organization that, since 1929, has overseen the annual Oscar awards and ceremony. Cinephiles will enjoy the photographic retrospectives in the lobby, as well as the vast collection of film-related books, periodicals, screenplays, photographs and posters at the Margaret Herrick Library,

located south of AMPAS in the **Fairbanks Center for Motion Picture Study** (333 S. La Cienega Boulevard, tel: 310-247 3000; open Mon–Tues, Thur–Fri 10am–6pm).

For a change of scenery, head west on Olympic Boulevard, past the sophisticated **Avalon Hotel** 🔞, whose sexy pool area attracts young starlets and movie-star hunks, and turn right on Spalding Drive for a look at the **Beverly Hills High School** (241 Moreno Drive), a well-landscaped complex of red-roofed white buildings, and the former site of the Beverly Hills Speedway.

Toward Wilshire are a number of exquisite hotels. Savor modern American cuisine at **The Peninsula** 🔞, sip a Lady Godiva cocktail at lovely **Maison 140** 🔞 or take a tour of the **Beverly Hilton** 🔞 at Santa Monica and Wilshire boulevards – once owned by producer Merv Griffin and now home to the annual Golden Globes awards show and Oscar Nominee Luncheon.

North of Wilshire, the stunning **Electric Fountain** 🔞 was funded with the help of actor Harold Lloyd's

Map on page 132

While staying at the Regent Beverly Wilshire, Dashiell Hammett wrote his final novel, The Thin Man (1934), which introduced detective Nick Charles. His wife, Nora, was based on Hammett's lover, playwright Lillian Hellman.

BELOW:
Elvis lived here.

Beverly Hills Hotel

When the Beverly Hills Hotel closed for a facelift, doomsayers forecast that it would never regain its old cachet. Upon reopening, though, few of the hotel's fans were surprised to discover there were plenty of people willing to pay large sums of money to frolic in its sumptuous rooms, dine in the famous restaurant or sunbathe in one of the secluded poolside cabanas.

The fact is that the "Pink Palace" is much more than a hotel, it's a legend – the place where Elizabeth Taylor honeymooned in one of the bungalows (her daddy once ran an art gallery in the lobby), and where reclusive resident Howard Hughes ordered pineapple upside-down cake from room service almost every night of his stay. Hughes rented four bungalows at the hotel: one for himself, another for his wife Jean Peters, a third for the blueprints of the *Spruce Goose*, the other for bodyguards and guests. One of his eccentricities was to order roast beef sandwiches delivered to a certain tree.

It was in the coffee shop in 1959 that Marilyn Monroe and Yves Montand romanced over afternoon tea. For a long time, Katharine Hepburn took lessons from the hotel's tennis pro and one day, after six sweltering sets, dived into the pool fully clothed. She was also known to curl up outside Spencer Tracy's locked door, waiting for him to let her in after a drinking bout. Greta Garbo chose the hotel as a hideaway in 1932, and Clark Gable checked in to dodge the press after separating from his wife.

When the world's wealthiest man, Hassanal Bolkiah, Sultan of Brunei, bought the hotel for $185 million in 1987, it was rumored that he would turn it into a private residence for himself, but over the years, he has instead invested in extensive renovations. The number of rooms was cut from 253 to 194; gilded ceilings were added to the lobby along with crystal chandeliers and rosebud lights. New additions included a kosher kitchen. Every room in the hotel has at least three phones and a butler-service button. Finally, 1,600 gallons (6,100 liters) of Beverly Hills Pink were computer-matched to old paint samples, so that the new extensions matched the colors of the old.

Some things, of course, stayed the same, particularly the Fountain Coffee Shop, with its original iron stools still bolted to the floor, and the familiar banana leaf-patterned wallpaper. The menu of the Polo Lounge, where big movie deals are still cut, features the Neil McCarthy salad, named for the polo-playing millionaire who died in 1972.

At first, the bar was called El Jardin but was rechristened when socialite and polo player Charles Wrightsman turned up with his team's silver trophy bowl. After that, bon-vivants W.C. Fields and John Barrymore were joined by Will Rogers and Darryl Zanuck, who dropped in after their matches. The lounge is open from 7am to 1.30am; jackets are suggested after 7pm.

In a town notorious for casual attire, decorum still prevails here. Mia Farrow was once turned away from the Polo Lounge because she was wearing pants, and rock manager Arnold Stiefel, who chose the place to sign up Guns N' Roses, recalled the waitresses being "in shock at all those people with things in their nose. I think it took the coffee shop at least six months to recover." ❏

LEFT: your suite awaits.

mother, and caused traffic jams when it was unveiled in the 1930s. It is the starting point of **Beverly Gardens Park** , a lengthy greenspace running along the north side of Santa Monica Boulevard, and all that remains of the bridlepath that, until the 1920s, stretched from Downtown's Biltmore Hotel to the Beverly Hills Hotel.

Today, the lovely 14 acre (5.6-hectare) strip has plants, trees, flowers, cacti and sculpture, including the landmark *Hunter and Hounds* statue, which was brought from France by a California banker in 1925. Every May and October since 1973 the park has hosted a popular art show, showcasing the photography, painting and ceramics of more than 200 artists.

The Witch's House

Among the expensive if unprepossessing bungalows north of tranquil Beverly Gardens Park, are a couple of architectural delights. At 516 N. Walden Drive, the bizarre, fairy tale **Witch's House** was built in 1921 as a set for silent films, before it was relocated to this site.

Three streets northeast, by contrast, is the snow-white **Church of the Good Shepherd** (505 N. Bedford Drive), the oldest church in Beverly Hills. The Good Shepherd has been the Catholic parish church for movie stars like Bing Crosby, witnessed the weddings of celebrities like Elizabeth Taylor, and was also where the funerals of Gary Cooper and Frank Sinatra were held.

If you continue in a northwesterly direction on Rodeo Drive, you'll easily spot the salmon-hued **Beverly Hills Hotel and Bungalows** *(see opposite)*, a remarkable site amid lush gardens and palm trees at Beverly Drive and Sunset Boulevard.

From JFK to John Wayne, many celebrities favored stayed here, and the hotel itself has been featured in films like *The Way We Were* (1973) and *American Gigolo* (1980). Modern guests enjoy a number of unusual amenities, from a classic pool to an expensive menswear boutique.

North of Beverly Hills are a number of outdoor gems. Hikers can explore **Franklin Canyon**, once used as a summer retreat by the family of oil baron Edward Doheny and now administered by the Santa Monica Mountains Conservancy. This 605-acre (245-hectare) park contains shaded meadows, picnic grounds, a lake, a wildlife pond, a nature center and 5 miles (8 km) of hiking trails.

Edward Doheny built another house north of Beverly Hills in the mid-1920s as a gift to his son. The 55-room **Greystone Mansion** (905 Loma Vista Drive, tel: 310-550 4654), which then cost nearly $4 million, certainly commands attention. Said still to be the largest house in Beverly Hills, the Gothic-style Greystone, its limestone walls, intricate woodwork and marble fireplaces, has frequently been featured in movies, including *Ghostbusters* (1984), *The Witches*

Maps on pages 132, 142

Beauty and the builders: the average Beverly Hills home has 4.12 bathrooms.

BELOW: the Witch's House was built in 1921 as a set for silent films.

*Oranges and statues
shield the rich and
famous of Beverly
Hills from the rest
of the world.*

BELOW: the Virginia
Robinson Estate.

of Eastwick (1987) and *X-Men* (2000). Although the historic estate is owned by the city, there are no organized tours of the manor, which is usually off-limits to visitors.

Sightseeing and picnicking, however, are encouraged in the tranquil 18-acre (7-hectare) park, filled with towering redwoods, sweeping lawns, sculpted gardens and panoramic city views (open daily 10am–5pm, in summer 6pm; free).

For a rare look inside the mansion, you can purchase tickets to one of the many events at Greystone, which include high-tea afternoons, intimate chamber concerts and an annual garden and design festival, where visitors are invited to enjoy wine tastings, watch demonstrations of glass-blowing and catch a glimpse of the 1920s interior designs.

Oldest house in the Hills

Slightly northwest of the Beverly Hills Hotel is another stupendous mansion. Probably the oldest home in Beverly Hills, the **Virginia Robinson Estate** ㉗ (1008 Elden Way, tel: 310-276 5367; open by appointment only Tues–Fri; charge) was built in 1911 for "the First Lady of Beverly Hills," whose family started the Robinsons-May department store chain. The blue-tiled pool and intimate beaux arts-style house (which is open to visitors) are delightful, but the tour mainly focuses on the gardens, full of blooming magnolias, kaleidoscopic flowers, king palm trees and fountains.

Just west of Beverly Hills lies the legendary **Playboy Mansion** ㉘ (10236 Charing Cross Road). Hidden cameras guard the gates, and the ornate house and sumptuous grounds can be seen only by those invited. It's impossible to avoid mention of Hugh Hefner's palace of hedonism when visiting Beverly Hills. Rumors rise like mist from this mythical estate, where voluptuous centerfolds are said to sunbathe naked by the pool, providing entertainment for the pipe-smoking bachelor who created the Playboy empire more than 50 years ago. In the 1990s, "Hef" was also the savior of the dilapidated Hollywood sign, when he led a movement for its restoration. ❏

Hef and the Playboy Empire

For the last half-century, "Playboy" has been a household name, evoking images of voluptuous centerfolds. The empire now encompasses publishing, TV, video, gaming and the Internet. The master behind the naughty bunnies, Hugh Hefner (aka, "Hef"), was born in 1926 to conservative parents. After working as a personnel manager and a promotion copywriter, he decided to start a sophisticated men's magazine that would challenge the country's puritanical heritage. Using private investments, he produced the first issue of *Playboy*, featuring the famous photo of Marilyn Monroe, in late 1953 and sold over 50,000 copies. Soon Hef purchased the first Playboy Mansion in Chicago. By 1971, the magazine was selling 7 million copies per month and Playboy Enterprises included clubs, resorts and casinos. Hef relocated to his Beverly Hills estate in 1975 and earned a star on the Hollywood Walk of Fame. Following a stroke in the 1980s, the world's most notorious bachelor married a Playmate and had two sons. Currently single again, the Playboy Mansion has become a fixture on the celebrity scene, and many film, TV and rock stars look forward to an invitation to the exclusive estate.

RESTAURANTS

Restaurants

blue on blue
9400 W. Olympic Boulevard.
Tel: 310-277 5221. Open: B, L
and D daily. $$$
When out-of-towners picture the Hollywood elite at play, this Beverly Hills oasis, inside the Avalon Hotel, is probably what they envision. Peaceful during the day and lively at night, the intimate restaurant looks onto a striking aquamarine pool. Trendsetters can sip mojitos poolside or savor caramelized fig salads and Atlantic black cod with Okinawa sweet potatoes and vanilla butter.

Crustacean Beverly Hills
9646 S. South Santa Monica Boulevard. Tel. 310-205 8990. Open: L and D Mon–Fri, D only Sat. $$$$
A culinary feast created by the An family from Vietnam, the restaurant includes a 'secret kitchen" within the main kitchen. Try the Ans' best family recipe: roasted crab and garlic noodles. It's delicate and delicious.

The Farm of Beverly Hills
439 N. Beverly Drive. Tel: 310-273 5578. Open: B, L and D daily. $$$
Farm-fresh cooking might seem out of place in Beverly Hills, but loyal locals swarm to this casual, rustic eatery just north of Rodeo Drive. Diners eat

together at communal tables in the pleasant dining room and enjoy innovative versions of California and American staples. Try the s'mores.

The Ivy
113 N. Robertson Boulevard. Tel: 310-274 8303. Open: L and D daily. $$$
With its inviting umbrellas, white-picket fence and vine-covered walls, this relaxing eatery is popular among Hollywood's power-brokers and has been featured in a few movies as a classic celeb hangout. Key deals are made over potent cocktails, fish, creative salads and inventive pastas.

Matsuhisa
129 N. La Cienega Boulevard. Tel: 310-659 9639. Open: L and D Mon–Fri, D only Sat–Sun. $$$$
Not the only sushi place in Beverly Hills, it's still one of the most popular. For nearly two decades, chef Nobu Matsuhisa's flagship restaurant has served innovative dishes to both celebrities and civilians in a casual, crowded setting.

Mr Chow
344 N. Camden Drive. Tel: 310-278 9911. Open: L and D Mon–Fri, D only Sat Sun. $$$$
Since 1974, this starkly-lit Asian eatery has enticed gourmets and A-list celebs with its energetic

vibe, attentive service and sophisticated Chinese cuisine.

Nate'n Al
414 N. Beverly Drive. Tel: 310-274 0101. Open: B, L and D daily. $$
Owned by the Mendelson clan for six decades, this popular, old-fashioned New York City-style deli will remind many patrons of their Jewish grandmother's kitchen. Even figure-conscious starlets find room for this modest institution's pastrami.

Spago Beverly Hills
176 N. Cañon Drive. Tel: 310-385 0880. Open: L and D Mon–Sat, D only Sun. $$$$
Hollywood's glitterati regularly haunt this epitome of Beverly Hills style, where first-rate service, fanciful decor and innova-

tive Californian-Eurasian cuisine are the standards for all others. Reserve weeks in advance.

The Stinking Rose
55 N. La Cienega Boulevard. Tel: 310-652 7673. Open: L and D daily. $$$
Unless you're a vampire, you'll appreciate the mounds of garlic at this whimsical Italian bistro. The pungent herb flavors everything here, including the neon ravioli and even the ice cream.

PRICE CATEGORIES

Prices for a three-course dinner per person with half a bottle of wine:
$ = under $25
$$ = $25–40
$$$ = $40–60
$$$$ = more than $60

RIGHT: garlic galore at the Stinking Rose.

BEL AIR AND BEYOND

**Serene, secluded and unmistakably sumptuous, LA's
rich and famous escape to the hideaways of
Bel Air and Brentwood for the gardens,
museums and architectural gems**

Movie stars and wealthy Angelenos seeking privacy turn from the fish-bowl of Hollywood to the secluded luxury they find in nooks like Bel Air and Brentwood. Visitors, too, appreciate the remote loveliness of these areas, as well as the cultural offerings in nearby Westwood and Century City.

Perennial flowers

Nestled in the canyons west of the more exclusive part of Beverly Hills, **Bel Air** ㉙ was the brainchild of Alphonso E. Bell, an imaginative oil baron who purchased more than 600 acres (243 hectares) of land in 1922. Planning a private, upscale neighborhood called "Bel Air Estates," he began with a Spanish Mission-style building to house his estate planning and sales offices, and enhanced the surrounding area with new roads, equestrian trails, exotic vegetation, a country club and stables.

For the next few decades, the community flourished, and by 1940 most of the lots had been sold. In 1946, Joseph Drown, a hotel entrepreneur from Texas, purchased Bell's office buildings and several acres of land, hired architect Burton Schutt to develop the pastoral hideaway now known as the **Hotel Bel-Air** ㉚ (701 Stone Canyon Road, tel: 310-472 1211), and transformed the

grounds into a sweet-smelling oasis of perennial flowers, palm trees, sycamores and redwoods. The haven was completed with the picturesque Swan Lake and a stunning pool, and the glamorous retreat soon became popular among famous dignitaries and Hollywood celebrities seeking seclusion, including Grace Kelly and Cary Grant.

Undisturbed by repeated ownership changes, the hotel still provides a luxurious setting for movie stars and non-celebs, and even if you're

Map on page 142

LEFT: a moment of privacy in a publicity-seeking city.
BELOW: the Chalon Suite at the Hotel Bel-Air has a private courtyard and fountain.

not staying in one of the romantic suites, a meal in the hotel's exquisite French-California restaurant *(see page 147)* or afternoon tea on the terrace will make a memorable visit.

Between the hotel and the Bel Air Country Club is another floral sanctuary, the **UCLA Hannah Carter Japanese Garden** ③ (10619 Bellagio Road, tel: 310-794 0320; open by reservation only Tues, Wed, Fri 10am–3pm; free), an intimate 1-acre (0.4-hectare) park set on a hillside and rife with vibrant flowers and koi-filled ponds. Inspired by the gardens of Kyoto, Japan, the garden is suffused with the Japanese garden spirit, with bridges, lanterns and a five-tiered pagoda. Visitors are welcome to tour the grounds, but food, drinks, cigarettes and pets are banned.

University district

The lovely campus of the 75-year-old **University of California at Los Angeles (UCLA)** – with over 170

UCLA 's Sculpture Garden features lovely works by Rodin and Matisse.

buildings and 39,000 students – invites visitors to attend various sporting events, concerts and plays. The main entrance to the college is on Hilgard Avenue, from which the **Franklin D. Murphy Sculpture Garden** ③, a 5-acre (2-hectare) park is reached. Over 70 sculptures are set in the garden, among them works by artists of the stature of Henri Matisse and Auguste Rodin. **Royce Hall** was the first building on campus and is now a concert venue, as is **Schoenberg Hall**, named after the composer who taught here in the 1940s. The **UCLA Planetarium** is a place for amateur and enthusiast astronomers to explore the cosmos through night sky shows and video presentations.

The **UCLA Fowler Museum of Cultural History** ③ (tel: 310-825 4361; open Wed–Sun noon-5pm, until 8pm on Thur; free), is located in the heart of UCLA's north campus. Originally established in 1963, the

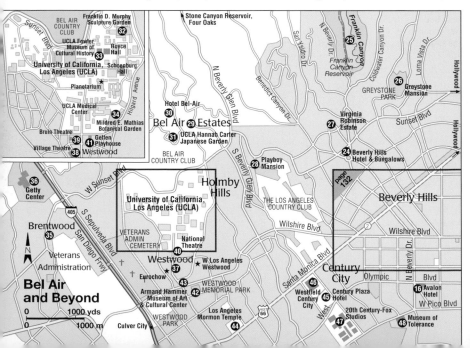

museum comprises more than 150,000 art pieces and 600,000 archaeological objects, with representations from the prehistoric, historic and contemporary cultures of Africa, Native America, Latin America, Asia and the Pacific. There are opportunities to study Peruvian textiles, Oaxacan masks, Balinese puppet theater and Indonesian baskets, as just a few examples.

For a more tranquil afternoon, visit the **Mildred E. Mathias Botanical Garden** ㉞ (tel: 310-825 1260; open daily 8am–4pm; free), a 7-acre (2.8-hectare) park that occupies the southeastern corner of campus. Almost 5,000 species of plants, many from tropical and subtropical regions, are bred, cultivated and tended by the gardeners here.

Brentwood

Brentwood ㉟, a wealthy community just west of the 405 freeway is well-known as the home of ex-football star O.J. Simpson. The world watched the slowest-ever car chase begin here, literally, as it occurred at the same time as an important world-

championship soccer match. Quintessential LA novelist Raymond Chandler lived here in the 1940s, and in August 1962, Hollywood sex symbol Marilyn Monroe died from a drug overdose in her bungalow on Helena Drive, under circumstances that still provide controversy.

Visitors are drawn to this exclusive area for the state-of-the-art **Getty Center** ㊱ *(see page 148)*, a gleaming white collection of Modernist-style buildings that became an integral part of LA's cultural scene in 1997. The fabulous complex contains a conservation institute, a bookstore and several impressive art galleries, which display a wide spectrum of work, including rococo-style furniture, Impressionist landscapes and mythological sculptures, though the center is thought by many visitors to be more impressive than the collection itself.

The 110-acre (45-hectare) site, which also houses a cactus garden, flowering maze and garden terrace café, offers visitors an oasis of order. Tours of the galleries, architecture and gardens are also available.

Map on page 142

UCLA alumni include Jim Morrison, Rob Reiner and Francis Ford Coppola.

BELOW: nannies push future LA power-brokers.

In June 1994, the bodies of Nicole Brown Simpson and Ronald Goldman were found outside a Brentwood condominium; O.J. Simpson, her ex-husband, was arrested and charged with the crime. In a trial that was televised worldwide, Simpson was acquitted.

BELOW: the most exclusive homes in Bel Air are hidden behind high walls and hedges.

Westwood Village

Back in the 1980s, **Westwood** ③⑦, a charming college town located near the intersection of Westwood and Wilshire boulevards and centered around the 420-acre (170-hectare) UCLA campus, was the ultimate pedestrian shopping area and the most popular place for young hipsters on the weekends.

Parking became impossible in this quaint enclave, as every restaurant, bar, boutique and movie theater benefited from the upscale West Side residents flocking here. The weekend party crowd eventually attracted more dangerous elements to the neighborhood, and events like the 1991 riot that flared up outside a theater showing *New Jack City* made people nervous of Westwood. The retreat led to an economic slump.

In recent years, however, "the Village" has had a renaissance of sorts. Restaurants like upscale **Eurochow** *(see page 147)*, in the hard-to-miss white dome building at Broxton and Westwood, and hotels like the stylish **W Los Angeles Westwood** have encouraged visitors back. Today, a range of shops, bookstores, cafés and bars and the largest concentration of movie theaters in any one place have all contributed to the revival here.

Like Grauman's Chinese Theatre and the El Capitan in Hollywood, three of Westwood's Mann theaters – the **Village Theatre** ③⑧ and the **Bruin Theatre** ③⑨ on Broxton Avenue, built in 1931 and 1937 respectively, and the newer **National Theatre** ④⓪ on Lindbrook Drive – regularly roll out the red carpet for star-studded movie premieres.

For live theater, there's the intimate **Geffen Playhouse** ④① (10866 Le Conte Avenue, tel: 310-208 5454), in a tranquil courtyard just south of UCLA. Constructed in 1929 by the Masons, the building became the Westwood Playhouse in 1975, with a production of Lillian Hellman's *The Little Foxes*.

Following a major gift from film producer David Geffen, the theater was renamed in 1996, and since then many famous faces have performed here, from Peter Falk to Annette Bening. Productions are usually of American classics, like the works of

Star Homes in Bel Air

Sellers of maps to movie-star homes are ubiquitous along the north stretch of Sunset. The maps promise more than they deliver, if only because so many mansions can be glimpsed only through hedges, high walls and locked gates. For anyone who wants to persevere, the best drive is up Benedict Canyon, where even non-star homes are spectacular. This was the playground of "old Hollywood," and the panorama from the intersection of Seabright and Tower Grove Drive – where Greta Garbo and John Gilbert cavorted in his Spanish-style house (demolished in 1986) – is breathtaking. Mary Pickford and Douglas Fairbanks, Jr entertained Tinseltown's elite at the legendary Pickfair (1143 Summit Drive) before it was torn down. Harold Lloyd's stunning 44-room Green Acres, with its 26 bathrooms and private golf course, was home to the actor until his death in 1971; for a short time it was a museum. Rudolph Valentino's Falcon Lair (1436 Bella Drive) can be glimpsed behind iron gates. Nearby, misleadingly numbered because it hides behind a blocked driveway, is the former Sharon Tate home (10050 Cielo Drive), scene of the 1969 murders by Charles Manson's cult.

Tennessee Williams, Arthur Miller and the more modern Sam Shepard. Recent upgrades included improved acoustics and a second theater that seats 117 people.

Marilyn Monroe's grave

Westwood's Old World architecture, from the Mediterranean Revival structures in the heart of town to the Romanesque buildings on UCLA's campus, adds to the peaceful ambience, and nowhere more than at **Westwood Memorial Park** **42** (also known as Pierce Bros Westwood Memorial Park, 1218 Glendon Avenue, tel: 310-474 1579). This cemetery at the southern edge of Westwood Village is the last and permanent home to a number of celebrities, including Marilyn Monroe, Natalie Wood, Dean Martin, Roy Orbison and "the odd couple," Jack Lemmon and Walter Matthau.

Just west of the cemetery, the **Armand Hammer Museum of Art and Cultural Center (AHMACC)** **43** (10899 Wilshire Boulevard, tel: 310-443 7000; open Tues–Sat 11am–7pm, until 9pm on Thur, Sun 11am–5pm;

charge), which was founded in 1990, originally featured galleries for Dr Armand Hammer's personal collections of Old Master paintings and drawings. Since 1994, UCLA has run the museum, and added collections from the university's Wight Art Gallery. Free lectures, readings, live music and lunchtime art talks are open to the public, and the works of Claude Monet and Mary Cassatt are here to be enjoyed.

Fox and Century City

Southeast of Westwood is the towering **Los Angeles Mormon Temple** **44** (10777 Santa Monica Boulevard, tel: 310-474 1549). Dedicated in 1956, the temple is open only to adherents, but visitors are welcome to explore the grounds and religious exhibits in the visitors' center.

Northeast along Santa Monica Boulevard, the sleek skyscrapers of **Century City** can be seen. In 1925, silent film star Tom Mix sold his private 176-acre (70-hectare) ranch, which lay between what would become Pico and Santa Monica boulevards, to William Fox, to

Map on page 142

Vintage vroom-vroom: a 1957 Chevy Bel Air convertible.

BELOW: a hideaway moment high in the hills above Hollywood.

Map on page 142

Welcome to the Museum of Tolerance.

BELOW: two views of Westwood.

expand his Fox Film Corporation from its tight quarters in Hollywood.

Five years later, bad financial decisions forced Fox out of his company, which was saved by a merger with Darryl Zanuck's 20th Century Films. 20th Century-Fox bought additional land and furthered its prestige with films like *The Grapes of Wrath* (1940) and *All About Eve* (1950).

In 1953, Zanuck introduced CinemaScope and produced movies with Marilyn Monroe, including *How to Marry a Millionaire* (1953), *Gentlemen Prefer Blondes* (1953), and *The Seven Year Itch* (1955). In the late 1950s, television, blacklisting and the studio's ever-swelling budget of *Cleopatra* (1963), forced the studio to rethink its finances; bosses decided on the commercial development of Century City.

Avenue of the Stars

By the 1980s, dignitaries like President Ronald Reagan were frequent guests of the **Century Plaza Hotel** 45 (2025 Avenue of the Stars), which still offers fine dining and luxurious rooms. Though landmarks like the Shubert Theatre have gone, Century City is still fashionable. The **Westfield Century City** 46 mall (10250 Santa Monica Boulevard), houses movie theaters and high-end stores like Godiva Chocolatier and Louis Vuitton. There is no on-street parking, so shoppers must either pay the stiff garage fee or buy enough loot for their parking to be validated.

Adjoining Century City is **20th Century-Fox Studios** 47 (10201 Pico Boulevard) to the south, a working film lot, with no public tours. Recent productions by Fox include *Moulin Rogue* (2001); *Mr & Mrs Smith* (2005) and television's *Buffy the Vampire Slayer* (1997–2003).

East on Pico, at Roxbury Drive, is the **Museum of Tolerance** 48 (9786 W. Pico Boulevard, tel: 310-553 8403; open Sun 11am–5pm, Mon–Thur 10am–4pm, Fri 10am–3pm; charge), which focuses on the Holocaust and the dynamics of racism in the US. There's also a video wall about the American civil rights struggle, and a re-creation of a 1930s pre-war Berlin café scene. ❑

RESTAURANTS

Bel-Air Bar & Grill

662 N. Sepulveda Boulevard. Tel: 310-440 5544. Open: L and D Mon–Fri, D only Sat–Sun. $$$

Between the Getty Center and the posh homes of Bel Air, this charming restaurant is surprisingly down-to-earth. Warm lighting and light jazz relax diners for eclectic dishes like chicken pot-stickers, Japanese pumpkin ravioli, shellfish bouillabaisse and all-American meatloaf.

Eurochow

1099 Westwood Boulevard. Tel: 310-209 0066. Open: D Tues–Sun. $$$–$$$$

Michael Chow, famous for his Mr Chow chain, transformed this landmark Westwood building into an Italian-Chinese restaurant. With a domed ceiling and stark-white furniture, this Mediterranean master-piece serves lobster spaghetti and great martinis, in style.

Hotel Bel-Air Restaurant

701 Stone Canyon Road. Tel: 310-472 5234. Open: B and D daily, L and T Mon–Sat, Br only Sun. $$$$

In picturesque gardens, this serene, romantic restaurant has perfected French country cuisine. The wine list is comprehensive and the menu exquisite, featuring seared foie gras with Cal-ifornia peaches and soft shell crabs in tomato-mustard cream.

Lunaria Restaurant and Jazz Club

10351 Santa Monica Boulevard. Tel: 310-282 8870. Open: L Mon–Fri, D Tues–Sat. $$$

Exotic landscapes on the walls and hot jazz in the air, this is Century City's most inviting European restaurant, where the cuisine combines flavors of Southern France and Northern Italy.

Moustache Café

1071 Glendon Avenue. Tel: 310-208 6633. Open: L and D daily. $$

In walking distance of UCLA, this romantic, bordello-like bistro presents French-influenced food from around the world. Sit outside on the patio.

Park Grill

2151 Avenue of the Stars. Tel: 310-277 1234. Open: B, L and D daily. $$$

This winning choice in Century City's Park Hyatt hotel showcases world cuisine in intimate, elegant surroundings. There's a spectrum of delicacies, from crab cakes and sushi rolls to coconut sorbet.

La Scala Presto

11740 San Vicente Boulevard. Tel: 310-826 6100. Open: L and D Mon–Sat. $$

A casual eatery in an upscale region just east of the main country club. This cozy Italian trattoria serves classics like spinach fettuccine, pesto chicken and veal parmigiana in an ivy-lined dining room with red leather booths.

Soleil

1386 Westwood Boulevard. Tel: 310-441 5384. Open: D Tues–Sun, Br only Sat–Sun. $$

The mauve-and-yellow awning beckons UCLA students and French and Italian cuisine fans to this charming bistro. The dinner menu has parmesan fondue and chicken Marsala, while the weekend brunch has a filling and ingenious menu.

Tongu

10853 Lindbrook Drive. Tel: 310-209 0071. Open: L and D Mon–Fri, D only Sat–Sun. $$$$

Some say the sushi is a bit pricey, but the gripes haven't stopped sashimi lovers and mischievous beauties from making this Westwood hotspot LA's hippest Asian fusion restaurant. Diners enjoy appetizers like marinated seaweed, and such entrees as sesame peppercorn-crusted tuna steak with sweet soy wasabi sauce.

PRICE CATEGORIES

Prices for a three-course dinner per person with half a bottle of wine:

$ = under $25
$$ = $25–40
$$$ = $40–60
$$$$ = more than $60

THE FABULOUS GETTY CENTER

It took more than a dozen years to create, and its architect, Richard Meier, was inspired by hill towns and Roman villas

The white city on the hill, high above and north of the intersection of the Santa Monica and San Diego freeways, has – as with all new architecture – drawn both praise and criticism. Detractors dislike its resemblance to an oversize refrigerator or a strip mall, while one admirer feels it is "too good for Los Angeles." Richard Meier, the Pritzker Prize-winning architect, described the site as the most beautiful he had built on, where light and landscape provided the cues for his design. The center, he says, "is both in the city and removed from it... evok[ing] a sense of both urbanity and contemplation." The views and sensation of space are peerless and, for many, more of an attraction than the art inside.

The collections are shown in five interconnecting buildings – the J. Paul Getty Museum – and the site includes six other buildings, with a research institute and library, an auditorium and a restaurant. Most offer breathtaking views of LA, the sea and the mountains. Between the museum and the research institute is a formal hill garden, designed by artist Robert Irwin.

The Getty Center, 1200 Getty Center Drive, tel: 310-440 7300. Free admission, but there's a charge for parking. Open Tues–Thurs and Sun; 10am–6pm; Fri–Sat, 10am–9pm. For more informantion go to: www.getty.edu/visit/

ABOVE: The two-story pavilions, arranged around an open courtyard of pools and rockery, give a sense of serene space far above the LA sprawl. The galleries use computerized window blinds to display the artworks in natural light.

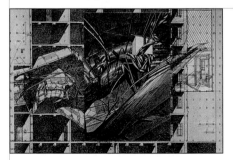

ABOVE: The Getty Center is a huge place with many galleries. An easy way to get around is to use a (free) GettyGuide, the hand-held multimedia system that provides maps and directions. It even looks like an orange iPod, so you don't feel like a lost, stupid tourist.

THE RECLUSIVE BILLIONAIRE

The Minneapolis-born oil billionaire J. Paul Getty always refused to fly, spent his last years in England, and never saw either the villa near Malibu that bears his name or the newer Getty Center. From the oilfields of Kuwait in May 1954, he telegraphed regrets that he could not attend the open-ing of the villa: "I hope this museum, modest and unpretentious as it is, will give pleasure..."

Getty inherited oilfields from his father and, employing his own considerable acumen and tal-ent, turned a thriving business into an immense empire, becoming America's first oil billionaire. Despite enormous wealth, Getty had a reputation for parsimony. In his British manor house he installed pay-phones, though he said it was because of the bills casual visitors were running up by calling, "uncles and third cousins in Caracas and Cape Town." He also explained his refusal to pay ransom to the kidnappers of his grandson, J. Paul Getty III, by saying that it would put his other 13 grandchildren in peril from extortionists.

One of the most telling stories concerns that of an electric pencil sharpener on the desk of an early curator of the Getty Villa. Getty admired this office luxury, then asked for an assurance that the curator would be meeting the cost personally.

ABOVE: The British-born artist David Hockney created the work *Pearblossom Hwy, 11–18th April 1986, #2* over eight days in the Antelope Valley outside Los Angeles. It is a mounted collage of 700 photographs (depicting the vast desert landscape), and was the first major work from LA-resident Hockney to enter the museum's contemporary collection.

LEFT TOP: This architectural drawing by Lebbeus Woods of a building façade, entitled *Berlin Free Zone*, was one of the museum's inaugural installations.

LEFT BOTTOM: Michelangelo Buonarroti's drawing of the Holy Family, *circa* 1530, was re-worked by the artist many times in a variety of different textures and styles.

LEFT: This exhibit is from the *Stammheim Missal*, a German manuscript created in Hildesheim *circa* 1170. Another treasure in the manuscript depart-ment is an illuminated psalter, an exceptional example of French Gothic work dating from the first decade of the 13th century.

SANTA MONICA, VENICE AND MARINA DEL REY

Three towns twinkle along the Pacific coastline. Santa Monica mixes urban chic with a beachtown vibe, Venice has a hippie aura and languid canals, while Marina del Rey is as sleek as the yachts in its harbor

Seekers of sun, sand, art and fashion will find much to please just a few steps from the ocean in the beachside communities that lie between Malibu and LAX, LA's international airport. Santa Monica, Venice and Marina del Rey have a breezy, clean-living vibe and a sizable swathe of amusements that can occupy visitors for days at a time.

Santa Monica

Santa Monica, the largest of the three towns, is actually an incorporated city, with wide, tree-lined boulevards, and a high proportion of rent-control apartments that have enabled a some of the less well-heeled residents to maintain tenure here in paradise.

Surrounded by Centinela Avenue, San Vicente Boulevard, the Santa Monica State Beach and Dewey Street, this seaside town began as a Mexican land grant in the 1820s and became, by the early 1900s, a charter city with picturesque avenues and parks, a public library, schools and two transcontinental railroad lines.

Although Santa Monica lost its bid to become the official Port of Los Angeles – bestowed on San Pedro down south – the city developed into a summertime resort town where people came to enjoy the piers, bathhouses and fine hotels. By the 1920s,

the aircraft industry had arrived, gambling ships had moored a few miles off the coast and Hollywood celebrities had built themselves gorgeous homes by the beach.

Since then, this refreshing near-metropolis has been popular with moviemakers. Many post-production houses and celebrity-owned production companies are based here, and films and TV shows, including *Get Shorty* (1995) and *Buffy the Vampire Slayer*, have been shot in the area. The city issues around 1,000 filming

Map on page 152

LEFT:
Santa Monica Pier.
BELOW:
shop for collectibles in these towns by the sea.

TIP

The Big Blue Bus, which costs around a dollar, goes through Santa Monica, Venice, Marina del Rey and LAX all the way to Westwood and Downtown LA; prepaid Little Blue Cards are a convenient way to travel. Tel: 310-451 5444.

permits a year. Luring visitors to places like the Third Street Promenade, Santa Monica Pier and Santa Monica Airport, the "Bay City" of Raymond Chandler's novels and terminus for historic Route 66 has come a long way in the last 185 years.

Visionary

South of Santa Monica, Venice and Marina del Rey – both smaller than their northern cousin and each within an unincorporated area of LA County – entice countless sunbathers, anglers, bicyclists, sightseers, artists and gourmets. Venice, over a century old

and famous for its Muscle Beach and bohemian boardwalk, owes its existence to Abbot Kinney, a visionary whose canal system may have failed (*see page 161*) but whose legacy survives with a trendy boulevard and an annual festival named after him.

Marina del Rey was also the brainchild of a dreamer, but although the vast tidal plain was conceived in the late 19th century by real estate speculator M.C. Wicks as a major commercial harbor, it wasn't until 1960 that the Army Corps of Engineers began dredging the area. By 1965, Marina del Rey had opened to the

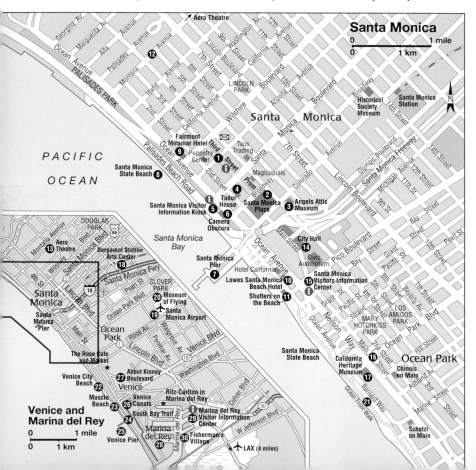

public, and today one of the world's largest man-made pleasure-craft harbors encompasses high-end restaurants, hotels, shops, parks, waterside promenades and public cruises.

Parks and promenades

Santa Monica has many fine attractions, but out-of-towners often make a beeline straight for the **Third Street Promenade ❶**. This three-block-long, pedestrian-only strip of bookstores, clothing boutiques, exclusive shops, casual eateries, boisterous pubs and street musicians is usually quitelively and crowded, especially on the weekends.

It's also fun. Sitting at an outdoor table on a soft tropical evening, with a cocktail and an exotic, organic tidbit to nibble on while observing the scene – which might include occasional tango dancers sashaying down the street – is as fine an introduction to the city as any.

Stretching from Wilshire Boulevard to Broadway, the tree-lined walkway was, until the late 1980s, a rundown retail area of discount stores. Today, despite a few homeless

people resting here and there, the promenade is one of the jewels of the city's recent revival. Places like Barney's Beanery and Yankee Doodle Billiard Club attract throngs of happy-hour hopefuls and after-dark party-seekers. Tourists find helpful information about attractions and events, as well as bus schedules and souvenirs, at the well-stocked **Santa Monica Visitor Information Cart** (open Wed–Sun 11am 6pm), located between Arizona Avenue and Santa Monica Boulevard.

Santa Monica Place ❷, a sparkling three-story galleria designed by famed architect Frank Gehry, anchors the southern end of the promenade. Flanked by Macy's and the Robinsons-May department stores and open every day, including Sunday, the dramatic glass-encased shopping center has a spacious food court, two roomy parking garages and trendy stores like Williams-Sonoma and Brookstone. The skylit California mall has been used as a backdrop for films including *Fast Times at Ridgemont High* (1982) and *Terminator 2: Judgment Day* (1991).

Santa Monica has many Art Deco buildings.

BELOW:
Ocean Avenue at dusk.

Angels in the attic

Downtown Santa Monica has a number of relatively inexpensive places to park, so it's a good idea to drive (or take the bus; *see tip on page 152*) and then hoof it; there are plenty of things to see and do within walking distance of the Third Street Promenade.

Two blocks northeast is the charming **Angels Attic Museum** ❸ (516 Colorado Avenue, tel: 310-394 8331; open Thur–Sun 12.30–4.30pm; charge), a two-story Victorian house erected in 1895 and reborn in 1984 as a world-class repository of antique dolls, dollhouses, miniatures and toys. For an added fee, patrons can savor afternoon tea and sandwiches in the sweetly scented garden or on the enclosed verandah.

Two streets northwest, on historic Route 66, is the interesting **Taos Indian Trading Co.** (403 Santa Monica Boulevard), a collection of fine turquoise jewelry, Native American pottery and traditional kachina dolls. Around the opposite corner is **Adamm's Stained Glass Studio & Art Glass Gallery** (1426 4th Street, tel: 310-451 9390), with a permanent display of work, including lamps and paperweights, from over 125 American glass artists. On the eastern side of the Third Street Promenade, the **Santa Monica Puppetry Center** (1255 2nd Street, tel: 310-656 0483) is a theater devoted to the art of small wooden people. Following the weekly shows, visitors can tour the workshop and museum, which displays over 400 puppets, marionettes and ventriloquist figures.

Homesick British ex-pats find some comfort (although no rain) at the **Tudor House** ❹ (1403 2nd Street), one of the best-known English tearooms in America. For over four decades, the Tudor House has sold British gifts and foods in its shop and served a variety of traditional meat pies, crumpets and scones, English tea sandwiches and daily afternoon tea in its quaint dining room. Just around the corner, there's no shortage of classic pub grub and British decor at the busy **Ye Olde King's Head** *(see page 163)*.

Santa Monica is keen on architecture and design; it's no coincidence that Thom Mayne, the 2005 winner

The Third Street Promenade is three blocks of shopping and streetlife. No cars allowed.

BELOW:
Hare Krishna festival by the beach.

of architecture's greatest prize, the Pritzker, is based here. All around this part of town are showrooms dedicated to bringing modern design to the home and the workplace, grouped together in an amorphous area called the **Design District**. Pick up a brochure from the Tourist Info Center to seek them out.

For evening entertainment, downtown Santa Monica has lots of laid-back bars and clubs. Theater lovers can enjoy contemporary performances at the **City Garage Theater** (1340 1/2 4th Street Alley, tel: 310-319 9939) or the **Promenade Playhouse at Piero Dusa** (1404 Third Street Promenade, tel: 310-656 8070). Magic enthusiasts can also look forward to Santa Monica's theater scene, which includes live shows at **Magicopolis** (1418 4th Street, tel: 310-451 2241).

Santa Monica Pier

This deceptively casual town embraces both a metropolitan sophistication and a beach-town atmosphere, but it's the coast that draws most of the spectators. Stretching from the northern border of Santa Monica to the historic municipal pier is the cliff-top **Palisades Park**, a eucalyptus-fringed green space along Ocean Avenue that looks out over views of ocean vessels in the distance and the solar-powered Ferris wheel on Santa Monica Pier below. It's also a romantic place to watch the sun set slowly over the mountains.

Although the park, bequeathed to the city in 1892 by Santa Monica's founders Colonel Robert Baker and Senator John P. Jones, has proven to be popular with the homeless (Santa Monica is "the home of the homeless," according to satirist Harry Shearer), it does have two sites, the **Santa Monica Visitor Information Kiosk ❺** (1400 Ocean Avenue; open daily 10am–5pm in summer, 10am–4pm in winter) and the free **Camera**

Obscura ❻ (1450 Ocean Avenue; open Mon–Fri 9am–4pm, Sat–Sun 11am–4pm), which has been documenting Santa Monica for more than 100 years. Turn the wheel of the rooftop turret and the city unfolds with 360° of seaside bliss.

Over the years, the archway at the end of Colorado Avenue has beckoned countless visitors down the hill and onto **Santa Monica Pier ❼**, the venerable boardwalk that has been a city landmark since 1909. Although the pier lost most of its original buildings and roller coasters long ago, was nearly demolished in the 1970s and was forced to undergo extensive restoration after a mid-1980s storm, it is now one of Los Angeles' most visited attractions. (Tip: the back staircase offers a prime Pacific view as the sun slips into the ocean.)

Besides a hands-on aquarium and **Pacific Park**, a fun zone of snack stands and amusement rides, the pier also has seafood eateries, souvenir carts, arcade games, street performers, caricaturists and fishermen. The crown jewel of the pier is the **Looff Hippodrome**, a national historic

Map on page 152

From 1924 to 1963, Santa Monica Pier was home to the La Monica Ballroom, a vast, ornate venue that hosted big-band concerts and some of the earliest national radio and television broadcasts.

BELOW: Santa Monica's answer to Rodeo Drive is Montana Avenue.

landmark whose whimsical, hand-carved **carousel** featured in *The Sting* (1973). The pier itself has been a backdrop in numerous movies, from *Funny Girl* (1968) to *Forrest Gump* (1994). Every summer, fans of the Santa Monica Pier gather for the Twilight Dance Series, free evening concerts that kick off at sunset.

Santa Monica State Beach is a clean stretch of white sand popular with anyone who loves outdoor living, from sunbathers to walkers to bicyclists on the nearby trail. Overlooking the beach are nearly two dozen hotels, many with panoramic views. For decades, visitors have enjoyed cocktails in the **Fairmont Miramar Hotel** ❾ (101 Wilshire Boulevard); the Koi Pond Lounge has been a playground for celebrities and politicians, from Jean Harlow to President Clinton, since 1921.

There's a good breakfast buffet at **Loews Santa Monica Beach Hotel** ❿ (1700 Ocean Avenue), while **Shutters on the Beach** ⓫ (1 Pico Boulevard) houses an art collection that almost rivals the ocean views outside the front door. Stop by the lobby for a brochure and read up on the works by artists like David Hockney and Roy Lichtenstein. Just south of the pier are two 14-ft (4-meter) "Singing Beach Chairs." These harmonically tuned chairs, designed with an oversized lifeguard look-out, are great perches for wave-watching.

Montana and Main

The Third Street Promenade isn't the only shopping avenue here. Amid its nicer homes at the city's northern end is Santa Monica's answer to Rodeo Drive, **Montana Avenue** ⓬, with 150 high-end stores displaying all manner of apparel, handicrafts and housewares. The attractive, tree-lined street is packed with local celebrities who traverse the 10-block, foot-friendly area in their Jimmy Choos (and pick up another few pairs in the process). Even non-shoppers head for Montana; **Strike-a-balance** (No. 1131) is a spa and yoga studio offering blissful massage treatments.

Two blocks northeast is the **Aero Theatre** ⓭ (No. 1328, tel: 323-466 3456), one of the few single-screen theaters remaining in Los Angeles. It

---

TIP

Health-conscious Santa Monica has three weekly farmers' markets – at Arizona and 3rd (Wed and Sat); at the Santa Monica Airport (Sat) and at Main Street and Ocean Park Boulevard (Sun).

BELOW:
it's a dog's life.

Map on page 152

was built in 1939 by aviation tycoon Donald Douglas as a 24-hour recreation facility for his employees during World War II. Today, patrons can sit back and savor films like *Roman Holiday* (1953) or *The Exorcist* (1973). The Aero is operated by the American Cinematheque, the organization that runs Hollywood's historic Egyptian Theatre *(see page 104)*. After catching a flick, grab a glass of organic juice and fresh sushi at the **Wild Oats Market** (No. 1425).

Back toward the southern end of town is Main Street, a charming shopping district just a couple blocks from the beach. If you're tired of walking, hop aboard the electric **TIDE Shuttle** and ride south along Main. Past the freeway and gleaming **City Hall 🄭**, you'll come to the walk-in **Santa Monica Visitor Information Center 🄯** (1920 Main Street, Suite B, tel: 310-393 7593; open daily 9am–6pm).

Five blocks farther down, the shopping and dining district of **Main Street 🄰** really begins. This is the place for Wolfgang Puck's **Chinois on Main** *(see page 162)* and Gover-

nor Schwarzenegger's former eatery **Schatzi on Main** *(see page 163)*. The stores are delightful and a tiny bit eccentric. There are jewelry-making workshops; photographs and paintings by female artists; and vintage clothing and linens. In a pretty courtyard complex at No. 2665, the **Eames Gallery** showcases the designs of Charles and Ray Eames, whose home and office furnishings have earned a place in New York's Museum of Modern Art.

Art and Aviation

Also on Main Street, the **California Heritage Museum 🄲** (2612 Main Street, tel: 310-392 8537; open Wed–Sun 11am–4pm; charge) displays Monterey furniture, California rainbow pottery and other regional decorative arts in a lovely, two-story house built in 1894 by architect Sumner P. Hunt for Roy Jones, the son of Santa Monica's co-founder.

A couple of miles east of the main tourist drag along the coast are two sites worth exploring, an arts center and an airport. Between Olympic Boulevard and Michigan Avenue, the

If it's too crowded to stretch out, you may end up like this. Life's a beach.

BELOW: get surf lessons or palm plants here.

TIP

In summer, you can attend free classical and pop music concerts in Marina del Rey's Burton Chace Park (tel: 310-305 9545) or tour the marina via an inexpensive water shuttle (tel: 310-628 3219).

BELOW:
tai-chi in the park is a very Californian sight.

Bergamot Station Arts Center (2525 Michigan Avenue; free) was once a train depot. Now it has been transformed into a dynamic arts complex, with over 30 art galleries, 10 shops and a cute café (closed Sunday). The centerpiece is the **Santa Monica Museum of Art** (tel: 310-586 6488; open Tues–Sat 11am–6pm; requested donation), which presents contemporary poetry journals, mixed media collages, watercolors and wire-crafted vessels.

Southeast of the station is another historic transportation hub, this one still functioning. The **Santa Monica Airport** ⑲, bordered by Bundy Drive and 23rd Street, is the oldest operating airport in LA County and the site of famous first flights by Charles Lindbergh, Amelia Earhart and Howard Hughes. In the 1920s, the Douglas Aircraft Company tested and built production aircraft here, including the military workhorse DC-3 Dakota. In its peak years, the Douglas plant employed over 40,000 workers, and the airport expanded significantly during World War II.

Modern-day visitors appreciate the historic setting when they attend monthly outdoor antiques markets, art shows, Halloween events, air races, concerts and two free public viewing areas of the runway. The **Museum of Flying** ⑳, a collection of vintage aircraft and Donald Douglas' personal effects, will soon reopen in its new location, a large hangar on the north side of the airport.

Venice Beach

Little more than a mile south of the Santa Monica Pier is the bohemian enclave of **Venice**. The most eye-popping way to savor this archetypical Southern California community is to stroll down **Ocean Front Walk** ㉑, the promenade that starts just south of the pier. Along this jumping beachside boardwalk, sun-burned rubbernecking tourists mingle with scantily-clad rollerbladers, rainbow-haired punks, daredevil skateboarders, hippie painters, tattoo artists, jugglers, mimes, fortune tellers and itinerant musicians.

From here, you can enjoy the sparkling ocean beyond **Venice City Beach** ㉒; shop for sunglasses, handmade jewelry, imported sarongs and leather boots; relish the mural-covered walls around you; relax at one of the red-checkered patio tables at the long-standing **Sidewalk Café**; or observe biceps flexing at nearby **Muscle Beach** ㉓ *(see page 51)*.

More active types can spend an hour or two on the beachside basketball and paddle tennis courts north of Muscle Beach. Some take their pleasure from a spin on the bicycle path that runs along the the Pacific Ocean, part of the lengthy 22-mile (35-km) **South Bay Trail** ㉔ winding from Santa Monica to Palos Verdes. You can rent a bicycle or a pair of in-line skates from one of the stores along Ocean Front Walk, Windward Avenue or Washington Boulevard.

Strollers can enjoy a pleasant trek amid the fishermen forever lining the

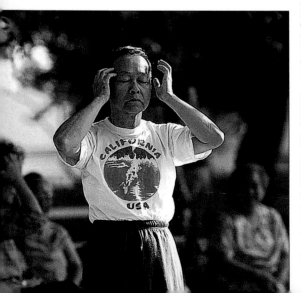

Venice Pier ㉕, a shadow of the three arcade-filled piers that once graced the coast, or beside the low-key but lovely **canals** ㉖ between Venice and Washington boulevards. The canals, all that remain of Abbot Kinney's breath-taking vision *(see page 161)*, are lined with vibrant flowers, verdant shrubs, colorful bungalows and bobbing canoes.

Abbot Kinney Boulevard ㉗, which many consider the heart of today's Venice, is east of Venice Beach. For over 20 years, the annual Abbot Kinney Festival – "the ultimate Venice block party" – has animated the boulevard with live music, performance artists, food booths and arts-and-crafts vendors. Day to day, however, the boulevard is still a trendy visit, densely packed with hip restaurants, bars and boutiques.

Foodies love French-inspired eateries like **Joe's** *(see page 162)*, **Lilly's** and **Jin Patisserie**, not to mention the delis, sushi joints and all-American restaurants. Music lovers enjoy live jazz at **Hal's Bar & Grill** *(see page 162)*, and shoppers take pleasure in the boulevard's antiques showrooms, funky clothing stores, art galleries and emporia for everything from incense to teapots.

If you're driving to Venice from Santa Monica, the most direct route is down **Pacific Avenue**, a road peppered with clothing shops, music stores and casual eateries, like the festive **Canal Club** at Venice Boulevard. One block west, along **Speedway**, are several small parking lots, though street parking is not as convenient as in Santa Monica.

Non-motorists can reach Venice by hopping aboard one of the many buses that run down Santa Monica's **Main Street** and end at **Windward Circle**, once the center of Abbot Kinney's Venice in the early 1900s, now a trendy residential neighborhood of historic bungalows, artists' lofts and small art studios.

Marina del Rey

South of Venice's Washington Boulevard is desirable **Marina del Rey** ㉘ – or the "Harbor of Kings" – upon which the surrounding community is dependent. The 400-acre (160-hectare) marina is a stark silhouette of gleaming white sailboats and million-dollar yachts against a backdrop of glistening sapphire waters; more than 6,000 private boats dock here.

Encircled by luxury resorts, high-rise condominiums, numerous restaurants and many miles of waterfront paths, the world's largest constructed yacht harbor has a casual, tropical flavor, enhanced by warm ocean breezes, year-round sunshine and the ambience of the surrounding streets that carry exotic names from far-off Pacific places like Fiji, Bali, Tahiti and Bora Bora.

Annual events entice travelers from far and wide to this small coastal community – festivals and attractions like the January boat show, April's Halibut Derby, the sailboat races from April to September, the Christmas-time boat parade and the spectacular 4th of July and New Year's Eve fire-

Map on page 152

Marina del Rey is a tranquil place for a stop-over when flying in or out of LAX.

BELOW: more than 6,000 private boats dock at Marina del Rey.

Map on page 152

In-line skaters play a part in the laid-back atmosphere of these coastal communities.

BELOW: sunset over Santa Monica.

works displays. Visitors also find daily diversions, from gourmet cuisine to harbor cruises.

Waterfront sunset

Cyclists enjoy up-close views of the marina on the continuation of the South Bay Trail as it heads east from Venice Pier, snakes along Washington Boulevard, Admiralty Way and Fiji Way and hugs Ballona Creek before veering toward Playa del Rey. On this picturesque route, stop at the **Marina del Rey Visitor Information Center** ❷⁹ (4701 Admiralty Way, tel: 310-305 9545; open daily) for details about attractions. Families are delighted by waterfront picnic areas like **Burton Chace Park**, **Admiralty Park** and **Mother's Beach,** a cove with bike rentals and volleyball courts. Lifeguards monitor the swimming here.

Shoppers are also catered for here with a few malls within walking distance of the six major hotels. Besides the **Marina Beach** and **Waterside** shopping centers and the **Villa Marina Marketplace**, the whimsical, brightly-hued Fisherman's Vil-

lage at the southern end of Marina del Rey, lures souvenir-seekers with a cluster of waterfront cottages and cobblestone paths resembling a New England seaport.

Not quite as weathered as the real thing, but with a 60-ft (18-meter) tall, non-working lighthouse, **Fisherman's Village** ❸⁰ entertains tourists with free weekend concerts, seafood and ethnic eateries. The view from here is charming, and might even include a bobbing sea lion or two. The village is the starting point for most sea-faring activities, like fishing excursions, narrated harbor tours, dinner cruises and whale-watching vessels (wintertime only). It's also the place to rent jet skis and kayaks.

By late afternoon, relax from all this activity and lounge in one of the waterfront restaurants or bars to savor a stunning sunset over cocktails. There's a range of cuisines, from high-end restaurants to Mexican cantinas. After dinner, as the stars hang low in the sky and twinkle over the sea, unwind in a cozy piano bar and uncover your skills at salsa or flamenco dancing. ❑

Tranquility by the Beach

Waves of bright flowers tumble over sagging fences, and ducks nestle under upturned boats on tiny jetties. Only a block away, traffic thunders ceaselessly along Pacific Avenue, but here in the wildlife sanctuary formed by the Venice canal system, all is tranquil.

The circulating system for the canals was a disaster, as the 30-inch (80-cm) pipes designed to flush sea water through gates on every tide failed, almost from the outset. More than 50 years of silt, dirt and refuse have reduced the once 4-ft (1.2-meter) high waterways to little more than knee-deep. But you can pick your way along rutted paths, over humpbacked bridges and past well-tended gardens, admiring the architecture, the birds and the flowers.

Over 85 years after the death of Abbot Kinney, some of his vision still remains along what is probably the nicest walk in urban Los Angeles. Venice began when Kinney acquired 160 acres (65 hectares) of marshland in 1902. His engineers' recommendation for the canals to be dug to reclaim the land gave him the idea to replicate Italy's city of Venice. After his workmen had spent three years digging the trenches, he had Japanese lanterns installed, imported gondolas, and encircled the entire area with a miniature railroad.

The opening (July 4, 1905) was attended by 40,000 people. Entertained by a large orchestra, they strolled in the square, modeled after the Venetian Piazza San Marco, and onto the 1,600-ft (490-meter) pier where the showpiece was the Ship Hotel. Wealthy visitors stayed in St Mark's Hotel, inspired by the Doge's Palace; the less affluent slept under canvas roofs in Villa City bordering the lagoon.

Mack Sennett shot Charlie Chaplin's second movie *(Kid Auto Races)* in Venice, Mary Pickford was rowed down the Grand Canal, Mabel Normand posed for pictures with a fish on her head and Carole Lombard hosted a memorable party on the pier. But gradu-

ally the resort began to lose its appeal and deteriorated, as low-grade boardwalk attractions replaced the earlier treats of performances by Sarah Bernhardt and the Chicago Symphony Orchestra.

Kinney's dream clouded, and he died in 1920. In 1925, after local residents voted to become part of LA, the main section of the canal was paved for the benefit of cars, and before the end of the 1920s, the Ohio Oil Company had erected a forest of derricks. By 1931, they were working 163 productive oil wells. Venice experienced a sharp decline, so much so that it was used as a stand-in for Los Robles, Mexico, during the filming of Orson Welles' 1958 film noir classic, *A Touch of Evil*.

The heart of today's Venice is Windward Circle, where a statue marks the site of the former lagoon. The continuation of Windward Avenue was once the Lion canal, and Market, Altair and Cabrillo streets follow the track of earlier waterways. During the heady Kinney years, there was a ticket office at the corner of Pacific and Windward for the Pacific Electric rail cars. At Ocean Front Walk, what was once the Hotel Stuart is now the Venice Beach Hotel. For a contemporary stroll by the canals, they are best viewed along Dell Avenue.   ❑

RIGHT: the canals were one man's exuberant folly.

RESTAURANTS, BARS & CAFÉS

Restaurants

Axe Restaurant
1009 Abbot Kinney Boulevard. Tel: 310-664 9787.
Open: L and D Tues–Fri, Br and D Sat–Sun. $$
A hip, artsy crowd is drawn to this organic California eatery (pronounced "ah-shay") on Venice's restaurant row. The open kitchen and stone tables are industrial-chic, but the cuisine is healthy and creative, like roasted artichokes, and tuna sashimi with lemongrass. Homemade ice cream, too.

Border Grill
1445 4th Street. Tel: 310-451 1655. Open: L and D daily. $$
Brought to you by the Food Network's "Too Hot Tamales," Mary Sue Milliken and Susan Feniger, this dynamic eatery showcases enticing Mexican cuisine. Amid vibrant murals, patrons can choose from a selection of wines or tequilas, and dishes like green corn tamales, roasted lamb tacos and portabello mushroom *mulitas*.

Chez Mimi
246 26th Street. Tel: 310-393 0558. Open: L and D Tues–Sat, D only Sun. $$–$$$
If you're lucky, Mimi Hébert will personally escort you to a table in one of the tree-shaded patios or tiny romantic dining rooms. The homestyle French cuisine is as perfect and as understated as the ambience.

Chinois on Main
2709 Main Street. Tel: 310-392 9025. Open: L Wed–Fri, D daily. $$$$
Still bustling 20 years after its opening, Wolfgang Puck's shrine to the cuisines of East and West lures Santa Monica residents with flavorful dishes that perfectly fuse the styles of Asia, France and California.

Hal's Bar & Grill
1349 Abbot Kinney Boulevard. Tel: 310-396 3105.
Open: L and D daily until 2am, Br Sat–Sun. $$$
Lively jazz performances, winning cocktails and simple American dishes entice Venice-area gadabouts. Sleek but comfortable, daring diners might be tempted by such innovations as fried squash blossoms, maple leaf duck breast and warm pear and cranberry bread pudding.

Harbor House Restaurant
4211 Admiralty Way. Tel: 310-577 4555. Open: L and D Sat–Sun, D only Mon–Fri. $$$
From the harborside patio, diners can gaze at the yachts of Marina del Rey while savoring steaks and seafood classics like jumbo shrimp, Maryland blue crab cakes, raw oysters, clam chowder, king salmon and Maine lobster.

Jer-Ne Restaurant + Bar
4375 Admiralty Way. Tel: 310-574 4333. Open: B, L and D daily, Br only Sun. $$$$
With its lovely prime waterfront location, the Ritz-Carlton's signature restaurant in Marina del Rey invites visitors to a smorgasbord of international flavors. Diners can trot the globe from their tables, with *huevos rancheros* for breakfast, a Korean tofu salad or a Kosher Reuben for lunch, and Iranian caviar, curried coconut shrimp, Berkshire pork sausages or Hawaiian swordfish for dinner.

Joe's Restaurant
1023 Abbot Kinney Boulevard. Tel: 310-399 5811.
Open: L and D Tues–Fri, Br and D Sat–Sun. $$$
Not your average neighborhood restaurant, chef Joe Miller's Venice-based haven is one of LA's finest examples of French-Californian cuisine. The atmosphere is refined but down-to-earth, much like the seasonal gourmet menu.

The Lobster
1602 Ocean Avenue. Tel: 310-458 9294. Open: L and D daily. $$$$
Glass walls and outdoor tables ensure stunning sunset views of the Santa Monica Pier and the ocean while diners savor award-winning seafood dishes, from lobster cocktails and grilled swordfish sand-

wiches to Maine sea scallops and peppercorn-crusted yellowfin tuna.

Mélisse
1104 Wilshire Boulevard. Tel: 310-395 0881. Open: D Tues–Sat. $$$$
This award-winning Santa Monica restaurant serves contemporary American-French cuisine in a warm, upscale setting. Inspired by Josiah Citrin, who worked with Wolfgang Puck, the menu has creations like parsley-crusted Dover sole with potato gnocchi and duck breast with figs and couscous. Desserts to-die-for, too.

Ocean Avenue Seafood
1401 Ocean Avenue. Tel: 310-394 5669. Open: L and D daily. $$$$
With a view of the Pacific, this seafood place and oyster bar celebrates the ocean in every sense of the word: Alaskan king crab legs, Caribbean ahi salad, shrimp fettucine, raw oysters – you name it, this Santa Monica gem has it. The wine list is comprehensive, and the desserts are great.

The Rose Café & Market
220 Rose Avenue. Tel: 310-399 0711. Open: B and L daily, Br only Sat–Sun. $
The casual dining room and sunny outdoor patio are rarely empty at this Venice café and bakery. When not noshing, be sure to check out the walls; artists have been displaying their work here for 25 years.

Schatzi on Main
3110 Main Street. Tel: 310-399 4800. Open: L and D daily, Br only Sat–Sun. $$$
Famous for its founder, Arnold Schwarzenegger, this Santa Monica eatery reflects the governor's journey from Austria to Hollywood. The menu features Austrian specialties like *Kaiserschmarrn* and California dishes like ahi sashimi salad. The restaurant is known, too, for its cigar-friendly bar and monthly Cigar Nights.

Ye Olde King's Head
116 Santa Monica Boulevard. Tel: 310-451 1402. Open: B, L and D daily, T only Sat. $$
The patterned carpet and painted landscapes recall the country inns of jolly ol' England in this pub by the sea. The Santa Monica institution has specialized in British fare like bangers and mash for the past 30 years. Afternoon tea, a gift shoppe, dart boards and imported beers are even more reasons to stop by for a pint.

Bars and Cafés

Baja Cantina, 311 Washington Boulevard, draws weekday beach lovers to the front patio for classic Mexican food, while young singles flock to this rowdy Marina del Rey bar on weekends.

The Brig, 1515 Abbot Kinney Boulevard, has recently been revamped, transforming the low-key pool hall into a swanky, softly-lit Venice lounge that still attracts the surfers, grad students and professionals.

The Circle Bar, 2926 Main Street, has enticed Santa Monica regulars for years. The dramatic den has red-lit walls, a circular bar and sexy singles on the dance floor.

Jin Patisserie, 1202 Abbot Kinney Boulevard, is an Asian-French pastry shop and tea garden in Venice. The patio tempts diners with salads, quiches and desserts.

The Veranda, 1910 Ocean Way, invites sand-and-sea lovers to the spacious lobby of Santa Monica's Casa Del Mar, where rattan seats and tall windows provide a relaxing setting for drinks and light food.

PRICE CATEGORIES

Prices for a three-course dinner per person with half a bottle of wine:
$ = under $25
$$ = $25–40
$$$ = $40–60
$$$$ = more than $60

NOTABLE NEIGHBORHOODS

From busy Koreatown to the hot clubs and cool bars of Silverlake, from the Latino roots of Los Feliz to the cosseted celebs of Malibu, here are areas of Los Angeles that are off the beaten path

A s residents, visitors and movie-goers know, Los Angeles is a sprawling metropolis with an overlapping freeway system, and it takes some orientation to adapt to. Made up of several independent cities like Santa Monica, and a number of destination regions like Hollywood, the City of Angels also has lesser-known neighborhoods and attractions – many of them close to more famous sites.

Not far from Downtown are four neighborhoods worth mentioning: as well as Echo Park *(see page 88),* there's Koreatown, Silverlake and Los Feliz. Nearly the same distance from Beverly Hills, but in opposite directions are Culver City and the Skirball Cultural Center. West of Santa Monica, and accessible via the famed Pacific Coast Highway (PCH), are sandy coastlines and acres of wooded canyons. Three of the most interesting communities in this tangled wilderness are Pacific Palisades, Topanga Canyon and, of course, magnificent Malibu.

Koreatown

Los Angeles has always been a cultural melting pot of ethnic neighborhoods like Chinatown, Little Tokyo, Thai Town and Little Armenia. **Koreatown** ❶, the largest Korean community in the US, is one

such neighborhood of Korean stores, restaurants and nightclubs.

Before driving to Koreatown, however, culture-seekers might first head want to head 2 miles (3 km) west on Wilshire and stop by the **Korean Cultural Center (KCCLA).** A combination museum, library and art gallery, this institution honors the history and culture of a nation known, in part, for colorful hanbok dresses, time-honored tea ceremonies, masked dance drama, pungent kimchi dishes, ginseng and

Map on page 166

LEFT: savoring an afternoon in Silverlake.
BELOW: a typical day in Koreatown.

L.A. UNIFIED SCHOOL DISTRICT STOP

Koreatown has many shopping and eating opportunities.

taekwondo. Another cultural institution, this one actually located in Koreatown, is east of the Wilshire/Western Metro station, the **Korean American Museum (KAM)** (3727 W. 6th Street, 213-388 4229; open Wed–Fri 11am–6pm, Sat 11am–3pm). Celebrating the legacy and future of Korean immigrants and their families, recent exhibits explored aspects of Korean American life, like small business ownership, religious practices and contemporary art.

As well as learning about Korean life, visitors can experience it first-hand in nearby teahouses, barbecue eateries and noodle shops, many of which line 6th and 8th streets, Wilshire Boulevard and Western Avenue. Night owls will also find plenty of entertainment in Koreatown, from pool halls and bowling alleys to multilingual karaoke bars. For shopaholics, the neighborhood has two enormous malls: the Kore-

atown Plaza and the Koreatown Galleria. The **Koreatown Plaza** (928 S. Western Avenue) is a three-level shopping center with a range of stores, from bakeries to clothing boutiques, and a food court serving up local staples, including *soon tofu* (spicy tofu casserole) and *pat-bing-su* (shaved ice).

The **Koreatown Galleria** (3250 W. Olympic Boulevard) is slightly more upscale than the Plaza, and provides an enormous inventory of clothes, jewelry, books and cosmetics, and several Korean eateries.

Silverlake

Hollywood is not, as some might believe, where the movie industry began on the West Coast. In fact, while Hollywood was still a quiet farming community, some of the earliest motion picture studios were springing up in parts of Silverlake, nearby Echo Park and an in-between area formerly known as

Notable Neighborhoods

0	5 miles
0	5 km

Edendale. Here, the Selig-Polyscope Company introduced cowboy legend Tom Mix to the screen. Near what is now Glendale Boulevard, the Mack Sennett Studios produced several movie classics starring Laurel and Hardy, the Keystone Cops and Charlie Chaplin. Nearby, in the late 1920s, Roy and Walt Disney created Mickey Mouse on Hyperion Avenue, at the Disney Bros. Studios.

Today, **Silverlake ❷** is a laid-back artistic community, known for eclectic boutiques, funky eateries, gay-friendly nightclubs and hilly streets lined with lovely Mediterranean and Craftsman-style homes. Five miles (8 km) northwest of Downtown and generally bounded by Sunset Boulevard on the south, Riverside Drive on the north, Hyperion Avenue on the west and Glendale Boulevard on the east, the community is centered around the picturesque **Silverlake Reservoir**.

Sunset Junction, the stretch of Sunset Boulevard between Maltman and Fountain avenues, beckons visitors to a variety of intimate cafés and offbeat shops, a farmer's market every Saturday morning and a yearly summertime street fair. Surrounding streets, like Hyperion Avenue and Silverlake Boulevard, also have eateries with sweet Latino pastries, and boutiques offering handmade clothing. But it's at night that Silverlake shows its true, rowdy colors. **Zen Sushi** (2609 Hyperion Avenue), for instance, provides live music and karaoke to accompany sashimi and teriyaki.

Locals flock for late-night sausages and beer to the **Red Lion Tavern** (2366 Glendale Boulevard), a German institution for more than 40 years. Silverlake also has its share of alternative bars, like the Moroccan-themed **Akbar**, and music clubs, including **Club Spaceland** (1717 Silver Lake Boulevard, tel: 323-661 4380), which is a live-rock venue, and has featured the likes of Beck and the Foo Fighters.

Los Feliz

Although natives debate the pronunciation of **Los Feliz ❸** (is it Los Feel-is or Los Fi-leez?), everyone seems to agree that this affluent

Several of Silverlake's streets retain the Scottish monikers (Rowena, Kenilworth, Ben Lomond, Locksley and Saint George) that they were given in the late 1800s, when the name of the hilly town was taken from Sir Walter Scott's novel "Ivanhoe."

Map on page 166

LEFT: sisterhood in Silverlake.
BELOW: poster-perfect in Koreatown.

The Dresden Room, Los Feliz, is a good place to hear late-night jazz.

BELOW: the Hollywood Entertainment Museum celebrates Liz Taylor, winner of a life achievement award from the AFI.

enclave, just east of Hollywood, is an enticing place to visit – or even better, to live. With well-landscaped mansions along Los Feliz Boulevard, key architectural landmarks, historic nightclubs and several entrances to Griffith Park, Los Feliz has plenty to tantalize the curious visitor. Architecture buffs will enjoy strolling the streets of Los Feliz, admiring the Spanish-style mansions and old-fashioned manors that populate the area. Fans of Frank Lloyd Wright will especially treasure this neighborhood; two of his architectural gems are here.

The **Ennis House** (2655 Glendower Avenue, tel: 323-660 0607), located on a hillside near the southern edge of Griffith Park, is a patterned-concrete masterpiece Lloyd Wright designed for Mabel and Charles Ennis in 1923. Resembling a Mayan temple, the Ennis House was the last of Wright's four textile-block houses erected in LA and, for some, his most monumental. Its airy rooms, colossal columns and enormous windows have featured in films such as *Blade Runner*. It is

currently in a terrible state, and in 2005 was added to the list of "America's most endangered historic places."

Heading south on Vermont Avenue, you'll arrive at Wright's second Los Feliz home, which is in a happier condition. On a hilltop in **Barnsdall Art Park** just west of Vermont, the **Hollyhock House** (4800 Hollywood Boulevard, tel: 323-644 6269; open Wed–Sun 12.30pm–3.30pm; charge) was built in the early 1920s for eccentric oil heiress Aline Barnsdall, who had originally bought the 36-acre (15-hectare) park as the site of an arts center and residence.

She lived here only a few years before donating the Mayan-style house and the surrounding acreage to the city of Los Angeles. Betwen 2003 and 2006, the house underwent a $10 million restoration. Even more was spent on the park, including replanting the 1,000 olive trees to recreate the look of the property from 1921.

As well as tours of the house, visitors can explore exhibits at the

The American Film Institute's 100 Best

Since 1967, the AFI has honored the art of cinema by training filmmakers (like David Lynch), preserving old films and holding annual awards ceremonies lauding the industry's top creators and performers with a Life Achievement Award. Recipients include Orson Welles, Alfred Hitchcock, Elizabeth Taylor, Clint Eastwood, Harrison Ford and Meryl Streep. In celebration of cinema's first century, the AFI produced a series of television programs called "AFI's 100 Years..." The documentaries, which contain movie clips and celebrity interviews, highlight the 100 best American movies, stars, comedies, thrillers, romances, songs, movie quotes and film scores. Although much-debated by film buffs, AFI's 100-best lists have determined the following top choices: *Citizen Kane* (1941) as the most notable film; Katharine Hepburn and Humphrey Bogart as the finest American screen legends; *Some Like It Hot* (1959) as the best comedy; *Psycho* (1960) as the best thriller and *Casablanca* (1942) as the best romance. "Over the Rainbow" was named the best song in a film. The number-one movie quote? Rhett Butler's farewell line: "Frankly, my dear, I don't give a damn."

nearby **Municipal Art Gallery** and also the **Junior Arts Center**.

From Los Feliz Boulevard, there are several entrances into **Griffith Park** ❹ (tel: 323-913 4688; open daily 6am–10pm), one of the largest urban parks in America (although most motorists prefer to enter the park from Crystal Springs Drive, via the main southern entrance just west of Interstate 5). The popular 4,210-acre (1,700-hectare) park offers hiking trails, picnic tables, an open-air theater, an observatory, a transportation museum, a city zoo and a Western heritage museum, something for just about every kind of recreation *(see page 184)*.

South of Griffith Park, the stunning **American Film Institute (AFI**; 2021 N. Western Avenue) towers over the sharp bend where Los Feliz Boulevard becomes Western Avenue. A long-standing film conservatory and preservation society, AFI hosts yearly awards shows and presents classic films, from *Casablanca* (1942) to *The French Connection* (1971), at both the ArcLight in Hollywood *(see page 109)* and the Skirball Cultural Center *(see page 171)*.

Along the neighborhood's main thoroughfares are art galleries, independent bookstores, cozy bistros, late-night diners and kitschy bars. Two standouts are the **Dresden Room** (1760 N. Vermont Avenue), where jazz musicians Marty and Elayne have entertained music buffs and night owls for more than 20 years, and the **Derby** (4500 Los Feliz Boulevard), a hip Hollywood throwback where swing, blues and bebop lovers feel at home.

Culver City

Overlooked by most Angelenos, **Culver City** ❺ is not devoid of culture. Roughly 4 miles (6.4 km) south of Beverly Hills, this city of nearly 40,000 people continues to expand its artistic heritage with ongoing art exhibits in Town Plaza and the recent move of the **Actors' Gang Theatre**, the bold company founded by Tim Robbins and other renegade artists in 1981, to the **Ivy Substation Theatre** (9070 Venice Boulevard, tel: 310 838 4264).

Three blocks southwest are two

SAVE THE ENNIS HOUSE!! In 2005, this Frank Lloyd Wright house was put on the list of America's most endangered historic places. To find out more or to make a contribution, go to: www.nationaltrust.org/ 11Most/2005/ennis. html

BELOW: Frank Lloyd Wright's Ennis House featured in the movie *Blade Runner.*

Chandler's City

Of all the writers whose work has been identified as quintessentially LA, Raymond Chandler is the one whose name is most often mentioned. Although director Billy Wilder once remarked that the only person who accurately caught the Californian atmosphere in prose "was an Englishman," Chandler was born in Chicago in 1888 and became a naturalized British subject only in his late teens.

Chandler was 25 when he arrived in Los Angeles, and had reached his early 40s before he sold his first magazine story. He had worked in a variety of professions – picking apricots, stringing tennis rackets and as office manager for an oil company, all the while moving from one address to another with his adored older wife Cissie.

In one 10-year period, he lived in nine different homes, a restlessness reflected in the nature of the cynical but soft-hearted Philip Marlowe. "When Marlowe has a problem," observed Elizabeth Ward and Alain Silver, authors of *Raymond Chandler's Los Angeles*, "he takes a drive around town... to look at the view and to look for answers."

Philip Marlowe was something new in

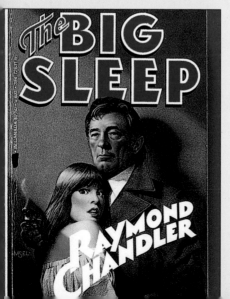

detective fiction – a wise-cracking knight errant with a neat turn of phrase and a humanity with which the reader could identify. To him LA was an ambiguous place. But it was a city Chandler understood well from "the violet light at the top of Bullock's green-tinged tower" to "that peculiar tomcat smell that eucalyptus trees give off in warm weather." He was indignant about the lack of appreciation that LA had for Hollywood. "It ought to consider itself damn lucky," he said. "Without Hollywood, it would be a mail-order city. Everything in the catalog you could get better somewhere else."

Marlowe was a favorite with the movies, portrayed by Dick Powell (*Farewell My Lovely*, retitled *Murder My Sweet*, 1944); Bogart (*The Big Sleep*, 1946); Robert Montgomery (*The Lady in the Lake*, 1947); James Garner (*Marlowe*, 1969); Elliot Gould (*The Long Goodbye*, 1973); and Robert Mitchum (*Farewell My Lovely*, 1975, and *The Big Sleep*, 1978).

Cary Grant never played the role, but was Chandler's vision of the perfect Marlowe. When he saw Humphrey Bogart's portrayal though, Chandler was satisfied. "As we say here," he wrote to his British publisher, "Bogart can be tough without a gun. He has a sense of humor that contains that grating undertone of contempt. Bogart is the genuine article."

Chandler's biographer Frank MacShane points out that, although they certainly had some characteristics in common, Marlowe was "not an extension of Chandler. They were both lonely men," he wrote in *The Life of Raymond Chandler*, "isolated in the nonsociety of California, and they held individualistic moral positions that were at odds with the standards of most of the people they associated with."

Long before his death in La Jolla in 1959, Chandler became disillusioned with Los Angeles. "I have lost LA," he wrote to producer John Houseman. "It is no longer the place I knew so well and was almost the first to put on paper. I have the feeling... that I helped to create the town and was then pushed out of it by the operators." ❑

LEFT: Robert Mitchum in Hollywood's *The Big Sleep*.

unusual institutions. The **Center for Land Use Interpretation** (CLUI) (9331 Venice Boulevard, tel: 310-839 5722; open Fri–Sun noon–5pm) produces a variety of public exhibits at the CLUI exhibit hall. Recent multimedia exhibits have covered topics like traffic control and submerged American towns.

A few doors down, the **Museum of Jurassic Technology** (9341 Venice Boulevard, tel: 310-836 6131; open Thur 2–8pm, Fri–Sun noon–6pm; charge) is a curious natural history museum with exhibits on the subject of the Lower Jurassic period. The museum's permanent collection and rotating exhibits feature odd creatures like the stink ant of the Cameroon rain forests and strange inventions like Hagop Sandaldjian's microminiatures.

The Heart of Screenland

Culver City, nicknamed "The Heart of Screenland," is best known as the longtime location of **Sony Pictures Studios**, on the former MGM lot between Washington and Culver boulevards. Classic films such as *The Wizard of Oz, Singin' in the Rain* and *National Velvet* were created on this lot, decades before it belonged to Sony. Movie lovers can take a two-hour walking tour of Sony (tel: 323-520 8687; tours available Mon–Fri 9.30am–2.30pm; charge), during which they will receive rare glimpses of Hollywood's Golden Age and today's state of-the-art film industry.

Like the Getty Center, the popular **Skirball Cultural Center** ❻ (2701 N. Sepulveda Boulevard, tel: 310-440 4500; open Tues–Wed noon–5pm, Thur noon–9pm; Fri–Sat noon–5pm; Sun 11am–5pm; charge) has a sprawling, isolated campus of its own, west of Highway 405. On the west side of Sepulveda, the Skirball's stunning arrangement of brick courtyards, blooming gardens and glass-and-concrete pavilions was designed by architect Moshe Safdic.

More than 400,000 people visit every year and enjoy rotating exhibits like George Segal's biblical sculptures or Myer Myers' silversmithing creations. The *Visions*

Map on page 166

Cat like cunning: to ensure a spot on the Sony Studios Tour, reserve ahead, bring a photo ID, and leave backpacks and video cameras in the car.

BELOW: the Skirball Cultural Center.

Sumptuous Southern California vegetation; Los Angeles has more green spaces than many first-time visitors realize.

BELOW:
the Self-Realization Temple – a calming place to visit.

and Values: Jewish Life from Antiquity to America exhibit traces of 4,000 years of Jewish history. The campus also includes a California Kosher restaurant, with outside dining tables and free music most sunny Saturday afternoons.

Pacific Palisades

Northwest of Santa Monica *(see page 151)* is an exclusive seaside community, where movie stars, including David Niven, Tom Cruise and Michael Keaton, have chosen to make their home – or at least one of their homes. Nestled between the ocean and the Santa Monica Mountains, **Pacific Palisades ❼** is a pleasant, affluent town that feels as though it's much farther away from Los Angeles than it actually is. Most LA visitors never take the opportunity to explore this residential area, but there are three tempting attractions here that can make it worth the journey.

Along the northeastern end of Pacific Palisades is the **Will Rogers State Historic Park ❽** (1501 Will Rogers State Park Road, tel: 310-454

8212; open daily 8am–sunset; parking fee), the movie star's former ranch and grounds, tucked away in the Santa Monica foothills adjoining Topanga State Park. Will Rogers, the most popular and highest paid Hollywood actor of the early 1930s, garnered fame as a trick roper, columnist, philosopher, radio personality and philanthropist. At his ranch, he loved to relax with family and friends and pursue his riding and roping interests. In 1944, nine years after his untimely death in a plane crash, the ranch became a state park.

To get here, motorists can head west from Highway 405 on Sunset Boulevard and turn right onto Will Rogers State Park Road. Although the 31-room ranch house and other structures in the park are currently being restored, visitors still love to enjoy the picnic grounds, watch weekend polo matches in summer, hike down the short Inspiration Point Trail for panoramic views of LA and participate in daily tours of the grounds (Tues–Sat 11am–2pm).

Equestrians use the riding and roping arena, and adventurous hikers, mountain bikers and horseback riders tackle the Backbone Trail, a rugged path that traverses the Santa Monica Mountains all the way to Point Mugu.

Back on Sunset, near the western edge of Pacific Palisades, the **Self-Realization Fellowship Lake Shrine** (17190 Sunset Boulevard, tel: 310-454 4114; open Tues–Sat 9am–4.30pm, Sun 12.30–4.30pm; free) offers a different kind of outdoor experience. The giant lotus archway welcomes everyone, of any religious faith, to this spiritual sanctuary. The 10-acre (4-hectare) site offers leisurely strolls through the gardens and around the tranquil lake, past swans, lotus flowers and a waterfall. The grounds include a small museum, a hilltop temple and a memorial to Mahatma Gandhi.

The place has an immensely calming effect on visitors, which was the intention of its founder, Paramahansa Yogananda, in 1950.

Not far from the Lake Shrine is the **Getty Villa** ❾ (17985 Pacific Coast Highway, tel: 310-440 7300, www.getty.edu; free, but timed tickets required for admission), a precursor to the Getty Center near Brentwood *(see pages 148–9)*. To get here, continue along Sunset until you reach the PCH, west of the Will Rogers State Beach.

The museum, which reopened in 2006 after a massive renovation, is centered around a reconstructed 1st-century Italian villa from Herculaneum. The original was buried in AD 79 by the eruption of Mount Vesuvius that engulfed Pompeii. Built from over 40 different types of marble, this "Pompeii by the Pacific" was bequeathed to the city by J. Paul Getty, the oil billionaire, who, astonishingly, didn't see it before his death. The Getty Villa houses Greek, Roman and Etruscan treasures and operates as a center for the study of classical antiquities.

Topanga Canyon

West of where Sunset Boulevard meets the Pacific Ocean is lovely **Topanga Canyon** ❿. Topanga Canyon Boulevard begins its serpentine path through **Topanga State Park** ⓫ (tel: 310-455 2465) and the **Santa Monica Mountains** ⓬, which together encompass about 150,000 acres (61,000 hectares). Although motorists could take this dizzying route all the way to Chatsworth in the San Fernando Valley, most stop along the way to take advantage of the 36 miles (58 km) of hiking trails snaking through the open chaparral and oak groves of Topanga State Park.

Bound by Topanga Canyon on the west and Rustic Canyon on the east, the 11,000-acre (4,460-hectare) park is the world's largest wildland within the boundaries of a major city. Long-distance hikers, mountain bikers, equestrians, campers and birders relish the rustic solitude. Nature lovers find marine fossils, a glimpse of a mountain lion, an incredible view of the Pacific, or simply explore the geologic forma

According to linguist John P. Harrington of the Smithsonian Institution, "Topanga" is an old Shoshonean word that means "above place" or "sky" – in reference to the location of the old village above Topanga Creek.

BELOW:
the Getty Villa reopened in 2006 after years of restoration.

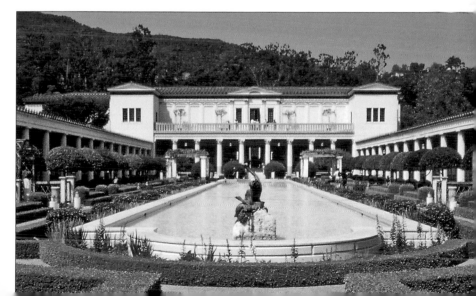

2005 marked the end of a 22-year battle by Malibu residents, headed by mogul David Geffen of DreamWorks, to keep the public away from the beach in front of their mansions. Celebs said to be opposed included Bob Dylan, Dustin Hoffman, Steven Spielberg and Tom Hanks. The winners: the public. Have fun.

BELOW:
Malibu.

tions and earthquake faults. Many of the park's trails can be accessed from Trippet Ranch, once a "gentleman's ranch" for weekend getaways from the city.

To get here, first drive through the small artists' village along Topanga Canyon Boulevard – which appears to be just a complex of shops and cafés – pass the post office and turn right on Entrada Road. The mountains have other trails accessible via Mulholland Drive.

The **Topanga Historical Society** (120 S. Topanga Canyon Boulevard, tel: 310-455 1969; open Wed 10am–1pm, Sun 1–4pm) organizes historical programs through the year. Culture lovers also enjoy the secluded town for live music most weekends at the **Abuelitas Mexican Restaurant** (137 S. Topanga Canyon Boulevard), and the Topanga Symphony's free orchestral concerts at the **Topanga Community House** (1440 N. Topanga Canyon Boulevard; 310-455 1980). Every Memorial Day weekend the Topanga Days Country Fair celebrates alternative, country and bluegrass music.

Magnificent Malibu

Beyond Topanga Canyon, the famous beach colony of **Malibu** ⑬ stretches 27 miles (43 km) to Ventura County. The movie stars live mostly in the northern sections, and access to some beaches is exclusive, but there are plenty of county beaches to enjoy.

Malibu Pier ⑭, was built by oil millionaire Frederick Rindge in 1905 and has been restored many times since then. From here, it's a short stroll to the **Malibu Lagoon State Beach**, with wildlife wetlands and beside which surfers play. Nearby, the **Adamson House** ⑮ (23200 Pacific Coast Highway, tel: 310-456 8432; open Wed–Sat 11am–3pm; charge) is a lovely 1929 Spanish-Moorish structure, decorated with tiles from the short-lived Malibu Potteries.

Frederick Rindge bought most of what is now Malibu (for $10 an acre) back in 1887 with the idea of creating an American Riviera. For years, the Rindges battled state and railroad interests to keep the area unsullied and virtually inaccessible.

But in 1926, Frederick's widow May was persuaded to allow the rental of oceanfront land (at $1 a foot) in what was called the **Malibu Movie Colony**.

Clara Bow and two of her lovers, Gary Cooper and John Gilbert, had cottages here, as did Gloria Swanson, Ronald Colman and Barbara Stanwyck. Those early $4,000 shacks grew more and more elaborate. Larry Hagman arrived in 1960 and paid $115,000 for his home; now the land alone exceeds half that much per oceanfront foot. These prices buy exclusivity to some degree – no wonder so many stars have made it home, including Robert Redford, Mel Gibson, Tom Hanks and Julie Andrews.

Farther west are a cluster of elegant Spanish-style buildings on a hillside above the coastline belonging to **Pepperdine University**, a respected Christian school on land formerly owned by John Wayne. He offered to donate it to USC for relocation, but the trustees opted to stay closer to the city center. Many visitors to Malibu come purely for the

beaches, and there are plenty to choose from. The largest beach, **Zuma**, is the least picturesque but has the most facilities. On the western end of Malibu, far below steep cliffs, there are a number of smaller, more interesting state beaches – like **El Matador** and **La Piedra** – connected by mysterious caves and filled with intriguing tide pools.

Green inferno

Beaches aren't the only landscape that Malibu offers. The backcountry behind Malibu has nature trails, campgrounds and appealing flora and fauna. Up Malibu Canyon, you'll soon come to the 4,000-acre (1,600-hectare) **Malibu Creek State Park** ⑯ (1925 Las Virgenes Road; open dawn to dusk), which was carved from a combination of ranches once belonging to Bob Hope, Ronald Reagan and 20th Century-Fox Studios.

Malibu Creek is a park with a movieland tradition – parts of *How Green Was My Valley* (1941) and *The Towering Inferno* (1974) were filmed in the foliage here. ❏

Map on page 166

Celeb-watching pelican in Malibu.

RESTAURANTS

The Edendale Grill

2838 Rowena Avenue. Tel: 323-666 2000. Open: D daily, Br only Sun. $$
Historic vibes resonate throughout this classic American eatery in Silverlake. Ensconced in the original hardwood floors, truck bay doors and pressed-tin ceiling of an elegantly restored 1924 firehouse, the grill is named for the valley that once housed LA's first movie studios.

Fred 62

1850 N. Vermont Avenue. Tel: 323-667 0062. Open: 24 hours daily. $
This retro Los Feliz diner features an old-fashioned ice cream fountain, booths resembling funky 1950s-era car seats and a creative American menu. Families, writers, tattooed artists and night owls, including Ben Stiller and Drew Barrymore, all feel at home here.

Gladstone's Malibu

17300 Pacific Coast Highway. Tel: 310-454 3474. Open: B, L and D daily. $$$
Near the ocean, this well-known restaurant serves the largest selection of fresh seafood on the West Coast. Visitors to Malibu savor dishes like crab Benedict and classic clam chowder.

Granita

23725 W. Malibu Road. Tel: 310-456 0488. Open: L Mon–Fri, D Tues–Sun. $$$$
A Wolfgang Puck classic, this Mediterranean-inspired restaurant gives the illusion of an under-

water oasis, with diffused lighting, undulating curves and textured glass. Situated in the Malibu Colony Plaza and popular with local residents and celebrities.

Soot Bull Jeep

3136 W. 8th Street. Tel: 213-387 3865. Open: L and D daily. $$
Faithful locals regularly swoop on this dim, smoky eatery in the heart of Koreatown.

● ● ● ● ● ● ● ● ● ● ● ● ● ●
Prices for a three-course dinner per person with half a bottle of wine: $ = under $25, $$ = $25–40 $$$ = $40–60, $$$$ = over $60

VALLEYS AND CANYONS

**Beyond Los Angeles and away from the crowds
are wide-open spaces, gracious towns,
fragrant gardens and Universal Studios,
one of the giants of the entertainment industry**

As with many major metropolises, there are two aspects to the city: the Los Angeles that tourists know and the Los Angeles that only residents can appreciate. Most out-of-towners come for the obvious places like Hollywood, the Sunset Strip and Beverly Hills. They probably hope to see Disneyland and the Pacific Ocean, from Malibu to Long Beach, and they might even have heard of Burbank (where *The Tonight Show* is taped) or Pasadena (home of the Rose Parade and Rose Bowl). Most, however, know little about the territories beyond the city limits, the "Valleys and Canyons."

When Angelenos refer to the Valley, they are usually talking about the **San Fernando Valley ❶**, the vast, flat expanse north of the Hollywood Hills, but there are two other notable valleys, the larger of which is the **San Gabriel Valley ❷**, which stretches east from downtown Los Angeles through the town of Pasadena, toward Riverside.

The third one is the smaller, more rural **Santa Clarita Valley ❸**, a fast-developing area to the north of the San Fernando Valley, best known for its enormous housing developments, numerous roadside produce stands, the William S. Hart Ranch in Newhall and the looming presence of its two theme parks, Six

Flags Magic Mountain and Six Flags Hurricane Harbor (*see page 211*), in Valencia.

Passes and canyons

Unlike the three northern valleys, LA's canyons are a bit more mysterious – rustic shortcuts that connect the city proper with its suburbs and hinterlands. To better understand these strange, meandering routes, it's helpful to know that some so-called canyons are actually passes – like the **Sepulveda Pass ❹**, which

Map on pages 180–81

PRECEDING PAGES:
Huntington Beach.
LEFT: pleasure is universal.
BELOW: rainbow at dusk in the Valley.

The LA Zoo is the only zoo on the West Coast to have a blue-eyed lemur.

connects the San Fernando Valley to West Los Angeles, and the **Cahuenga Pass** ❺, through which the Hollywood Freeway travels on its way from Universal City to Hollywood. When locals refer to the "canyons," they're usually referring to **Laurel Canyon** ❻, a haven for musicians (Joni Mitchell, the late Frank Zappa), which is the link from West Hollywood to Studio City, or **Coldwater Canyon** ❼, the road that joins Beverly Hills to Sherman Oaks.

Farther west, there's **Topanga Canyon** ❽ and **Malibu Canyon** ❾, both of which are dramatic routes from the Valley to the Pacific, paved strips that have created local territorial wars by giving Valley surfers direct access to ocean waves annexed by the wealthy residents of Malibu for their exclusive use (or so they thought). Between Cahuenga Pass and Malibu Canyon are several smaller, more secluded canyons.

Along the northern edge of the **Santa Monica Mountains** ❿, between the canyons and beyond, is a wonderful, dizzying road called **Mulholland Drive** ⓫. This is the spine that separates the Valley from the city. Beginning at Cahuenga Pass, Mulholland Drive meanders for 50 miles (80 km), occasionally lined with lavish homes, sometimes hugged by speeding Porsches and always offering sensational views, day or night.

Between the San Diego Freeway and Topanga Canyon, Mulholland is largely unpaved, a glorious dirt road off of which are a multitude of trails that allow weekend hikers access to a semi-wilderness just minutes away from the busy city.

San Fernando Valley

At the nexus of the valleys and canyons is the great spreading girth of the San Fernando Valley, an enormous bedroom community. Primar-

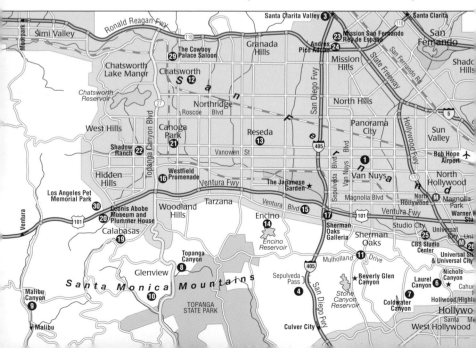

Map
on pages
180–81

ily rural until the 1870s, the Valley as a defined area came about when the great *ranchos* were subdivided and the transcontinental railroad jumpstarted a real-estate boom, creating towns like **Chatsworth** ⑫ and **Reseda** ⑬. Today, roughly 2.4 million people live in the San Fernando Valley, which means that, were it a separate city, it would be the fourth largest in the United States, topped only by New York, Los Angeles and Chicago.

Defining the Valley

Physically, the Valley is easy to define, bounded by the Santa Monica Mountains and Hollywood Hills to the south, the Ventura County line to the west and the San Gabriel Mountains to the north and east. But to identify the Valley solely in terms of geographic boundaries is to ignore a way of life that's grown up in and around it, something that has become a metaphor for American

life in the 21st century. Though the Valley is constantly evolving, it has always embraced a sense of classic suburbia, a land of hyperbolic malls, upscale condominiums, pastel-colored boulevards and endless, endless freeways.

Still, it would be unwise to oversimplify the Valley. Although it might once have been easy to dismiss it as a suburban community over the hill from the "real" Los Angeles, city dwellers don't hear too many wisecracks about "Valley girls" anymore.

By the time the new millennium began, the San Fernando Valley had turned into a significant destination of its own, with diverse and high-end stores, desirable mansions in the hills above **Encino** ⑭, and an infrastructure of comfort and security that would seem to make a journey into Los Angeles redundant. Many residents feel that the San Fernando Valley is a fine place to be, and,

Los Angeles County has a population of 9.9 million.

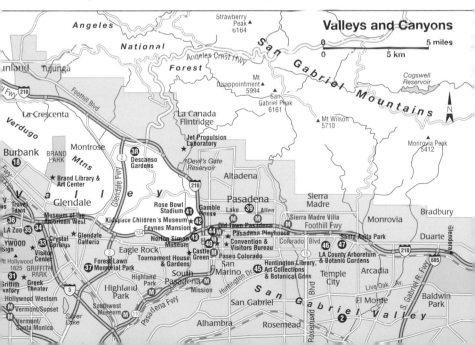

TIP

Visit the 1978 flagship location of Jerry's Famous Deli, an LA institution, at 12655 Ventura Boulevard in Studio City (tel: 818-980 4245). The truly enormous menu offers everything from Reubens to tiramisu.

BELOW: Hindu Temple in Malibu Canyon.

despite stressful commuter traffic, the area is improving all the time. With countless delis, ethnic eateries and stylish restaurants, dining is pleasant indeed. Shopping is abundant and easy, thanks to a combination of streets like **Ventura Boulevard** ⓯ and malls like the **Westfield Promenade** ⓰ in Woodland Hills, the smaller **Sherman Oaks Galleria** ⓱ and **Burbank Town Center** ⓲. Parking is convenient, in contrast to the rest of Los Angeles. In short, the desert that evolved into a suburb has evolved into a string of distinct cities, each with attractions that entice residents and might just be of interest to out-of-towners, too.

Historic homes

With sparkling new shopping malls and so many modern houses, the San Fernando Valley would seem an unlikely destination for history buffs. But there are actually several worthy historic sites here.

On the western end of the Valley, just south of the Ventura Freeway, the community of **Calabasas** ⓳

maintains the **Leonis Adobe Museum** ⓴ (23537 Calabasas Road, tel: 818-222 6511; open Wed–Sun 1–4pm, at 10am on Sat; charge), a Monterey-style adobe ranch house dating to around 1845. Adjoining the adobe museum is the **Plummer House**, once the oldest home in Hollywood until it was relocated here in 1983.

A little farther north, **Canoga Park** ㉑ shelters the two-story house and 13-acre (5-hectare) park that was once just a tiny fraction of expansive **Shadow Ranch** ㉒ (22633 Vanowen Street, tel: 818-883 3637), the prosperous ranch of a wheat farmer named Albert Workman, who bought the property in 1869. Supposedly the site of the first eucalyptus trees in Southern California, the Workman Ranch was renamed "Shadow Ranch" because of the shadows that these tall trees cast on the residence.

Northeast of the ranch, just south of where the 405 splits from I-5 is **Mission Hills**, with some of the oldest structures in the Valley. These are on the grounds of the **Mission San Fernando Rey de España** ㉓ (tel: 818-361 0186; open daily 9am–4.30pm; charge), founded in September 1797 as the 17th in a string of 21 Spanish missions along the California coast. The mission's convent buildings have been restored and are open to the public; the chapel, destroyed in the 1971 Sylmar earthquake, has been replaced by a replica.

Between the mission and the 118 freeway is the **Andres Pico Adobe** ㉔ (10940 Sepulveda Boulevard, tel: 818-365 7810), a lovely home originally built in 1834, modified many times since and now the headquarters of the San Fernando Valley Historical Society.

Soon after the start of the 20th century, the Valley become a major center for the motion picture indus-

try. Companies like Universal, Warner Bros and Disney were drawn to the area by the huge expanses of available space, accessible via the rough-hewn Cahuenga and Sepulveda passes, down which cattle and sheep use to be driven to market in Los Angeles. The Universal Studios lot, in fact, sits on what was once a 230-acre (93-hectare) chicken ranch.

When Carl Laemmle, a German immigrant, threw a bash to open the studio in 1915, his guests included Buffalo Bill Cody and Thomas Edison. In more recent years, NBC TV opened a vast facility in "Beautiful Downtown Burbank" (a phrase made famous by Johnny Carson on TV's *The Tonight Show*). In 1963, CBS moved into the old Republic Studios lot in Studio City, forming the **CBS Studio Center** ㉕.

Biggest tourist draw

Universal City, east of Lankershim Boulevard, is home to the famous **Universal Studios** ㉖ theme park (hours vary; charge; *see page 190*), unquestionably the single biggest draw in the San Fernando Valley, and the second biggest attraction in the Southland, after Disneyland.

Families and childlike grown-ups come here to experience heart-pumping rides and shows based on Universal blockbusters like *Back to the Future* (1985), *Backdraft* (1991), *The Mummy* (1999) and *Van Helsing* (2004). Of course, the most popular attraction is the **Studio Tour**, which takes visitors through the world's largest working movie studio, offering glimpses of special effects and sound stages.

For a more in-depth tour, there's the **VIP Experience** (tel: 818-622 5120; reservations required), during which visitors can explore a prop warehouse and sound mixing rooms, walk through a working sound stage and see legendary movie sets normally closed to the general public. Afterward, take a stroll through **Universal CityWalk**, a vibrant, neon-lit promenade containing souvenir shops, assorted eateries, music clubs and a multiplex movie theater.

A short drive away in **Burbank** is

Sherman Oaks Galleria of "Valley Girl" fame now has more offices than stores, but its food court is good for lunch in the sun.

Map on pages 180–81

BELOW: cruising Mulholland Drive.

Warner Bros Studios ㉗ (3400 Riverside Drive), home of the *Harry Potter* films and the television series *ER*, among many others. Warner Bros offers a comprehensive peek behind the scenes of a studio – the **VIP Studio Tour** (tel: 818-972 8687; available Mon–Fri 8.30am–4pm, longer hours May–Sept; children under 8 not allowed; charge), a two-hour journey through backlot streets, working sound stages, craft shops, wardrobe departments and recognizable sets (like the "White House" from television's *The West Wing*), ending at the **Warner Bros Museum**, a good place to buy *Harry Potter* and *Friends* memorabilia.

Northeast along Alameda Avenue is **NBC TV Studios** ㉘ (tel: 818-840 3537; available Mon–Fri 9am–3pm; weekends and extended hours during summer; charge), with a 70-minute tour that has fewer bells and whistles than the one at Universal. Nevertheless, a walk through one of America's most famous studios, known for such long-running soap operas as *Days of Our Lives* and prime-time classics like *Sanford and Son*, leaves visitors with a good sense of the rigors involved in putting together a television show. The tour includes a look at various behind-the-scenes departments and, perhaps, any shows currently being taped. Afterward, many opt to join the long line for admittance to *The Tonight Show with Jay Leno*.

Griffith Park

Although some people might head for the Valley to watch country-and-western dancers at the funky **Cowboy Palace Saloon** ㉙ in Chatsworth, or to visit the graves of celebrity pets like Hopalong Cassidy's horse at the **Los Angeles Pet Memorial Park** ㉚ in Calabasas, most head south to frolic in the largest urban park in the United States, 4,210-acre (1,700-hectare) **Griffith Park** (tel: 323-913 4688; www.laparks.org; open daily 6am–10pm).

Effectively separating Hollywood and Downtown Los Angeles from Burbank and Glendale, the park was donated to the city by Colonel Griffith J. Griffith, a Welsh immigrant whose will stipulated that his former estate should become a place of leisure for the people of Los Angeles. On an average weekend, more than 50,000 visitors come here for a variety of activities, including hiking and horseback-riding trails, and, as Griffith wished, for rest and relaxation.

Because of its enormous size, the park is best described by areas. On the southern end, the entrance from Vermont Avenue leads to the outdoor, 5,700-seat **Greek Theater** (tel: 323-665 1927), which has open-air concerts in summer; the **Bird Sanctuary**, basically a hiking trail through a heavily wooded area; and the **Griffith Observatory** ㉛, in an incredible hilltop setting that provides some of the finest panoramic views of Los Angeles. In 2006, the observatory reopened with

Bugs welcomes you to the Warner Bros VIP Studio Tour.

BELOW: the Hollywood sign gets a facelift, November, 2005.

a state-of-the-art planetarium and its fantastic 1935 murals restored. Some visitors might immediately recognize the observatory – it's been featured in many films, from *Rebel Without a Cause* (1955) to *Jurassic Park* (1993).

From the observatory, hikers can attempt a closer view of the famous **HOLLYWOOD sign** ㉜, perched high atop Mount Lee, from where in 1923 the sign read "HOLLYWOOD-LAND" to promote a new subdivision in the wooded hills above Downtown (the word "LAND" was removed in 1949). The massive sign, nearly 45 ft high and 450 ft across (14 meters by 137 meters), blinked with 4,000 lightbulbs then, making it the most eye-catching marketing scheme of its time. In 1932, a despondent young actress named Peg Entwistle jumped to her death from the letter "H."

Today the sign is a protected historic landmark, with gates, security cameras and park rangers making it impossible to get close enough to touch. It can, however, be seen in the distance from different points around LA *(see page 103)*.

To explore the eastern half of Griffith Park, use the entrance from Los Feliz Boulevard, just west of the Golden State Freeway, which leads into the **Crystal Springs** ㉝ picnic grounds, with its miniature railroad, and also to the **Visitor Center**. Down an incline opposite the center, young children love the 80-year-old, red-and-white-striped **Griffith Park Merry-Go-Round** (open daily during summer 11am–5pm, weekends only Sept-May; charge), with nearly 70 finely-carved, leaping horses and a soundtrack of old-time marches and waltzes.

The northern entrance, near the intersection of Interstate-5 and the 134 freeway, leads to **Zoo Drive**, and to two of the park's most popular attractions. Visible from both nearby

freeways is the Mission-style **Museum of The American West** ㉞ (tel: 323-667 2000; open Tues– Sun 10am–5pm; charge), part of the Autry National Center. The museum has several absorbing displays, including Western sculptures, clips from vintage movies, firearm collections and artifacts like clothing and holsters from Wyatt Earp, Teddy Roosevelt and Annie Oakley. Next door is the **Los Angeles Zoo** ㉟ (tel: 323-644 4200; open daily 10am–5pm; charge), home to more than 1,200 animal species, some of which are endangered.

At the western end of Zoo Drive is **Travel Town** ㊱ (tel: 323-662-5874; open Mon–Fri 10am–4pm, Sat–Sun 10am–5pm; free), an outdoor transportation museum that has become an interactive graveyard of antique locomotives, freight and passenger rail road cars, cabooses and trolley cars.

Even more interesting are the real graveyards that serve as bookends of Griffith Park, the two branches of **Forest Lawn Memorial Park** ㊲ (open daily 8am–5pm), one west of

Map on pages 180–81

Resident of the Los Angeles Zoo, one of 1,200 animal species.

BELOW: the Griffith Observatory dates from 1935; be sure to look at the lovely murals inside.

South of San Marino is the Mission San Gabriel Arcángel, the fourth Spanish mission founded along El Camino Real. Relocated in 1775 to evade soldiers, the mission became very prosperous, producing crops of wheat, corn and beans as well as soap, tallow, hides, wine and woven goods.

BELOW: Laurel Canyon Dog Park.

the park in the Hollywood Hills, the other east in **Glendale**. Both cemeteries contain full-sized replicas of famous churches, like Boston's Old North Church and Scotland's Wee Kirk o' the Heather. The Hollywood park has patriotic statues relating to America's history, while Glendale's features a dramatic stained-glass replica of Leonardo da Vinci's *The Last Supper*.

In addition, several celebrities are buried at Forest Lawn. The Hollywood Hills branch is the final resting place for Buster Keaton, Liberace and Lucille Ball, and the Glendale branch contains the graves of Mary Pickford, Nat "King" Cole and Humphrey Bogart.

For another fine outdoor experience, travel north past Glendale to **La Cañada Flintridge** and the fragrant **Descanso Gardens** ❸❽ (tel: 818-949 4200; open daily 9am–5pm; charge), a 160-acre (64-hectare) oasis of rose bushes, camellias, oak woodlands and chaparral hillsides. Visitors can also view art displays in the Boddy House Gallery, enjoy lunch in the Santolina

Café and stop by the gift shop for lanterns, watercolors, nature books and collectibles. Just east of the gardens, adventurous nature lovers can embark on a lengthy, sometimes harrowing journey into the **Angeles National Forest** via the serpentine **Angeles Crest Highway**.

San Gabriel Valley

Due east of the San Fernando Valley is the San Gabriel Valley – at the heart of which is the lovely city of **Pasadena** ❸❾, home to two of Southern California's most important scientific institutions – the California Institute of Technology (Cal Tech) and the Jet Propulsion Laboratory (JPL). Pasadena rose to prominence as a resort for Midwesterners, who came by train every snowy winter. At the height of its popularity in the late 1880s, the town had hotel rooms for 35,000 guests, at grand old piles like the seven-story **Castle Green** ❹⓪, a Moorish-Spanish-style building that opened in 1899. Today, this national historic landmark houses condominiums; its lobby and grounds are in demand by film crews.

Whether you approach Pasadena from Glendale via the 134 freeway or from La Cañada via the 210, you'll pass the Arroyo Seco gorge, home to the **Brookside Golf Course** and the huge **Rose Bowl Stadium** ❹❶ (tel: 626-577 3100). The **Rose Parade**, which is broadcast on TV across America, dates from New Year's Day, 1890. It was known as the "Battle of the Flowers," a ritual with flower-strewn horses and a chariot race. Since 1916, the race has been replaced by a football game, the annual Rose Bowl played between college teams.

Opposite the stadium is the hands-on **Kidspace Children's Museum** (tel: 626-449 9144; open daily 9.30am–5pm; charge). Southeast of the Rose Bowl, history and

Map on pages 180–81

art lovers will appreciate four fine structures. The first, the **Gamble House** ㊷ (4 Westmoreland Place, tel: 626-793 3334; open Thur–Sun noon–2pm; charge), is the work of American Arts and Crafts architects Charles and Henry Greene. Called a "symphony of wood," the national historic landmark was built for the Gamble family (of Procter & Gamble) and doubled as Doc Brown's house in *Back to the Future* (1985).

Not far away, the **Pasadena Museum of History** (470 W. Walnut Street, tel: 626-577 1660; open Wed–Sun noon–5pm; charge) is part of the Fenyes estate, with lovely landscaped grounds. Inside are displays about old Pasadena and a Finnish folk-art museum. Tours can be arranged of the **Fenyes Mansion**, filled with 15th and 16th-century European art and furniture. It's a wonderful reminder of the "Millionaire's Row" of the past.

Just across the 134 freeway is the **Norton Simon Museum** ㊸ (tel: 626-449 6840; open Wed–Mon noon–6pm, Fri until 9pm; charge), a collection of fine art by masters like Rembrandt, Reubens, Cézanne, Van Gogh and Picasso. Farther south is the **Tournament House** (391 S. Orange Grove Boulevard, tel: 626-449 4100; tours available Feb–Aug), an Italian Renaissance mansion once owned by chewing-gum manufacturer William Wrigley Jr. The gardens are open daily. The house is the headquarters of the Tournament of Roses Association.

For anyone interested in shopping and dining, take the time for a stroll through **Old Town Pasadena** ㊹, a restored cluster of bookstores, boutiques, eateries, bars and coffee-houses, encompassed by Pasadena and Marengo avenues and Holly and Green streets.

West on Colorado Boulevard, is the cream-colored **Paseo Colorado**, an outdoor shopping mall with upscale stores and restaurants. For a more complete listing of Pasadena's shops, watering holes and attractions, pick up a visitors guide at the **Pasadena Convention & Visitors Bureau** (171 S. Los Robles Avenue, tel: 626-795 9311; open Mon–Fri 8am–5pm, Sat 10am–4pm).

California is the largest producer of roses in the nation.

BELOW: the Rose Bowl is played between college football teams.

Map
on pages
180–81

*The hot streets of LA
feel far away when
visiting cool, green
Huntington Gardens.*

The **Pacific Asia Museum** (46 N. Los Robles Avenue, tel: 626-449 2742; open Wed–Sun 10am–5pm, Fri until 8pm; charge) provides an engrossing look at 5,000 years of art and artifacts from Asia and the Pacific Islands – from Chinese jade vessels to carved Tibetan Buddhas.

The nearby **Pasadena Museum of California Art** (tel: 626-568 3665; open Wed–Sun noon–5pm; charge) is, not surprisingly, dedicated to works of art featuring the Golden State, as well as creations from California-based animators, painters and photographers. Theater lovers will enjoy the **Pasadena Playhouse** (39 S. El Molino Avenue, tel: 626-356 7529), the State Theatre of California and the place where thespians like William Holden, Eve Arden and Raymond Burr began their careers.

Pasadena isn't all that the San Gabriel Valley has to offer. In the town of **San Marino** is the **Huntington Library, Art Collections and Botanical Gardens** 45 (tel: 626-405 2100; open summer: Tues– Sun 10.30am–4.30pm; winter: Tues–Fri noon–4.30pm, Sat–Sun 10.30am–

4.30pm; charge). Established in 1928 by railroad tycoon Henry Huntington, the 150-acre (61-hectare) site entices visitors with Chinese and Japanese gardens (14 gardens in all); a Gutenberg Bible; an original manuscript of Chaucer's *The Canterbury Tales;* and paintings by Edward Hopper and Thomas Gainsborough.

If you're a television or movie fan, **Arcadia** has two recognizable landmarks. The **Los Angeles County Arboretum & Botanic Garden** 46 (tel: 626-821 3222; open daily 9am–5pm; charge), a lush 127-acre (51-hectare) park filled with plants from around the world, includes the lake where TV's *Fantasy Island* was filmed. Concerts are often held here in the garden, a sweet-smelling experience during the summer months.

On the opposite side of Baldwin Avenue is the 70-year-old racetrack **Santa Anita Park** 47 (tel: 626-574 7223), the site of Seabiscuit's last winning race and a featured location in the 2003 Oscar-nominated film named after the legendary horse. Tours by tram are available during race season. ❑

The Man Who Brought the Water

When young William Mulholland rode through the San Joaquin Valley on horseback, arriving in LA in 1877, he "fell in love at first sight," he later recalled. "The country had the same attraction for me that it had for the Indians. It was so attractive to me that it at once became something about which my whole scheme of life was woven, I loved it so much."

Since arriving in the United States as a deckhand in 1872, the 22-year-old Irishman had worked on steamers in the Great Lakes, toiled on sidewheelers on the Colorado River and searched for gold in Arizona. But the service he performed for his newly adopted home – bringing a water supply across 240 miles (390 km) of deserts and mountains – is what enabled Los Angeles to become a major city and why he is memorialized by the spectacular road that bears his name. From the Cahuenga Pass, Mulholland Drive winds for 50 miles (80 km) along the Santa Monica Mountains, providing breathtaking views of the city at many lookout points, sometimes in the shadow of lovely mansions, often in more deserted areas.

One day soon after his arrival, Mulholland became intrigued by the technique of a well-digger and asked so many questions that he was offered a job as the man's assistant. This post eventually led to his working as a *zanjero* – a man responsible for keeping the water flowing – for the city's water department, which he eventually came to head. He spent his nights reading books on mathematics, hydraulics and geology.

By 1900, with the population at 170,000, it was clear that Los Angeles' growth would be limited unless additional water supplies could be found. This problem had also been preoccupying Mulholland's predecessor, Fred Eaton. The men teamed up in a project to syphon off water from the Owens Valley.

Through 1904's blistering summer, the pair trekked through the area, devising a plan to bring the valley's water through a concrete-lined aqueduct, 53 miles (85 km) of tunnels and 12 miles (19 km) of "inverted steel syphons." They promised that the project could be completed within 10 years and would cost the city $24.5 million, an estimate that proved to be astonishingly accurate; the water arrived on time and $40,000 under budget. "Here it is, take it," was Mulholland's comment as he pressed the button to start the water flowing.

There was a dark side to the story. Eaton tried to extort $1 million for land in the Owens Valley – land that Los Angeles wanted for a reservoir – and the Owens Valley ranchers who had been led to believe that the government was acquiring land rights in order to improve it, suddenly awoke to the realization that the big city 250 miles (400 km) away was about to turn their valley into a dustbowl (the film *Chinatown* used this story as a sub-plot). To his credit, Mulholland seems to have acted only from the purest of motives. He ended his friendship with Eaton over the latter's profiteering.

Before he died in 1935, William Mulholland had built the city's water department into the world's largest wholesaler of water, serving almost 10 million people in 100 communities spread over 4,000 sq. miles (10,400 sq. km). ❑

RIGHT: William Mulholland.

UNIVERSAL STUDIOS

A studio tour, rides and the lively CityWalk – Universal is a fun "behind the scenes" peek into Hollywood movie magic

The Universal Studios tour started in 1912 when, for 25¢, guests visited the sets of movies in production. In 1930, the studio won its first "Best Picture" Oscar for *All Quiet on the Western Front,* but by that time the tours had been suspended. Universal became the maestro of monsters, unleashing Bela Lugosi's *Dracula* and Boris Karloff's *Frankenstein* to great success. Later celluloid stars and masterpieces included Basil Rathbone as Sherlock Holmes; Abbott and Costello, and Alfred Hitchcock's *Psycho, The Birds* and *Topaz.* More "Best Picture" Oscars went to *The Sting, The Deer Hunter, Out of Africa,* and *Schindler's List.* The studio tour resumed in 1961, and has become more popular with each passing year. To book a privileged VIP tour, telephone 818-622 5120.

ABOVE: You'll get face to face with a 30-ft (9-meter) King Kong as he stalks through New York and sends your tram flying.

ABOVE: The ever-evolving CityWalk now has B. B. King's Blues Club, a Hard Rock Cafe, the Rumba Room nightclub, a 3D IMAX theater, an amphitheater where stars perform, and virtual racing.

ABOVE: Universal was the last studio home for Hitchcock, the director of classic thrillers like *Vertigo,* starring James Stewart and Kim Novak.

LEFT: Frankenstein and fellow monsters have been known to roam the theme park.

STEVEN SPIELBERG – THE LEGEND

Steven Spielberg and Universal Studios have a long association. For years, the director worked from a hacienda on a corner of the studio lot, a gift from former Universal chairman Lew Wasserman. Asked why he spent over a million dollars on the gift, Wasserman said it was "less than the profits of *E.T.* in Brazil alone."

Spielberg films for Universal include *Jaws*, *E.T.*, *Jurassic Park* and *Schindler's List*. The LA-educated boy-wonder directed *Close Encounters of the Third Kind*, *Raiders of the Lost Ark*, *The Color Purple* and *War of the Worlds*. His company produced *Back to the Future* and the animated *Who Framed Roger Rabbit*. After years of being just nominated, Spielberg finally won two Oscars in 1994, both for *Schindler's List*, and another in 1999 for *Saving Private Ryan*. Paramount outbid Universal to buy DreamWorks, co-owned by Spielberg, in late 2005.

BELOW: It's all make-believe as you visit sets and props from Universal films like *Jaws*, *E.T.*, *The Mummy* and *War of the Worlds*. Just don't go in the water...

ABOVE: Jurassic Park: The Ride is just one theme-park thrill; there's an 84-ft (26-meter) drop into the Jurassic Jungle where Velociraptors and Tyranosaurus await. The *Psycho* house is on a hill behind the Bates Motel, the *Shrek* attraction is in 4D with 3D glasses, while buses cruise through the devastation of Spielberg's *War of the Worlds*.

THE SOUTH BAY

The South Bay epitomizes Southern California:
wide sandy beaches, surfing and the
ever-shining sun, laid-back people
and casual or coastal-chic communities

Early 20th-century travelers and chroniclers found it easy to dismiss the rarely-visited coastal hamlets of the South Bay, but times have changed. Today's South Bay is what the Beach Boys were exporting to the world in songs like "Surfin' USA," which was based on their own observations at Manhattan Beach. Average daytime temperatures here are 60°–80°F (16°–27°C) all year round. Everyone seems to be on in-line skates, riding a bicyle, playing volleyball, swimming, shopping or eating seafood. These are classic South Bay pastimes, the epitome of health and hedonism

Marshes to horses

The South Bay begins with **Playa del Rey ❶**, where the beaches are sheltered by breakwaters and offer gentle waves. Behind the beach is **Del Rey Lagoon** (open dawn to dusk), a quiet little park surrounding a saltwater pond. The lagoon is part of what was once an extensive marshland where local Chumash Indians used to hunt duck before the Spanish arrived. Some remnants of the marshland remain in the **Ballona Wetlands** east of the community, and both marsh and lagoon attract geese, herons and other birds that use the coast as a major flyway on their winter routes from Canada to Mexico.

South of Playa del Rey is **Dockweiler State Beach**, probably one of the loneliest stretches in the South Bay, as it lies directly beneath the flight path for departing jets from **Los Angeles International Airport (LAX) ❷**. South of the airport is **El Segundo ❸**, the headquarters of Mattel, the company that created the impossibly proportioned Barbie doll, and which spawned an empire of dollhouses, toy cars and minature designer clothes. El Segundans might be proud of their family oriented

Map
on page
194

LEFT:
looking north over
Malaga Cove, the Palos
Verdes Peninsula.
BELOW: waiting
for that perfect wave.

Long Beach

49 Six Flags Magic Mountain

27 Long Beach Area Convention & Visitors Bureau

World Trade Center

First National Bank Building

LINCOLN PARK

Broadway

Ocean Center Building

Historical Society of Long Beach 28

The Pike at Rainbow Harbor 30

Pacific Coast Club

Villa Riviera

29 Long Beach Convention & Entertainment Center

MARINA GREEN PARK

RAINBOW LAGOON PARK

Island Grissom

Shoreline Lagoon 32

Shoreline Village 31

Aquarium of the Pacific

Downtown Long Beach Marina

Queensway Bay

Scorpion Submarine

Queen Mary 33

Long Beach

0 ___ 1000 yds
0 ___ 1000 m

Santa Catalina Island

1 Playa del Rey
Ballona Wetlands

2 Los Angeles International Airport (LAX)

3 Dockweiler Beach

El Segundo

7 Manhattan Beach

11 Redondo Beach Performing Arts Center

8 Hermosa Beach

The Lighthouse Café

Hermosa Beach Playhouse

The Comedy & Magic Club

9 Redondo Beach

13 Torrance

Alpine Village

12 Home Depot Center

39 Rancho Los Cerritos Historic Site

Knott's Berry Farm Theme Park 48

Anaheim 46

King Harbor Marina

Redondo Beach Pier

Redondo Beach

10 Riviera Village

15 Malaga Cove

16 La Venta Inn

14 South Coast Botanic Garden

24 Railroad Museum

25 General Phineas Banning Residence Museum

Drum Barracks Civil War Museum

Long Beach Playhouse 36

Richard & Karen Carpenter Performing Arts Center

E. B. Miller Japanese Garden 38

37

Rancho Los Alamitos

Garden Grove 47

Gondola Getaway 40

Bolsa Chica Ecological Reserve

17 Point Vicente Interpretive Center

19 Wayfarers Chapel

Abalone Cove Shoreline Park

Vincent Thomas Bridge

Los Angeles Maritime Museum

Ports O'Call Village 23

Fort MacArthur Museum & Korean Bell of Friendship

21

Point Fermin Park & Lighthouse

20 Cabrillo Beach

22 Cabrillo Marine Aquarium

26 Long Beach Museum of Art

35 American Art (MoLAA)

34 Belmont Shore

Belmont Pier

41 Seal Beach

Alamitos Bay

Huntington Harbor

Huntington Beach Playhouse

Huntington Beach 42

Drilling Islands

San Pedro Bay

International Surfing Museum 44

Huntington Beach Pier 43

45 Santa Catalina Island

PACIFIC OCEAN

The South Bay

0 ___ 5 miles
0 ___ 5 km

neighborhood, but visitors often find the odors from the nearby Chevron refinery and Hyperion sewage treatment plant too unpleasant to bear.

East of LAX is **Inglewood ❹**. The 18,000-seat **Forum ❺**, at Manchester Boulevard and Prairie Avenue, was once home to the pro basketball Lakers and the pro hockey Kings; now it's become a top concert arena, featuring acts like Eric Clapton and the Rolling Stones. **Hollywood Park ❻** (1050 S. Prairie Avenue) features thoroughbred racing from late April to mid-July and from early November to mid-December. The grounds, which were opened in 1938, include two lakes, a pub and deli, a sports bar and a 24-hour casino.

The beach communities

For many Angelenos, the *real* South Bay – the one illustrated in books, films and songs about Southern California's fun-loving beach lifestyle – begins south of El Segundo with a trio of beachside communities. The first is **Manhattan Beach ❼**, once a sleepy town and now a prime residential area. In the late 1990s,

wealthy families fled the valleys and headed for this valuable enclave, where smog is blown inland by the ocean breezes and few earthquakes have occurred. The hills are filled with million-dollar homes, and the streets are lined with shops, restaurants and bars.

Out-of-towners can enjoy a breezy stroll along the lengthy **Manhattan Beach Pier**, at the end of which is the red-roofed **Roundhouse Marine Studies Lab and Aquarium** (tel: 310-379 8117; open Mon–Fri 3pm–sunset, Sat–Sun 10am–sunset; free), where families can glimpse swell sharks, moray eels, sea anemones and rare octopuses.

Fishing is permitted all year on the pier, but anglers aren't the only ones delighted by the balmy climate. Volleyball enthusiasts can't get enough of the beach here, and surfers often catch a few waves nearby. Before heading to the next town, unwind with a beer and some grub at the popular **Shellback Tavern**, a 50-year-old watering hole not far from the pier.

A half-mile (0.8 km) south is the small town of **Hermosa Beach ❽**,

Map on page 194

Sealed with a sun-drenched kiss.

BELOW: hanging on Huntington Beach: "Surf City USA."

where the streets are densely packed with early California-style beach bungalows, and the surfing culture attracts fairly young, bohemian residents. Besides the pristine beaches, the jewel of Hermosa Beach is the **Pier Avenue Promenade**, an outdoor pedestrian mall of sidewalk cafés, restaurants and bars that lies between Hermosa Avenue and the Strand.

Here, you'll spot more than a few healthy bodies showing off sun-kissed tans as they roller-blade, skateboard or bike along the boardwalk to and from the **Hermosa Beach Pier**. You can rent bicycles and blades near the pier, watch vigorous games of beach volleyball, try boogie-boarding in the surf or risk a swim in the usually frigid waters.

At night, Hermosa Beach really lights up, especially around the promenade. In addition to boisterous taverns and cantinas, the promenade has two hotspots for music lovers, the **Lighthouse Café** (tel: 310-376 9833), an Asian-style restaurant and landmark jazz joint from the 1940s, and **Sangria** (tel: 310-376 4412), a lively eatery and nightclub that dishes up Spanish tapas, flamenco shows and live Latin jazz six days a week. On the corner of Hermosa Avenue and 10th Street is the **Comedy & Magic Club** (tel: 310-372 1193), where *The Tonight Show*'s host, Jay Leno, regularly tests new material. Northeast of the club is the award-winning **Hermosa Beach Playhouse** (tel: 310-372 4477); the 500-seat theater presents off-Broadway productions each season.

Redondo Beach

South of Hermosa Beach is **Redondo Beach ❾**, the largest of the three communities. The most visited part of town centers around **King Harbor**, which contains a yacht club, several shops and more than a few eateries. Nearby is the **Redondo Beach Marina**, where visitors can rent kayaks, charter gondolas, board glass-bottomed boats or, between mid-December and March, take whale-watching excursions.

Just south, the renovated **Redondo Beach Pier** is popular with strollers and fishermen hoping to hook halibut, sea bass, yellowtail or albacore.

Festivals include the Manhattan Beach Fair in October and the twice-yearly Fiesta Hermosa!

BELOW:
volleyball tournament on Hermosa Beach.

Redondo also has eclectic shops, seafood restaurants, music clubs and free concerts on summer evenings.

Farther south, between Catalina Avenue and Palos Verdes Boulevard, is the **Riviera Village** ⓾, a six-block, Mediterranean-style hamlet of art galleries, beauty salons, boutiques and bistros. Theater lovers should head northwest to the **Redondo Beach Performing Arts Center** ⓫ (1935 Manhattan Beach Boulevard, tel: 310-937 6607), home of the Civic Light Opera of South Bay Cities and the Distinguished Speaker Series, where guests have included Maya Angelou and Walter Cronkite.

For anyone with more time, consider two entertainment complexes to the east: the **Home Depot Center** ⓬ (18400 Avalon Boulevard) in **Carson City**, home of the LA Galaxy pro soccer team, and the kitschy **Alpine Village** (833 W. Torrance Boulevard) in **Torrance** ⓭, a collection of German-style restaurants and markets and site of the annual Oktoberfest celebration, the largest in Southern California. There's great food, imported bands and hilarious contests each night in September and October.

Palos Verdes Peninsula

The **Palos Verdes Peninsula** is dotted with expensive homes, many with stables in their backyards, so it's no surprise that Donald Trump chose this spot in which to build the **Trump National Golf Course**. It's an impressive facility, complete with lakes and waterfalls.

Earlier property developers invited the sons of Frederick Law Olmsted (who designed New York's Central Park) to landscape the area, and rows of the eucalyptus trees that they planted can still be seen throughout the peninsula. Palos Verdes is known for the **South Coast Botanic Garden** ⓮ (26300 Crenshaw Boulevard, tel: 310-544 1948; open daily 9am–5pm; charge), a former landfill where

the 87 acres (35 hectares) now encompass shaded paths, a man-made lake and sections of flowers, herbs, vegetables and fruit trees.

Beyond the botanic garden, a tour of the peninsula really begins with **Malaga Cove** ⓯, where the Spanish Renaissance-style plaza contains a replica of a famous European fountain. The attractive 1930s-era library (2400 Via Campesina; open Mon–Sat) displays century-old images of Palos Verdes and is located beside a charming English garden. The nearby **La Venta Inn** ⓰ (796 Via Del Monte), a restored 1920s-style Spanish villa, is the oldest building on the peninsula and was once a retreat for celebrities like Charles Lindbergh and Gloria Swanson.

Farther south along **Palos Verdes Drive** – the main thoroughfare along the peninsula's edge – natural history buffs can garner a lesson at the **Point Vicente Interpretive Center** ⓱ (tel: 310-377 5370; open daily 10am–5pm; free), currently being renovated. Located next to the **Point Vicente lighthouse**, the small museum has illuminating displays on

Map on page 194

TIP

The South Bay Trail provides views of the coast from Playa del Rey, through Redondo Beach, to the Palos Verdes Peninsula. There are plenty of bike shops, restrooms and cafés, but remember to obey the traffic laws of each village.

BELOW: Point Vicente lighthouse.

local geology, flora and fauna and is, with binoculars and great patience, an excellent place to spot whales, dolphins and pelicans.

Palos Verdes Drive turns sharply here, leading visitors eastward along the southern portion of the peninsula, toward the **Abalone Cove Shoreline Park** (open daily; parking charge), which has two beaches, tide pools and incredible cliff-top views. Opposite the park is the **Wayfarers Chapel** ⓳, conceived in the 1920s by followers of the 18th-century theologian Emanuel Swedenborg.

This tranquil sanctuary, crafted from glass, stone and redwood, was designed by Frank Lloyd Wright's son, Lloyd Wright, and has been a landmark on top of the Palos Verdes cliffs since 1951. Open to everyone and popular for weddings, this "tree chapel," as it is called, is accessible via a spectacular winding drive along the rocky coastline.

Veering south toward the coast, visitors will come across Paseo del Mar, which curves alongside **Point Fermin Park** ⓴, with its pretty Victorian (1874) lighthouse (open

Mon–Sat 1–4pm). A favorite place for joggers, the park is also popular with amateur pilots who bring their radio-controlled model airplanes to ride the sea breezes. Across the road is Angels Gate Park, interesting for the pagoda-like pavilion that houses the **Korean Bell of Friendship**, an enormous bell donated by the Republic of Korea to celebrate America's bicentennial in 1976. Angels Gate Park is also the site of the **Fort MacArthur Museum** ㉑ (tel: 310-548 2631; open Tues, Thur, Sat–Sun noon–5pm; free), a collection of military photos, drawings and memorabilia housed in an old army base that was used to defend the Los Angeles Harbor from 1914 to 1974.

Going for grunion

Beyond the Palos Verdes Peninsula is **San Pedro** ㉒, once famous among sailors for its bars and brothels and now the **Port of Los Angeles**. Every September, the world's largest lobster festival lures hundreds of shellfish enthusiasts to enjoy Maine lobster (good prices) and live entertainment. A recently opened pedestrian waterfront promenade has further rehabilitated the town's image.

At the southern end of San Pedro, the **Cabrillo Marine Aquarium** (3720 Stephen White Drive, tel: 310-548 7562; open Tues–Fri noon–5pm, Sat–Sun 10am–5pm; free) offers tours through the tide pool area, while the Aquatic Nursery raises young sea animals like grunion, garibaldi – the state marine fish – and white sea bass.

Driving north, past rows of bobbing sailboats in the Cabrillo Marina, you'll encounter the **22nd Street Landing**, home to the West Coast's largest privately-owned diving and fishing fleets; whale-watching excursions depart from here, too.

A little farther north, the **Ports O'Call Village** ㉓, a promenade of cobblestone streets, specialty shops and restaurants, presents a contem-

---

TIP

The Cabrillo Marine Aquarium organizes beach clean-ups, dive-a-thons, film screenings, weekend fairs, whale fiestas, Baja expeditions, trips to the Channel Islands and floating lab experiences. Call 310-548 7562 for more info.

BELOW:
climb aboard
the *Queen Mary*.

porary take on a 19th-century New England-style seaside town. From here, you can participate in an educational harbor cruise or head north to the **Los Angeles Maritime Museum** (Berth 84, tel: 310-548 7618; open Tues–Sun 10am–5pm; free), a restored Streamline Moderne building that currently houses California's largest collection of ship models, navigational equipment, Native American nautical artifacts and ship figureheads, plus exhibits about tall ships, surfing, commercial shipping, recreational sailing, the Navy and the whaling industry. Sightseers can board a **trolley** – which runs on the original tracks of the famous Red Cars that once blanketed the region – and ride between the Ports O' Call and other sites.

For anyone with more time, there is a trio of intriguing attractions north of San Pedro. In **Lomita**, the charming **Lomita Railroad Museum** ㉔ (2137 W. 250th Street, tel: 310-326 6255, open Thur–Sun 10am–5pm; charge) showcases miniature locomotives and actual railroad cars such as a 1910 Union Pacific caboose. In

Wilmington is the **General Phineas Banning Residence Museum** ㉕ (401 E. M Street, tel: 310-548 7777; tours available Tues–Thur 12.30–2.30pm, Sat–Sun 12.30–3.30pm; free), the elegant Greek Revival home of the pioneer who initiated some of the earliest Western stagecoach routes. South of the residence is the **Drum Barracks Civil War Museum** (1052 Banning Boulevard, tel: 310-548 7509; tours available Tues–Thur 10am–1pm; Sat–Sun 11.30am–2.30pm; charge), Los Angeles' last remaining military facility from the Civil War era.

Long Beach

The beautifully illuminated 6,500-ft (1,980-meter) long **Vincent Thomas Bridge** connects San Pedro with the city of **Long Beach** ㉖, which can also be reached from Downtown LA by using the Metro Blue Line. Your first stop should be the **Long Beach Area Convention & Visitors Bureau** ㉗ at One World Trade Center for a free visitor guide. Nearby are the **Historical Society of Long Beach** ㉘ (110 Pine Avenue, tel: 562-

Map on page 194

Sailing along the South Bay.

BELOW:
Wayfarers Chapel, designed by Frank Lloyd Wright's son, Lloyd Wright

Every September, San Pedro is home to the world's largest lobster festival.

BELOW: the Port of Los Angeles.

495 1210), which stores thousands of archival photographs and documents and holds an annual tour of historic cemeteries; and the **Long Beach Convention & Entertainment Center** ㉙ (300 E. Ocean Boulevard), a venue for the Long Beach Symphony Orchestra and the Long Beach Ice Dogs hockey team.

Just south of here is the main tourist area. West of the shops, chain restaurants and family entertainment of **The Pike at Rainbow Harbor** ㉚ and the charming 19th century-style **Shoreline Village** ㉛ is the popular **Aquarium of the Pacific** ㉜ (100 Aquarium Way, tel: 562-590 3100; open daily 9am–6pm; charge). The aquarium has over 12,500 species from three aquatic regions – Southern California and the Baja, the Tropical Pacific and the Northern Pacific – and lots of exhibits on scaly friends like blue whales, bamboo sharks, rainbow lorikeets and sea jellies. Home to the world's largest coral reef exhibit, the aquarium also shows an animated 3-D film that traces creatures through their habitats, from glaciers to rainforests.

Queen Mary

From the aquarium, you can take the **Aquabus**, a 40-ft (12-meter) long water taxi, to Long Beach's best attraction, the *Queen Mary* ㉝ (tel: 562-435 3511; open Mon–Thur 10am–4.30pm, Fri–Sun 10am–5pm; charge), a handsome ocean liner moored at the southern end of the Queens Highway. The Cunard Lines' Scottish-built ship made its maiden voyage across the Atlantic in May 1936 and carried many of Hollywood's elite to Europe until the outbreak of World War II, when it was used as a troopship and painted gray so it could not be seen at night.

By the 1950s, air travel was luring away travelers, and in 1967 the city of Long Beach purchased the *Queen Mary* for $3.5 million, which has since become a major tourist attraction. The Art Deco interior has been beautifully restored; 365 of its cabins have become hotel rooms; and the remaining decks are open for tours. In addition to three fine restaurants, there are fast-food stands, an elegant bar with occasional live music, and dinner theater on the weekends.

Moored next to the *Queen Mary* is the huge Soviet nuclear submarine, the *Scorpion*, which can also be visited.

East Village Arts District

In recent years, Long Beach has become popular with artists, as creative types have sought the inexpensive loft and studio space that Santa Monica and Venice used to provide. The **Long Beach Museum of Art** ❸ (2300 E. Ocean Boulevard, tel: 562-439 2119; Tues, Sat–Sun 11am–5pm, Wed–Fri 11am–9pm; charge) deserves credit for promoting art in the city. It is located inside a stately 1912 mansion, with a new pavilion dramatically perched on top of a bluff overlooking the Pacific Ocean.

Long Beach is also home to the **Museum of Latin American Art (MoLAA)** ❸ (628 Alamitos Avenue, tel: 562-437 1689; open Tues–Fri 11.30am–7pm, Sat 11am–7pm, Sun 11am–6pm; charge), in the city's East Village Arts District. Established in 1996, MoLAA is the only museum in the western US to exclusively showcase contemporary Latin American art.

Anyone interested in theater will be happy to be here, as Long Beach also nurtures a thriving theater scene. Close to the downtown area, the 99-seat **Edison Theatre** (213 E. Broadway, tel: 562-432 1818) is home to the California Repertory Company, a graduate training program for theatrical actors, designers and technicians. Near the intersection of Anaheim Street and the PCH is the **Long Beach Playhouse** ❸ (tel: 562-494 1014), a 75-year-old landmark that presents modern dramas and comedies, classic productions, experimental works and traditional musicals in two separate theaters.

On the campus of the **California State University (CSU) at Long Beach**, the **Richard and Karen Carpenter Performing Arts Center** ❸ (6200 Atherton Street, tel: 562-985 7000) provides space for over 1,000 patrons to enjoy concerts, film screenings, Broadway favorites and cabaret shows. Before or after any of these events, the public is invited to view a permanent display of awards and memorabilia from the popular singing duo, the Carpenters.

Map on page 194

TIP

The *Queen Mary* "First Class Package" includes a self-guided tour of the ship and the adjacent Soviet nuclear submarine, the *Scorpion*, which patrolled the Pacific Ocean during the Cold War. Call 562-435 3511 for tickets.

BELOW: industry in Long Beach.

On the western edge of CSU's campus is the **Earl Burns Miller Japanese Garden** (1250 Bellflower Boulevard, tel: 562-985 5930; open Tues–Fri 8am–3.30pm, Sun noon–4pm; free), a small, lovely sanctuary dedicated in 1981. Sprawling east of the campus is the **Rancho Los Alamitos Historic Ranch and Gardens** (6400 Bixby Hill Road, tel: 562-431 3541; open Wed–Sun 1–5pm; free), dating from Colonial times. Anyone who chooses to visit can join a guided tour, amble through the gardens or participate in programs about Native American culture, landscape design or agricultural skills.

A few miles northeast of the ranch lies the **El Dorado Nature Center** (7550 E. Spring Street, tel: 562-570 1745; open Tues–Sun 8am–5pm; free), a spacious wildlife habitat and interactive museum, which hosts nature walks and classes that demonstrate the relationship between the environment and subjects like games, art, tools and health. At the northern end of Long Beach, the **Rancho Los Cerritos Historic Site** (4600 Virginia Road, tel: 562-570 1755; open

When people think of the South Bay, they think of fish, sea and most of all – surfing.

BELOW: grab a gondola to explore Naples island.

Wed–Sun 1–5pm; free) has flowering fruit trees, subtropical orchards, a research library and a Monterey-style adobe that was built in 1844.

The communities farther east are also worth exploring. In **Belmont Shore** , you can fish from the pier, shop for eclectic goods along 2nd Street or take a romantic cruise through the canals of picturesque **Naples island** via Gondola Getaway (tel: 562-433 9595), established in 1982 as the first US company to offer Venetian-style gondola cruises.

Farther along, **Seal Beach** is a quaint seaside community catering to anglers, bikers, surfers, kite lovers and shoppers. Two side-by-side preserves, the **Seal Beach National Wildlife Refuge** (tel: 562-598 1024) and the **Bolsa Chica Ecological Reserve** (tel: 714-846 1114) in Huntington Beach, offer limited access to critical habitat for migratory waterfowl, raptors and shorebirds.

Huntington Beach , which recently trademarked the title "Surf City USA," has plenty of diversions – most of them involving waves. There's **Huntington Beach Pier** , California's longest municipal pier, punctuated by the distinctive, red-roofed Ruby's Surf City Diner, and the **International Surfing Museum** (411 Olive Avenue, tel: 714-960 3483; open Thur–Mon noon–5pm, daily in summer; charge), a tribute to surfing films and music, surfboards and memorabilia, from trophies to posters. Nearby are the **Surfing Walk of Fame** and the **Surfing Hall of Fame**. The US Open of Surfing, plus 36 other competitions, are held in Huntington every year.

Catalina Island

Santa Catalina Island lies approximately 22 miles (35 km) offshore and is accessible from San Pedro or Long Beach by various methods, including the *Catalina Express* ferry (tel: 800-481 3470) or

Island Express Helicopters (tel: 800-228 2566). Catalina is so close to Los Angeles that, on smog-free days, the island can be seen from the mainland. There are only two ports, the principal town of Avalon and the smaller Two Harbors.

Avalon, one of early Hollywood's most popular film sets, has a 1920s feel, helped by the fact that walking is encouraged and few cars are allowed. The first stop should be the **Green Pleasure Pier**, from which various boat tours depart and where the **Catalina Island Chamber of Commerce & Visitors Bureau** (tel: 310-510 1520) provides free information about island activities, lodging and dining.

Along the beachfront, **Crescent Avenue** has the Victorian turret of **Holly Hill House** at one end and the brick-red rotunda of the Art Deco **Casino Ballroom** at the other. The Casino, home of the big bands in the 1930s and '40s, was once used for Hollywood screenings and now houses the **Catalina Island Museum** (tel: 310-510-2414; open daily 10am–4pm; charge), covering centuries of island history, from Native Americans to Hollywood celebrities.

Beyond the intimate city of Avalon, Catalina is almost as undeveloped as when the first Spanish conquistador set foot here more than 400 years ago. Visitors can rent bicycles or take a bus tour of the island's interior, where it's usually possible to glimpse some of the island's buffalo.

About 2 miles (3.2 km) west is the **Wrigley Botanical Garden** (tel: 310-510 2595; open daily 8am–5pm; charge), the centerpiece of which is the 1930s-era **Wrigley Memorial**. William Wrigley Jr, the chewing-gum mogul, used to own the island. His mansion is now the **Inn on Mount Ada**, a gorgeous bed-and-breakfast with grand views. At the opposite end of town is another fine building, the **Zane Grey Pueblo Hotel**, former home of the celebrated "Western" author. Although not as interesting as Avalon, **Two Harbors** does have the **Banning House Lodge**. The house was built in 1910 as a summer home for the famous Banning family. It is now a delightful inn with wonderful views. ❏

Map on page 194

Santa Catalina Island has been home to various peoples for the past 7,000 years, including native Pimungans in the 1500s, Russian sea otter hunters in the 1800s and big-band musicians in the swing-era 1940s.

BELOW:
Catalina Island was one of early Hollywood's most popular film sets.

THEME PARKS

Sunshine is the key to theme park success, and there's plenty of both in Southern California. Disneyland, Knott's Berry Farm and Six Flags Magic Mountain are all just a short distance from Los Angeles

The Los Angeles area is not just the center of filmmaking, it's also the birthplace of the modern-day theme park. This is no coincidence – after all, each industry uses similar tools and talents to create make-believe environments that evoke feelings of laughter, awe or fear among spectators and participants. Walt Disney not only capitalized on this symbiotic relationship, he invented it, and as a result, Disneyland is the "godfather" of theme parks.

Ironically, Disneyland is not the first in the US – that honor belongs to Knott's Berry Farm. Both parks are in **Anaheim** ⑯, southeast of LA. Anaheim was a German farming community in the late 1800s and is now a premier tourist destination. Northwest of Los Angeles, in a town called Valencia, is another park: Six Flags Magic Mountain. Collectively, the three parks require at least a week to explore, so expect to stay awhile or make multiple trips to sunny Southern California.

Birth of a mouse

As Walt Disney once said, "it all began with a mouse" – Mickey Mouse, that is, born in 1928, the offspring of Walt's imagination. Walt came to California in 1923 and set up shop in the back of a Hollywood realty office with his brother Roy. Based on the success of their short animated films, Walt, ever the entrepreneur, led the company into riskier ventures – feature films and, eventually, televison.

By the 1950s, the company had a large Burbank studio and a collection of awards (including Oscars). Walt soon envisioned a little 8-acre (3-hectare) park next to their studio lot where employees could relax and tourists could take pictures with sculptures of Mickey and Minnie

Map on page 194

LEFT: Knott's Barry Farm.
BELOW: teens usually like the scary rides – go for Disney's California Screamin'.

Mouse, Donald Duck, Pluto, Goofy and the gang. Walt's dream began to grow: soon he was pitching financiers to support his plans for a much larger theme park, but there were no takers. So Walt turned to Leonard Goldenson, head of ABC Television, who backed the fantastical notion.

Disneyland

In 1955, after several years of design and months of construction, the transformation of 80 acres (32 hectares) of orange groves into a Magical Kingdom was finished. **Disneyland** ⓐ (tel: 714-781 4565; seasonal opening hours; charge; www.disneyland.disney.go.com) opened its gates, and in poured 3.8 million visitors in the first year.

Walt often stated that he was more concerned about the quality of Disneyland's experience than its profitability. Little did he realize that Disneyland, and its cousins in Florida, Paris, Tokyo and Hong Kong, would become the most important and most profitable share in his corporate kingdom.

Some might wonder why Disneyland has become such a worldwide phenomenon. Well, it doesn't hurt that the park's lovable characters have been woven into the fabric of many cultures or that the entire Disney fantasy is sustained through painstaking attention to minutiae – whether in the sophisticated animation of Walt's films or the vitality of his first theme park.

More intimate than Florida's Walt Disney World, the original Magic Kingdom rewards with small, unexpected pleasures, such as throwing pennies in the wishing well at the Snow White Grotto, watching doves circle the Sleeping Beauty Castle or pulling the sword from the stone and being declared England's ruler.

There's no sign stating "the original," but Walt's first-born is the official home of his characters, which, while the world changes, continue to bring joy and familiarity to children everywhere. But the park hasn't stagnated – Disney bosses have been careful not only to maintain its pristine operation, but also to introduce new attractions.

TIP

Disneyland has plenty of places to eat, but two winners are the "Minnie & Friends" breakfast buffet at the Plaza Inn on Main Street, USA, and the atmospheric Blue Bayou, a fine Cajun-Creole restaurant in New Orleans Square.

BELOW:
Toon Town
at Disneyland.

Satellite Attractions

Disneyland, Knott's and Six Flags aren't the only family-friendly destinations within driving distance of Los Angeles. In Buena Park, the Medieval Times Dinner & Tournament (tel: 888-935 6878) lures patrons into a European-style castle, where they can enjoy roasted chicken dinners amid jousting matches. Not far away, the Pirate's Dinner Adventure (tel: 714-690 1497) transports guests to the 1800s with a beef feast and a musical adventure aboard a Spanish galleon. Toward the 210 freeway in San Dimas lies California's largest water park, Raging Waters (tel: 909-802 2200), which offers summertime attractions like a lazy river and steep slides. To the east, in the town of Perris, is the Orange Empire Railway Museum (tel: 951-657 2605), the largest collection of passenger cars, locomotives and streetcars in the West, some of which can be ridden. In Newport Beach is the Newport Harbor Nautical Museum (tel: 949-675 8915), which houses models of Chumash Indian canoes, steamships and modern yachts. Farther south toward San Diego, Carlsbad's LEGOLAND (tel: 760-918 5346) delights kids with over 50 rides and attractions, including LEGO-brick replicas of famous US landmarks.

Since 1955, the most ambitious development has been the creation of the **Disneyland Resort**, which includes an improved **Magic Kingdom**, the 55-acre (22-hectare) Disney's California Adventure theme park, a huge shopping, dining and entertainment center called Downtown Disney and three hotels. These are the original **Disneyland Hotel**, the contemporary **Paradise Pier Hotel** and the luxurious, Craftsman-style **Grand Californian** – all of which have pools, eateries, a health club and a private entrance into Disney's California Adventure.

To really enjoy the Disneyland experience, it's important to allow enough time to explore all the attractions, shows, stores and cafés that you want to see, without cramming too much into a single day.

Although it's virtually impossible to do everything in one trip to Anaheim, set aside at least two full days, mainly because major attractions like **Space Mountain**, the **Indiana Jones Adventure** and **Big Thunder Mountain Railroad** must, in order to avoid long lines, be visited early

in the morning or late at night. If you plan to see **Disney's California Adventure**, you'll have to add at least one more day to your vacation.

As with Disneyland, the park is divided into separate themes – although instead of names like **Tomorrowland** and **Frontierland**, these salute various aspects of the Golden State, from the boardwalk games of **Paradise Pier** to the **Twilight Zone Tower of Terror** in the **Hollywood Pictures Backlot**.

In addition, there's the **Grizzly River Run** (where you'll probably get soaking wet); an interactive animation studio; an Art Deco-style theater that hosts Broadway-size shows; and a ride that soars high above California landmarks like the Golden Gate Bridge and Yosemite National Park.

If you need a break from kid-focused attractions, take a stroll through **Downtown Disney**, which sits between the two theme parks and features plenty of restaurants, boutiques and other attractions. Options include the House of Blues restaurant and concert hall, Ralph

Map on page 194

Marching to Mickey Mouse's tune.

BELOW:
Cup and Saucer ride at Disneyland.

Brennan's Jazz Kitchen, the La Brea Bakery Café, the ESPN Zone Sports Arena and a dozen 1920s-style AMC movie theaters. And, yes, with stores like the Build-a-Bear Workshop and LEGO Imagination Center, even kids will find plenty of things to do.

Fast tips

There are almost as many ways to "do Disneyland" as there are visitors. But whatever your taste or pace, here are a few helpful ideas to get you organized and away from the crowds.

Consider the season: Although the park stays open later in summer and presents more special events then, crowds are heaviest from mid-June to late August, and the heat can be unbearable. Also try to avoid major holidays, like Easter, Labor Day, the 4th of July, Memorial Day, Thanksgiving and Christmas, when two-hour waits for rides are common. January to May can be a quieter time, as can September to mid-December. Just remember that it often rains in winter, and the park closes early in autumn.

Japanese-American Boy Scout out for a day of fun.

BELOW: theme parks can be tiring for kids, so be sure to allow plenty of time.

Be selective: If you only have one day to spend in the park, don't try to see all the rides, performances and musical acts. Use a map and plan your route ahead of time.

Be early: Arrive at the main gate at least 45 minutes before opening time. You can cover a lot of ground with a head start, and guests are often ushered into Main Street before the rest of the park opens, meaning you can purchase maps, rent strollers, procure entertainment schedules, visit with some of the costumed characters, have a bite at the Blue Ribbon Bakery and still be at the blockade at the end of Main Street ahead of the late-morning rush into Disneyland.

Reverse your thinking: Many first-timers try to see attractions in geographical order, but this can lead to long lines and undue headaches. You can avoid some of the congestion by following an unorthodox plan of attack. For instance, you should see popular attractions or go on rides early in the day, late at night or during a parade or special event, which lures away other participants.

Ideally, you could visit Fantasyland and Tomorrowland during the morning, save activities like shopping and dining for the afternoon and explore Adventureland, Frontierland and New Orleans Square at night, when the mystique of attractions like the Haunted Mansion are heightened.

Use FASTPASS: This system saves your place in line at certain key attractions while you enjoy less-crowded rides. To utilize this service, head to one of the participating rides (which includes Autopia, Splash Mountain, the Indiana Jones Adventure, the Haunted Mansion and a few rides in California Adventure). Check the "Return Time" display, insert your admission ticket or passport and hold onto your FASTPASS ticket until it's time to return.

Knott's Berry Farm

Roughly 6 miles (10 km) from Disneyland, in next-door Buena Park, is **Knott's Berry Farm** (tel: 714-220 5200; hours vary by season. www.knotts.com), America's first theme park. Like Disneyland, its original concept was more humble than the current park. In 1920, Walter and Cordelia Knott began selling fresh berries and homemade preserves from a roadside stand. Later, Cordelia added fried chicken dinners to the menu, and soon Knott's was such a popular destination that Walter decided to build an authentic "Ghost Town" and offer pony rides to entertain the impatient and hungry patrons.

Even though Knott's has grown tremendously over the years and was eventually sold to the Cedar Fair amusement group, the park still embraces its charming berry-farm and Old West California roots. For instance, the 1880s era Ghost Town buildings aren't just movie facades; they were transported from mining towns in Kansas, Arizona and other Western states. Visitors can still enjoy Cordelia Knott's fried chicken and boysenberry pie at the Mrs Knott's Chicken Dinner Restaurant in the **California MarketPlace**, which features a variety of clothing, collectibles and "vittles".

Currently, the park is divided into six themed areas. **Ghost Town** is the heart and soul of Knott's, where there's an original Butterfield Stagecoach and a narrow-gauge steam train to ride. You can also pan for gold at the mine and working sluice; test the first-ever electronic shooting gallery; witness "shoot 'em up" gunfights; or watch a can-can show in the rowdy saloon.

History buffs can look at real Old West artifacts in the Western Museum or watch blacksmiths, woodcarvers and spinners create souvenirs to take home. If thrill rides are what you're after, look no farther than the **GhostRider**, one of the world's longest and tallest wooden roller coasters.

In **Indian Trails**, browse or buy Native American arts and crafts; study authentic tepees and totem poles; and watch daily perfor-

Map on page 194

TIP

If you want to visit Knott's Berry Farm and Hurricane Harbor as well as Knott's Soak City and Magic Mountain, consider staying in Buena Park or Valencia, respectively. Be sure to ask about combo tickets at each theme park.

BELOW: Knott's Berry Farm was the first theme park in the US.

mances by costumed dancers, singers and musicians. A 19th-century river is the setting for **Wild Water Wilderness**, which features the exhilarating (and drenching) **Bigfoot Rapids** ride, and the multi-sensory **Mystery Lodge** history and special effects show.

Fiesta Village is is place to find mariachi bands, the wicked **Montezooma's Revenge** and **Jaguar!** roller coasters, as well as the 19th-century **Dentzel Carousel**. Teens hang out at **the Boardwalk**, which celebrates Southern California's beach lifestyle with the wild **Supreme Scream**, **Boomerang**, **Rip Tide** and **Perilous Plunge**, the tallest and steepest water ride anywhere around.

Camp Snoopy is kiddie headquarters for smallfry, with more than 30 rides, climbing forts and bouncy inflatables. Check out the shows at the **Camp Snoopy Theatre**, where kids will delight in seeing adult-size versions of their favorite Peanuts Gang characters.

An adjacent waterpark, **Knott's Soak City**, contains more than 20 water-based rides and attractions, all inspired by California's 1960s-era surfing culture, bearing names like Malibu Run and Laguna Storm Water Tower. The park is geared toward families and preteens, with the exception of a few high-speed slides. Soak City is open only during the summer, from late May to September.

Navigating through Knott's

Although you could cover the major attractions, shows and restaurants of Knott's Berry Farm in a single day, the same crowd-evading rules apply to this park as to Disneyland. If you arrive at least 45 minutes before the official opening time, you can beat the mid-morning rush and grab some breakfast in the California MarketPlace.

If your gang is ready for roller coasters, head for GhostRider, Boomerang or Supreme Scream right away, before the crowds build. Anyone in charge of young children, should peruse Ghost Town and then head into Camp Snoopy, which, if the kids have a say in the matter, will be your headquarters at least until lunchtime.

In peak summer months, temperatures can get pretty high, so you should probably save cooler attractions, such as the dampening Timber Mountain Log Ride or air-conditioned Dinosaur Discovery Center, for the mid-afternoon. Remember that large groups of kids from summer camps often leave the park by late afternoon, so if you're not particularly hungry, dinnertime is a good time to join leaner crowds on the medium-scare rides.

It's helpful, too, to note that on days when the park is open later in the evening (as in the summer months), tickets are half-price after 4pm. Not only is this cheaper, it still allows enough time to see all the major attractions.

Six Flags Magic Mountain is home to 16 world-class roller coasters and 11 different world records, including the world's fastest suspended boomerang coaster, the world's only hairpin drop coaster and the first looping coaster ever built.

BELOW: kids and cuddly friend.

Six Flags Magic Mountain

If you had to choose just one word to capture the spirit of each of these three theme parks, it would probably be "fantasy" for Disneyland, "history" for Knott's and "screams" for Magic Mountain. **Six Flags Magic Mountain** ㊾ (tel: 661-255 4100; hours vary by season; www.sixflags.com), once a small amusement park in the middle of nowhere, has developed quickly. Located in Valencia, about 40 minutes north of Hollywood and about 90 minutes from Disneyland, the park is less family-oriented than the others and tilted more toward teenagers and hardcore roller-coaster enthusiasts.

Monster coasters

Magic Mountain means BIG, SCARY rides. The people behind Six Flags love to build the biggest, the fastest and the scariest, and the main reason tourists come is to scream through the thrills. One of the best rides is **Scream**, a floorless train with seven 360° inversions, including a 150-ft (46-meter) drop at the start. **Tatsu** dares you to "fly at the speed of fear." **Riddler's Revenge** is "the world's tallest and fastest stand-up coaster;" while **Superman the Escape** is the first to reach speeds of 100 mph (160 km/h).

When evening rolls around, you might care to stroll over to **Gotham City Backlot**, which gains added mystery in the dark. Because Magic Mountain is "Scream City," you can be guaranteed a scary ride or two; try **Batman the Ride**, which whips you through harrowing corkscrew bends and vertical loops.

Little kids are not left in the dark, however, because there are water rides and **Bugs Bunny World**, complete with Looney Tunes favorites like Bugs, Sylvester and Tweety, especially for them. Children also enjoy **Hurricane Harbor** (tel: 661-255 4100), the adjacent summertime water park that offers adult thrills, too. On a hot day in the desert, the harbor provides great relief with its 20-plus lagoons and water slides, including the **Tornado**, a six-story funnel that drops raft riders from 75 ft (23 meters) in the air. ❑

Map on page 194

The 4th of July holiday pulls in the crowds, so try to visit at a different time.

BELOW: getting happy while getting wet at Magic Mountain.

TRANSPORTATION

GETTING THERE AND GETTING AROUND

GETTING THERE

By Air

The area's largest airport, **Los Angeles International Airport (LAX)**, extends along LA's western coast, roughly 20 minutes from Downtown. Heavy freeway traffic and tight security measures at the airport can slow your progress, so it's essential that you allow plenty of time if you're catching a flight. Serving more than 60 domestic and international airlines, LAX (tel: 310-

AIRLINES

Aeromexico: 800-237 6639
Air Canada: 888-712 7786
Alaska Airlines: 800-252 7522
American Airlines: 800-433 7300
British Airways: 800-247 9297
Continental Air: 800-523 3273
Delta Airlines: 800-221 1212
Northwest: 800-225 2525
Southwest: 800-435 9792
United: 800-864 8331
US Airways: 800-428 4322
Virgin Atlantic: 800-821 5438

646 5252) is the world's fifth busiest passenger airport.

Smaller airports in the vicinity include the **Bob Hope Airport** (tel: 818-840 8840) in Burbank, 20 minutes northwest of Downtown; the **Ontario International Airport** (tel: 909-937 2700), an hour east of LA; the **Long Beach Airport** (tel: 562-570 2600), 30 minutes southeast of Downtown; and the **John Wayne Airport** (tel: 949-252 5200) in Santa Ana, an hour south of Los Angeles.

By Sea

San Pedro is LA's official port, and its **World Cruise Center** is one of the busiest passenger complexes on the West Coast. Cruise lines operate excursions from the port, including harbor cruises, whale-watching trips and ferries to Catalina Island.

By Rail

The city's 65-year-old downtown train station, **Union Station**, still has its original lavish furnishings. **Amtrak** (tel: 800-872 7245) provides transportation throughout Southern California, via eight different routes, including *California Zephyr, Capitol Corridor, Coast Starlight, Pacific Surfliner, San Joaquins, Southwest Chief, Sunset Limited* and *Texas Eagle.*

By Road

Southern California has a massive, intertwining freeway system that can be convenient if you have ample patience and can decipher maps. The major routes are listed here, but you can receive additional information from the **Automobile Club of Southern California** (tel: 213-741 3686 or 888-874 7222).

The principal north-south byways in LA are **Interstate 5** (which connects Canada to Mexico via Sacramento, Los Angeles and San Diego), **Interstate 15** (which begins at the Canadian border and traverses San Bernardino and San Diego), **US Highway 101** (which borders the Pacific Coast, passes through San Francisco and ends in downtown LA) and **State Highway 1** (which hugs the coast from San Diego to San Francisco).

The principal east–west byways are **Interstate 8** (which splits from Interstate 10 and ends in San Diego), **Interstate 10** (which starts in Florida and ends in Santa Monica) and **Interstate 40** (which connects Tennessee with Barstow, California).

Other important LA freeways are **Interstate 210** (San Fernando to Pomona), **Interstate 405** (San Fernando to Santa Ana), **Interstate 605** (Monrovia to Long Beach), **State Highway 110** (Pasadena to Long Beach), **State Highway 55** (Anaheim to Newport Beach), **State Highway 57** (Pomona to Santa Ana), **State Highway 60** (downtown LA to Riverside), **State Highway 91** (Torrance to San Bernardino), **State Highway 710** (East LA to Long Beach) and **State Highway 105** (LAX to Norwalk).

Without a vehicle, visitors can still reach LA via private buses. The **Greyhound Lines** bus company (tel: 800-231 2222) brings tourists to Southern California from all over the US. LA, Hollywood, Glendale, Pasadena, Long Beach and Anaheim all have Greyhound terminals.

GETTING AROUND

On Arrival

To/From the Airport

Public transportation is on **LAX**'s lower level, which is where arriving passengers claim baggage. At this level, there are stops for taxis, LAX shuttles, buses, hotel and rental car courtesy trams and shared-ride vans in front of each airline terminal.

Hopping in an unlicensed taxi at LAX should be avoided if at all possible. Los Angeles' cabs are expensive – more so than in most cities in the United States – and are almost never found driving the streets looking for customers. Taxis can be found at airports, train stations, bus terminals and major hotels or ordered by calling **Bell Cab** (tel: 310-207 6888) or **Taxi Co-op** (tel: 310-715 1968).

An average fare from LAX to Downtown is around $40. At LAX, there is an official line and greeter for licensed taxis outside each terminal baggage claim area. Passengers will be presented with a ticket stating typical fares to major destinations. Only authorized taxis with an official seal on each vehicle are permitted into the airport. Free shuttle buses run regularly to parking lots and other key locations in the airport. "A" shuttles transport travelers between terminals for airline connections. "C" shuttles take passengers to the **LA County Metropolitan Transportation Authority (MTA) Bus Center**, where they can board city buses serving the LA area, including Santa Monica's Big Blue Buses. "G" shuttles offer transportation to the MTA's **Aviation Station** on the Metro Rail Green Line. Tourists can wait for any of these shuttles, with their luggage, beneath the blue LAX Shuttle Airline Connection signs which are found on the Lower/Arrival Level islands in front of each terminal.

Passengers can obtain local transit information for bus and rail lines by telephoning 800-266 6883.

Shuttles from the airport are reasonably priced, the fare depending on your destination. Among the companies operating 24 hours daily are **Prime Time Shuttle** (tel: 800 733 8267) and **SuperShuttle** (tel: 310-782 6600 or 800 258 3826). Call them from the terminal *after* you have your bags to let them know you are waiting.

Free parking lot shuttles, major rental car companies, door-to-door vans, hotel courtesy trams, local buses and taxis also provide transportation for passengers at the Bob Hope, Ontario, Long Beach and John Wayne airports.

CRUISE LINES

Celebrity Cruises: 800-647 2251
Crystal Cruises: 800-804 1500
Disney Cruise Line: 800-951 3532
Norwegian Cruise Line: 800-327 7030
Princess Cruises: 800-774 6237
Radisson Seven Seas Cruises: 877-505 5370
Royal Caribbean Cruise Line: 866-562 7625

Orientation

Initially, most visitors are overwhelmed by the sheer size of Los Angeles and the crowded nature of its roadways, but with patience and a detailed street map, you can navigate through this sprawling metropolis. While most major US cities are centered around a distinct downtown area, LA is a patchwork quilt of various incorporated cities and unincorporated areas. Although several major thoroughfares – including Sunset, Santa Monica and Wilshire boulevards – run from Downtown, through assorted enclaves, all the way to the coast, the best way to experience the city is neighborhood by neighborhood.

Core areas, such as Hollywood and Santa Monica, offer reliable public transportation, but the most convenient way to explore LA is via car. Except during rush hour, the freeways are the quickest way to get from one end of town to the other.

Public Transportation

Unlike Chicago and New York, LA is notorious for its lack of public transportation, although the recently expanded Metro Rail system has certainly helped. The 400-mile (640-km) system of bus, light-rail and subway transportation facilities will not be fully in

SPECIAL PASSES

Daily fares and all-day passes for LA's buses and light-rail trains are quite inexpensive, but you can save money by purchasing monthly passes for individual lines. The new monthly **EZ Transit Pass** provides unlimited riding on several different local routes such as the MTA bus and rail system, DASH, Foothill Transit, Long Beach Transit and the Santa Monica Big Blue Bus. Call 800-266 6883 for more information.

place until 2009, but plenty of **MTA** buses and trains are already available throughout the city. For information and schedules, visit www.mta.net or call 800-266 6883.

By Bus

Various bus lines serve the cities and unincorporated areas of LA County. Besides the MTA, which provides a variety of bus routes throughout LA, the city offers **DASH** shuttle service (tel: 213-808 2273) around Downtown and to surrounding locales like Chinatown, Boyle Heights, Los Feliz, Hollywood, San Pedro and Van Nuys. Other reliable lines include the **Burbank Bus** (tel: 818-246 4258), which runs from downtown Burbank to the Bob Hope Airport; **Foothill Transit** (tel: 626-967 3147), which provides transportation throughout the San Gabriel Valley; **Long Beach Transit** (tel: 562-591 2301); and the **Santa Monica Big Blue Bus** (tel: 310-451 5444).

By Subway and Train

Currently, the MTA's light-rail system can transport passengers from Pasadena to LAX. The relatively new **Metro Gold Line** begins in Pasadena, passes through Chinatown and terminates at Union Station, from where the **Metro Red Line** subway travels to Wilshire Boulevard, Hollywood, Universal City and

North Hollywood. The **Metro Blue Line** starts at the 7th Street Metro Center and ventures down into Long Beach, while the **Metro Green Line** takes passengers from the Norwalk Station to LAX and Redondo Beach.

   Metrolink (tel: 800-371 5465) offers train services between places as far afield as Oxnard, Burbank, Lancaster, San Bernardino, Anaheim and Oceanside. Metrolink fares, which can be pricier than Metro tickets, depend on the distance of your chosen route.

Private Transportation

By Taxi

Taxis are reasonable if traveling short to medium-length distances. They are not advisable for lengthy trips because of the prohibitive fares – remember that LA is quite enormous. Taxi cab services offer roughly the same prices, and if you are going a long distance, such as from LAX to downtown LA, you can usually get the cab driver to give a fixed rate. Taxis should be reserved at least an hour in advance. See *On Arrival* for taxi phone numbers.

By Limousine

For a more comfortable form of transportation, try a limousine. Options include **The Black Label Co.** (tel: 310-765 4294), **Carey Limos** (tel: 310-665 5100), **Chauffeur's Unlimited** (tel: 310-645 8711), **Diva Limousines** (tel: 310-278 3482) and **ITS** (tel: 310-845 1230).

By Car

The most efficient way to traverse LA is to rent a car. You can rent one at the airport, your hotel or any car rental agency. Car rental companies all charge basically the same rates, and some deliver the cars directly to you. Consult the phone directory for the agency nearest you. Most require that you be at least 25 years old and possess a valid

driver's license and credit card. Foreign travelers might need to produce an international driver's license. If you are insured in the US, you usually do not have to purchase insurance from the rental company. If not, read the rental agency's insurance policy carefully before purchasing car insurance.

Car Rental
Advantage: 800-777 5500; www.arac.com
Alamo: 800-462 5266; www.alamo.com
Avis: 800-331 1212; www.avis.com
Beverly Hills Rent-A-Car: 800-479 5996; www.bhrentacar.com
Be a star in an exotic, classic or luxury car.
Budget: 800-527 0700; www.budget.com
Dollar: 800-800 3665; www.dollar.com
Enterprise: 800-261 7331; www.enterprise.com
Hertz: 800-654 3131; www.hertz.com
National: 800-227 7368; www.nationalcar.com
Thrifty: 800-847 4389; www.thrifty.com

By Water

A variety of boat excursions leave regularly from San Pedro and Long Beach, including **Catalina Express** (tel: 800-481 3470), **Catalina Classic Cruises** (tel: 800-641 1004) and **Catalina Explorer** (tel: 877-432 6276). Marina del Rey offers a few ocean cruises as well. Contact a travel agent for other companies, schedules and prices.

By Bicycle

Santa Monica, Venice, Marina del Rey, Manhattan Beach and other South Bay communities have a variety of bike and skate rental shops along the coast. For terrific views of the ocean, visitors can rent a bicycle in any one of these seaside towns and take a ride on the coastal South Bay Bicycle Trail that runs from Malibu to Palos Verdes.

A CCOMMODATIONS

SOME THINGS TO CONSIDER
BEFORE YOU BOOK THE ROOM

Choosing a Hotel

Like most major US cities, Los Angeles has many types of accommodations, from inexpensive chain motels to chic bed-and-breakfasts by the sea. The most pricey hotels are often attractive historic landmarks and typically have the best access to shopping, public transportation and conciergcs who will arrange theater tickets, tours and other matters. Because of LA's spread-out nature, you might want to choose a hotel wherever you plan to spend much of your time, thereby saving you the anxiety and expense of car, bus or taxi rides. Many of LA's tourist

MOTEL/HOTEL CHAINS

Best Western: 800-528 1234
Comfort Inn: 800-228 5150
Days Inn: 800-329 7466
Doubletree: 800-222 8733
Econolodge: 877-424 6423
Embassy: 800-362 2779
Holiday Inn: 800-465 4329
Motel 6: 800-466 8356
Quality Inn: 800-228 5151
Ramada: 800-272 6232
Red Roof Inn: 800-733 7663
Super 8: 800-800 8000
Travelodge: 800-578 7878
Vagabond Inn: 800-522 1555

information offices can help you with your selection.

The following list of lodging options, grouped by location, represents a sampling of the best LA hotels in the budget-to-luxury price range, plus a few alternative accommodations. With the exception of "Luxury," these categories are not permanent. When making reservations, ask specifically about special weekend or corporate rates and package deals. Receptionists for US reservation services often quote expensive rates, but many hotels offer an ever-changing variety of discounts and promotions. Also bear in mind that you can often find good deals online through websites like www.orbitz.com and www.priceline.com.

Regardless of your plans and the time of your visit, you should reserve lodging beforehand; most hotels have 1-800 reservation numbers, which are free if called within the US.

When you call, you'll probably have to give a credit card number to guarantee your reservations. Ask about the establishment's refund policy on deposits and try to secure a guaranteed late arrival, just in case your flight is delayed at the airport or your 40-minute limo ride from LAX turns into a two-hour traffic nightmare.

There are definitely parts of LA where no one would want to be stranded late at night without a hotel room.

Be sure to specify if you want a room where smoking is allowed, but be warned: there are more non-smoking than smoking rooms available. If you're lucky, you may get a balcony.

Apartment Rentals

LA has a number of extended-stay apartments, which may prove cheaper than a hotel if you are planning a long visit; as they have kitchen facilities they also

BELOW: most hotels have pools.

mean you can prepare your own meals. Here are a few:

Archstone Citrus Suites, 1915 Ocean Way, Santa Monica, tel: 310-943 7200, www.archstone apartments.com

Best Western Marina Pacific Hotel & Suites, 1697 Pacific Avenue, Venice Beach, tel: 310-452 1111, www.mphotel.com

Embassy Hotel Apartments, 1001 Third Street, Santa Monica, tel: 310-3941279, www.embassyhotelapts.com. A fantastic 1927 Mediterranean-

style building a few blocks from the beach. Popular with actors, poets and musicians, so be sure to book ahead.

Hotel Bamboo, Beachwood Canyon, Hollywood Hills, tel: 323-962 0270, www.athomela.com

SeaCastle Apartments, 1725 Ocean Front Walk, Santa Monica, tel: 310-917 1998, www.theseacastle.com

The Villas at Park La Brea, 5555 W. 6th Street, Los Angeles, tel: 888-580 8742, www.thevillas-plb.com

Alternative Accommodations

• For quaint B&Bs, contact B&B Finder at 888-469 6663.

• For youth-oriented hostels, visit www.hiusa.org or contact the LA Council of Hostelling International USA in Santa Monica at 310-393 3413.

• For campgrounds, contact the California Department of Parks and Recreation at 916-653 6995 or Catalina Island Camping at 310-510 0303.

DOWNTOWN/DOWNTOWN ENVIRONS/ MIRACLE MILE AND BEYOND

Luxury

Millennium Biltmore Hotel
506 S. Grand Avenue
Tel: 213-624 1011,
1-800-245 8673
Fax: 213-612 1545
www2.millenniumhotels.com
Between the Central Library and Pershing Square stands this luxurious downtown landmark, opened in 1923 and frequented by kings, presidents and Hollywood celebrities ever since. With an opulent interior reminiscent of European palaces, the renovated Biltmore tempts patrons with gorgeous suites, a Roman-style pool, a boisterous sports bar and two gourmet restaurants.

The Westin Bonaventure Hotel & Suites
404 S. Figueroa Street
Tel: 213-624 1000,
1-888-625 5144
Fax: 213-612 4800
www.starwoodhotels.com

Situated amid Downtown's skyscrapers, this extravagant hotel, a frequent movie backdrop, makes a striking statement with its five glass cylinders and soaring atrium. Besides a heated pool and high-speed Internet access in all rooms, it offers a New York-style steakhouse and a revolving lounge.

Expensive

Los Angeles Marriott Downtown
333 S. Figueroa Street
Tel: 213-617 1133,
1-888-236 2427
Fax: 213-613 0291
www.marriott.com
Close to the Walt Disney Concert Hall, this upscale hotel lures travelers beyond its landscaped grounds, into its vibrant lobby and guest rooms. The hotel's American pub, California café and

Continental restaurant provide innumerable dining options.

The New Otani Hotel & Garden
120 S. Los Angeles Street
Tel: 213-629 1200,
1-800-639 6826
Fax: 213-622 0980
www.newotani.com
Not far from LA's Civic Center, this Little Tokyo hotel has 434 deluxe guest rooms, a lovely half-acre Japanese garden, a dramatic lounge and three restaurants, including a sushi and tempura bar. Holiday buffets and traditional festivals take place here all year.

The Standard Downtown LA
550 S. Flower Street
Tel: 213-892 8080
Fax: 213-892 8686
www.standardhotel.com
Hotelier André Balazs, the man behind West Hollywood's Chateau Marmont, converted a 12-story office building

into this hip, colorful joint. Trendy, retro decor – from funky art in the lobby to vintage chairs in the rooftop bar – create a unique atmosphere that resembles a futuristic film set.

Wilshire Grand Los Angeles
930 Wilshire Boulevard
Tel: 213-688 7777,
1-888-773 2888
Fax: 213-612 3989
www.wilshiregrand.com
This elegant Downtown hotel offers more than just free Internet access, boutiques and a 24-hour fitness center; it also has four good restaurants that could entice patrons to stay longer, to try them all.

Inexpensive

Farmer's Daughter Hotel
115 S. Fairfax Avenue
Tel: 323-937 3930,
1-800-334 1658
www.farmersdaughterhotel.com
A family-operated icon for over three decades, this friendly, 66-room hotel exudes countrified charm with its denim bedspreads, gingham curtains and comfy rocking chairs. Conveniently located opposite the Grove and the Farmers' Market, it's also just a stroll away from Wilshire's Museum Row.

Figueroa Hotel
939 S. Figueroa Street
Tel: 213-627 8971,
1-800-421 9092
Fax: 213-689 0305
www.figueroahotel.com
Providing a sharp contrast to Downtown's ultra-modern convention center to the south, this intimate hotel invites guests into a golden interior reminiscent of Morocco. A cacti-surrounded pool and exotic suites, with authentic cushions, rugs and drapes, create the air of an oasis amid LA's concrete desert. The Figueroa is popular with writers and artists and anyone with an artistic inclination.

Miyako Hotel
328 E. 1st Street
Tel: 213-617 2000,
1-800-228 6596
Fax: 213 617 2700
www.miyakoinn.com
This lovely Asian hotel, situated in the same block as Little Tokyo's Japanese Village Plaza, has tastefully decorated guest rooms. Shiatsu massages are available, or if you prefer you can unwind in the karaoke bar.

Budget

Comfort Inn
1710 W. 7th Street
Tel: 213-616 3000,
1-877-424 6423
Fax: 213-483 6971
www.choicehotels.com
True to its name, this is a comfortable hotel located just west of Downtown and less than a mile from the LA Convention Center. Guests, who include business travelers, can access fax and copy machines, voice mail, free parking and an outdoor heated pool.

GuestHouse International Inn
7721 Beverly Boulevard
Tel: 323-692 1777,
1-800-214 8378
Fax: 323-692 1770
www.guesthouseintl.com
In the shadow of the gargantuan CBS Television City, home of The Price Is Right, this no-frills hotel promises simple comfort and little touches like complimentary coffee and newspapers, baths and microwaves.

Vagabond Inn
3101 S. Figueroa Street
Tel: 213-746 1531,
1-800-522 1555
Fax: 213-746 9106
www.vagabondinn.com
A stone's throw from USC's campus, this on-the-cheap hotel caters to business travelers and families, with its free parking, Internet access, heated pool and pet-friendly rooms.

PRICE CATEGORIES

Price categories are for a double room for one night, usually with a Continental breakfast:
Luxury: over $300
Expensive: $200–300
Inexpensive: $100–200
Budget: under $100

HOLLYWOOD/WEST HOLLYWOOD

Luxury

Hollywood Roosevelt Hotel
7000 Hollywood Boulevard
Tel: 323-466 7000,
1-800-950 7667
Fax: 323-462 8056
www.hollywoodroosevelt.com
Recently renovated, Hollywood's most legendary hotel was the site of the first Oscars ceremony in 1929. With its elegant Art Deco trimmings, palm-shaded pool and fine restaurant, this historic landmark transports guests to the Golden Age of Hollywood, when greats like Clark Gable and Marilyn Monroe stayed here. Its location is stellar, too – Grauman's Chinese Theatre is just across the boulevard.

Mondrian Hotel
8440 Sunset Boulevard
Tel: 323-650 8999,
1-800 697 1791
Fax: 323-650 5215
www.morganshotelgroup.com
Creating a modern urban fantasy, this sophisticated resort tantalizes guests with its dreamy lobby, light-filled bedrooms, stunning Asia de Cuba restaurant, sexy Skybar lounge and relaxing Agua Spa. This WeHo hotspot captures the Sunset Strip vibe and serves as a popular rendezvous for people in the movie industry.

Sunset Marquis Hotel and Villas
1200 Alta Loma Road
Tel: 310-657 1333,
1-800-858 9758
Fax: 310-657 1330
www.sunsetmarquishotel.com
Hidden amid lush gardens in a quiet cul-de-sac south of the Sunset Strip, this delightful hotel presents over 100 gorgeous suites and a dozen Mediterranean style villas. The secluded property includes a state-of-the-art screening room, two heated swimming pools and the Whiskey Bar, a movie-star magnet.

Sunset Tower Hotel
8358 Sunset Boulevard
Tel: 323-654 7100,
1-800-225 2637
Fax: 323-654 9287
www.sunsettowerhotel.com
With 74 elegant rooms and suites, this historic, Art Deco tower presents views of the Hollywood Hills through floor-to-ceiling windows. Here guests can pamper

themselves at the Argyle Salon & Spa and enjoy Old Hollywood features like the wood-paneled Tower Bar. Modern amenities include flat-screen TVs and i-Pod stations.

Expensive

Chateau Marmont
8221 Sunset Boulevard
Tel: 323-656 1010,
1-800-242 8328
Fax: 323-655 5311
www.chateaumarmont.com
Located above the border between Hollywood and West Hollywood, this castle-like 1920s-era mansion has long been a refuge for Hollywood's elite, including Natalie Wood and Keanu Reeves. There are 63 luxurious suites and bungalows, including the penthouse, which offers panoramic views of the city.

Hyatt West Hollywood
8401 Sunset Boulevard
Tel: 323-656 1234,
1-800-233 1234
Fax: 323-650 7024
www.hyatt.com
The "rock & roll Hyatt" and the "Riot Hyatt" are two monikers that have been given to this chic hotel. With fashionable rooms and views of the Sunset Strip, there's also high-speed wireless Internet, an A-list restaurant, a fitness center, a heated rooftop pool and proximity to hot nightclubs, including Chi, downstairs.

Le Montrose Suite Hotel
900 Hammond Street
Tel: 310-855 1115,
1-800-776 0666
Fax: 310-657 9192
www.lemontrose.com
Nestled on a residential

street south of the Sunset Strip, this celebrity hideaway offers 133 newly renovated suites with sunken living rooms, cozy fireplaces and DVD players. Kitchenettes, private balconies, in-suite massages and currency exchange are also available, and guests can expect such touches as fresh fruit, mineral water and homemade cookies.

Renaissance Hollywood Hotel
1755 N. Highland Avenue
Tel: 323-856 1200,
1-800-468 3571
Fax: 323-856 1205
www.renaissancehollywood.com
The cornerstone of the Hollywood & Highland Center, this hotel is a great place to view the Hollywood sign. With 637 rooms, this elegant high-rise has a multi-lingual staff, a business center, secretarial and child care services, a laundry valet, a rooftop pool and the eclectic Twist restaurant.

The Standard Hollywood
8300 Sunset Boulevard
Tel: 1-323-650 9090
Fax: 1-323-650 2820
www.standardhotel.com
Cool and trendy, this West Hollywood sister establishment to the Standard Downtown has crisp and modern guestrooms and as gorgeous a view of LA from the rooftop as the hipsters who stay here could hope for.

Inexpensive

The Grafton on Sunset
8462 Sunset Boulevard
Tel: 323-654 4600
Fax: 323-654 5918

www.graftononsunset.com
Hip and lovely, this West Hollywood joint features 103 rooms and five specialty suites, all decorated with feng sui appeal and including organic bath products, video and music CD libraries and daily newspapers. The romantic pool and Balboa steakhouse are classic Hollywood.

Hollywood Orchid Suites
1753 Orchid Avenue
Tel: 323-874 9678,
1-800-537 3052
Fax: 323-874 5246
www.orchidsuites.com
Located directly behind the Chinese and Kodak theaters, this collection of junior, executive and deluxe suites provides convenient kitchenettes, full kitchens and guides to local restaurants and attractions. Rates and occupancy rise during the Academy Awards.

Magic Castle Hotel
7025 Franklin Avenue
Tel: 323-851 0800,
1-800-741 4915
Fax: 323-851 4926
www.magiccastlehotel.com
With the price of a spacious room, studio or suite in this long-standing hotel comes pastries from the Susina Bakery, coffee via Wolfgang Puck, discounted meals at the Yamashiro restaurant and the option of visiting the Magic Castle, a private magicians' club.

Ramada Plaza Hotel and Suites
8585 Santa Monica Boulevard
Tel: 310-652 6400,
1-800-845 8585
Fax: 310-652 2135
www.ramadaweho.com
Guests can expect com-

fortable rooms and suites, an outdoor heated pool and in-room features like irons, refrigerators, coffeemakers, hair dryers and safes, but the real treat of this afforable hotel is its close proximity to the Sunset Strip and West Hollywood's Pacific Design Center.

San Vicente Inn and Resort
845 San Vicente Boulevard
Tel: 310-854 6915,
1-800-577 6915
Fax: 310-289 5929
www.sanvicenteinn.com
Close to all "Boystown" hotspots, West Hollywood's only gay resort attracts couples and friends with the secluded atmosphere of its historical cottages. There's a clothing-optional pool, hot tub and steam room.

Budget

Dunes Inn Sunset
5625 Sunset Boulevard
Tel: 323-467 5171
Fax: 323-461 1720
www.dunesla.com
This small motel, just east of the 101, offers clean rooms, affordable prices, free parking, satellite TV and close proximity to the Metro Red Line and the Hollywood Walk of Fame.

Holloway Motel
8465 Santa Monica Boulevard
Tel: 323-654 2454,
1-888-654 6400
Fax: 323-654 2454, x260
www.hollowaymotel.com
Located in the heart of West Hollywood, this motel is a real bargain. The price of a room includes breakfast, on-site parking, cable TV, voice mail and built-in room safes.

BEVERLY HILLS/BEL AIR AND BEYOND

Luxury

The Beverly Hills Hotel
9641 Sunset Boulevard
Tel: 310-276 2251,
1-800-283 8885
Fax: 310-887 2887
www.beverlyhillshotel.com
Set in lush gardens with graceful palm trees, the historic "pink palace," a symbol of old Hollywood glamour, has lured movie stars for decades. Gorgeous bungalows, a classic swimming pool and the popular Polo Lounge are a few reasons why.

The Beverly Hilton
9876 Wilshire Boulevard
Tel: 310-274 7777,
1-800-445 8667
Fax: 310-285 1313
www.hilton.com
This world-famous hotel and home of the annual Golden Globe Awards tempts movie stars and others with lavish penthouse suites, in-room spa services, an Olympic-sized pool and Trader Vic's, a top Polynesian restaurant.

Hotel Bel-Air
701 Stone Canyon Road
Tel: 310-472 1211,
1-800-648 4097
Fax: 310-476 5890
www.hotelbelair.com

BELOW: Hotel Bel-Air arch

This 1920s hotel has 91 exquisite guest rooms and suites amid lush gardens, coastal redwoods and towering palms. Today's guests enjoy the same privacy as did Grace Kelly and Cary Grant.

Hyatt Regency Century Plaza
2025 Avenue of the Stars
Tel: 310-228 1234,
1-800-233 1234
Fax: 310-551 3395
www.centuryplaza.hyatt.com
A Century City landmark, this hotel has nearly 700 guest rooms and suites. Patrons should make time for the stunning Breeze restaurant, with seafood and sushi bars.

The Regent Beverly Wilshire
9500 Wilshire Boulevard
Tel: 310-275 5200,
1-800-545 4000
Fax: 310-274 2851
www.regenthotels.com
Anchoring exclusive Rodeo Drive, this classic Beverly Hills hotel has a star-studded history. Nearly 400 rooms and suites, complete with marble bathrooms and down pillows, offer the ultimate in luxury.

Expensive

Avalon Hotel
9400 W. Olympic Boulevard
Tel: 310-277 5221,
1-800 670 6183
Fax: 310-277 4928
www.avalonbeverlyhills.com
A hideaway near the southern edge of Beverly Hills, this hip hotel entices young Hollywood stars with its luminous pool and inventive restaurant. Its stylish

rooms, suites and penthouse studios evoke the "patio lifestyle" of 1950s-era California.

The Crescent Hotel
403 N. Crescent Drive
Tel: 310-247 0505
Fax: 310-247 9053
www.crescentbh.com
Italian sheets, flat-screen TVs, gourmet snacks and the eclectic Boé restaurant welcome guests to this European-style hotel in Beverly Hills.

Luxe Hotel Sunset Boulevard
11461 Sunset Boulevard
Tel: 310-476 6571,
1-866-589 3411
Fax: 310-471 6310
www.luxehotels.com
Not far from the Getty Center, this graceful hotel has superior rooms and suites, a full-service spa, an on-site tennis court and wireless Internet access.

Maison 140 Beverly Hills
140 Lasky Drive
Tel: 310-281 4000,
1-800-670 6182
Fax: 310-281 4001
www.maison140beverlyhills.com
This intimate blend of French and Asian style offers guests designer bed linens, flat-screen televisions, in-room spa treatments, European antiques and intriguing artwork. The dramatic Bar Noir serves great cocktails.

Inexpensive – Budget

Brentwood Motor Hotel
12200 Sunset Boulevard
Tel: 310-476 9981,
1-800-840 3808
www.bmhotel.com

Cozy and reasonably priced, this hotel is well located not far from the Getty Center and UCLA. Built in 1947, the bungalow style building houses 20 quaint, brick-walled rooms. Free parking.

Hotel Beverly Terrace
469 N. Doheny Drive
Tel: 310-274 8141,
1-800-842 6401
Fax: 310-385 1998
www.hotelbeverlyterrace.com
Many of the rooms here have Asian-inspired touches like butterfly paintings, bamboo art and sage green tones. Tropical plants and colorful lanterns surround the pool, and there's a good Italian restaurant.

Hotel Del Flores
409 N. Crescent Drive
Tel: 310-274 5115
Fax: 310-550 0374
www.hoteldelflores.com
This vintage hotel offers clean rooms, color TVs, microwaves and low rates in the heart of Beverly Hills.

PRICE CATEGORIES

Price categories are for a double room for one night, usually with a Continental breakfast:
Luxury: over $300
Expensive: $200–300
Inexpensive: $100–200
Budget: under $100

SANTA MONICA/VENICE/MARINA DEL REY/LAX

Luxury

Casa Del Mar
1910 Ocean Way
Tel: 310-581 5533,
1-800-898 6999
Fax: 310-581 5503
www.hotelcasadelmar.com
A 1920s-era lobby, with floor-to-ceiling windows and a striking bar, beckons guests into this opulent hotel by the sea. The Santa Monica landmark features a spectacular restaurant and nearly 130 elegant rooms, where ocean views, jacuzzis and period furnishings are the norm.

The Fairmont Miramar Hotel
101 Wilshire Boulevard
Tel: 310-576 7777,
1-866-540 4471
Fax: 310-458 7912
www.fairmont.com
For over 80 years, this Santa Monica retreat, nestling amid lush grounds above the ocean, has lured Hollywood celebrities, from Greta Garbo to Barbra Streisand. Guests will encounter gorgeous suites and bungalows, a California-style restaurant, an outdoor whirlpool and a day spa.

Loews Santa Monica Beach Hotel
1700 Ocean Avenue
Tel: 310-458 6700,
1-800-235 6397
Fax: 310-458 6761
www.loewshotels.com
From the four-story glass atrium, the stunning palm-lined pool, the sleek hotel restaurant and many of the sumptuous rooms, guests can view the hotel's true highlight – a

dramatic sunset over the Pacific. 24-hour room service, a fitness center, professional babysitters and bike rentals also available.

The Ritz-Carlton Marina del Rey
4375 Admiralty Way
Tel: 310-823 1700,
1-800-241 3333
Fax: 310-823 2403
www.ritzcarlton.com
This luxurious, waterfront hotel houses a romantic restaurant with bold international cuisine and over 300 elegant guest rooms, some with amazing views of sailboats.

Shutters Hotel on the Beach
1 Pico Boulevard
Tel: 310-458 0030,
1-800-334 9000
Fax: 310-458 4589
www.shuttersonthebeach.com
Facing the Pacific Ocean, this classic beachside establishment rejuvenates guests with its cozy lobby, tranquil spa, stylish seafood restaurant and airy bedrooms. Artworks from masters like David Hockney and Roy Lichtenstein adorn walls throughout the hotel.

Expensive

Channel Road Inn
219 W. Channel Road
Tel: 310-459 1920
Fax: 310-454 9920
www.channelroadinn.com
This fully restored 1915 manor, located one block from Santa Monica's beaches, promises romantic ocean or garden views in each of its 14 rooms and suites, some of

which also contain fireplaces, jacuzzis, sunny decks or canopy beds.

The Georgian Hotel
1415 Ocean Avenue
Tel: 310-395 9945,
1-800-538 8147
Fax: 310-656 0904
www.georgianhotel.com
Towering over the intersection of Ocean Avenue and old Route 66, this Art Deco landmark once entertained Clark Gable and Carole Lombard. Today, the elegant hotel lures guests into 84 contemporary rooms and suites, which include such amenities as wireless Internet, Aveda body products and, sometimes, ocean views.

Sheraton Gateway Hotel LAX
6101 W. Century Boulevard
Tel: 310-642 1111
Fax: 310-642 4048
www.starwoodhotels.com
Just minutes from LAX, this hotel welcomes business and leisure travelers with amenities like free airport shuttles, ergonomic desk chairs, in-room movies, a coffeeshop and two restaurants.

Inexpensive

The Cadillac Hotel
8 Dudley Avenue
Tel: 310-399 8876
Fax: 310-399 4536
www.thecadillachotel.com
Standing along the northern end of Venice Beach Boardwalk, this Art Deco hotel offers glorious ocean views and a college-dorm atmosphere, from its pool table to its casual lounge. Erected in

1905, this pink and turquoise building was once Charlie Chaplin's summer home.

Embassy Suites Hotel LAX North
9801 Airport Boulevard
Tel: 310-215 1000,
1-800-362 2779
Fax: 310-215 1952
www.embassysuites.com
Every two-room suite in this LAX-area hotel is appointed with amenities like sleeper sofas, microwave ovens and high-speed Internet access. Complimentary, cooked-to-order breakfasts and, later, California cuisine in the garden atrium.

Foghorn Harbor Inn
4140 Via Marina
Tel: 310-823 4626,
1-800-423 4940
www.foghornhotel.com
Perched along Mothers Beach in Marina del Rey, this intimate 23-room hotel offers free shuttle service to and from LAX, satellite television, 24-hour coffee in the lobby and incredible marina views. Every room has either a patio or a balcony. Perfect for in-transit passengers to and from LAX.

The Hotel California
1670 Ocean Avenue
Tel: 310-393 2363,
1-866-571 0000
Fax: 310-393 1063
www.hotelca.com

Dating to 1948 and close to the Santa Monica Pier, this vintage and popular hotel has ocean views, tropical murals, hardwood floors, Egyptian cotton sheets and free WiFi.

Inn at Venice Beach
327 Washington Boulevard
Tel: 310-821 2557,
1-800-828 0688
Fax: 310-827 0289
www.innatvenicebeach.com
Guests of this lovely inn in Venice can relax in the cobblestoned courtyard and savor a complimentary breakfast of fresh pastries, fruit and assorted coffees and teas. All 43 airy rooms and suites include private baths, free local calls and wireless Internet access.

The Venice Beach House
15 30th Avenue
Tel: 310-823 1966
Fax: 310-823 1842
www.venicebeachhouse.com
Built in 1911 by friends of the founder of Venice, this nine-room B&B is situated amid a tranquil garden not far from the beach. All rooms have cable TV and high-speed Internet, but each has its own unique theme. High-end inexpensive, bordering on expensive.

Budget

Bayside Hotel
2001 Ocean Avenue
Tel: 310-396 6000,
1-800-525 4447
Fax: 310-396 1000

www.baysidehotel.com
Cozy rooms, comfy beds, oversized desks and ocean views await guests at this affordable Santa Monica hotel, not far from the beach.

Days Inn Santa Monica
3007 Santa Monica Boulevard
Tel: 310-829 6333,
1-800-591 5995
Fax: 310-829 1983
www.smdaysinn.com
Hotel guests might be a couple of miles from Santa Monica's beaches, but the in-house sauna, rooftop spa and swaying palm trees are all quintessential California at a very affordable price.

Travelodge Hotel at LAX
5547 W. Century Boulevard

Tel: 310-649 4000,
1-800-421 3939
Fax: 310-649 0311
www.travelodgelax.com
This clean, affordable hotel offers travelers a free breakfast buffet, heated pool, 24-hour restaurant and gift shop. Good for airline passengers and has free shuttles to Manhattan Beach.

Venice Beach Cotel
25 Windward Avenue
Tel: 310-399 7649
Fax: 310-399 1930
www.venicebeachcotel.com
Located on the Venice boardwalk and close to Muscle Beach, this cool youth hostel has a friendly staff, daily housekeeping service, free boogie board rentals and no curfew.

AROUND DISNEYLAND

Luxury–Expensive

Disneyland Hotel
1150 Magic Way
Tel: 714-778 6600,
1-877-700 3476
Fax: 714-956 6597
www.disneyland.com
Steeped in magical history, Disneyland's original hotel invites families, home after a long day in the adjacent theme parks, to relax with complimentary movies, assorted pools, several restaurants and comfortable beds.

Disney's Grand Californian Hotel
1600 S. Disneyland Drive
Tel: 714-635 2300,
1-877-700 3476
Fax: 714-300 7300
www.disneyland.com
With an exclusive entrance to Disney's

California Adventure, this Craftsman-style resort has 745 rooms and suites, 24-hour room service, a Napa Valley-style restaurant, a redwood-themed pool and extras like cribs, mini-bars, in-room safes and comfy robes.

Hilton Anaheim
777 Convention Way
Tel: 714-750 4321,
1-800-801 8241
Fax: 714-740 4460
www.anaheim.hilton.com
Close to Disneyland and Knott's Berry Farm, this 15-story complex offers high-speed wireless Internet, complete business services, a poolside grill, a sports lounge, an Italian restaurant and a world-class fitness center that includes a pool, spa and basketball gym.

Inexpensive–Budget

Candy Cane Inn
1747 S. Harbor Boulevard
Tel: 714-774 5284,
1-800-345 7057
Fax: 714-772 5462
www.candycaneinn.net
Adjacent to the Disneyland Resort, this award-winning boutique hotel presents flowering gardens, refreshing pools, down comforters, shuttle service to the theme parks and a poolside breakfast buffet. You might forget to go to Disneyland itself.

Jolly Roger Inn
640 W. Katella Avenue
Tel: 714-782 7500,
1-888-296 5986
Fax: 714-782 7619
www.jollyrogerhotel.com
Families will appreciate this modest hotel, with

its spacious guest rooms, free parking, laundry facilities, a gift shop, access to the Disney Channel and free shuttle service to nearby Disneyland.

PRICE CATEGORIES

Price categories are for a double room for one night, usually with a Continental breakfast:
Luxury: over $300
Expensive: $200–300
Inexpensive: $100–200
Budget: under $100

ACTIVITIES

THE ARTS, NIGHTLIFE, KIDS, EVENTS, SHOPPING, SPAS, SPORTS AND TOURS

As first-time visitors to Los Angeles soon learn, LA is one gigantic city, filled with a multitude of unique neighborhoods, millions of inhabitants and countless attractions and activities, from art galleries to sightseeing tours. Day or night, you can bet that there's something happening somewhere. Publications like the *LA Weekly*, *LA Stage* magazine, *Los Angeles* magazine and the *Los Angeles Times*' "Calendar" section provide current listings of local events, and websites like www.la.com, www.losangeles.city search.com and www.seemyla.com also make planning easier. In addition, you can contact LA INC., the city's official convention and visitors bureau, at 213-689 8822 or other area tourist information offices for a calendar of events and advice on things to do in each neighborhood.

THE ARTS

Theater

Although LA is known as the center of the filmmaking universe, most cultural enthusiasts, including many Angelenos, don't think much of the city's theater scene. While it's no Chicago or New York City, perhaps, LA has a ton of

theaters, presenting everything from large-scale Broadway musicals to avant-garde one-person shows. In fact, LA is often the spawning ground for actors eventually headed to Broadway, and resident troupes frequently include famous film stars, enjoying a brief hiatus from the cameras for a more intimate turn in a 99-seat Equity-waiver playhouse.

In addition to the intimate theaters that line Santa Monica Boulevard and other major roads – such as the **Lee Strasberg Theatre Institute** (7936 Santa Monica Boulevard, tel: 323-650 7777, www.strasberg.com) – there are several more prominent institutions. The Music Center's **Ahmanson Theatre** and **Mark Taper Forum**, for instance, present productions from the Center Theatre Group (135 N. Grand Avenue, Downtown, tel: 213-628 2772, www.taperahmanson.com). Also located Downtown are the **REDCAT** (631 W. 2nd Street, tel: 213-237 2800, www.redcat.org) for innovative musical theater and the 880-seat **Aratani Japan America Theatre** (244 S. San Pedro Street, tel: 213-680 3700, www.jaccc.org) for traditional Japanese performances.

In the Hollywood area, there are several landmark theaters, including the **Pantages Theatre** (6233 Hollywood Boulevard, tel:

323-468 1770, www.broadwayla.org), a 75-year-old movie palace that now presents world-class Broadway musicals, and the **Kodak Theatre** (Hollywood & Highland Center, tel: 323-308 6300, www.kodaktheatre.com), which hosts holiday shows and musical events. Nestled in the Hollywood Hills, the **Ford Amphitheatre** (2580 Cahuenga Boulevard East, tel: 323-461 3673, www.fordamphitheatre.org) provides an intimate outdoor space for various daring and classic productions.

Farther west, the **Geffen Playhouse** (10886 Le Conte Avenue, tel: 310-208 5454, www.geffenplayhouse.com) has an eclectic mix of musicals, classic plays and brand-new works. In Santa Monica, the **Santa Monica Playhouse** (1211 4th Street, tel: 310-394 9779, www.santamonica playhouse.com) presents family shows and holiday cabarets, while **Highways, Inc.** (1651 18th Street, tel: 310-315 1459, www.highwaysperformance.org) offers brazen, ethnic performances involving dance, music and stories. Down in Culver City, there's also the **The Actors' Gang Theater** (9070 Venice Boulevard, tel: 310-838 4264, www.theactorsgang.com), founded in 1981 by a group of renegade artists, including Tim Robbins, and further east you'll find the **Pasadena Playhouse** (39 S. El Molino Avenue, tel: 626-356 7529, www.pasadenaplayhouse.org), the state's official theater.

Dance

Live dance performances – from visiting ballet presentations to experimental dance shows – occur in venues throughout Los Angeles County all year long. The top venues include:

The Music Center/Performing Arts Center of Los Angeles County
135 N. Grand Avenue, Downtown
Tel: 213-972 7211.
www.musiccenter.org
Each season, the Dorothy Chandler Pavilion and Ahmanson Theatre host various dance troupes, including the Miami City Ballet and the Alvin Ailey American Dance Theater.

UCLA Live
405 Hilgard Avenue, Westwood
Tel: 310-825 4401.
www.uclalive.org
An assortment of dance troupes, from Japanese ensembles to French ballet companies, perform regularly in UCLA's Royce Hall.

The **REDCAT** (tel: 213-237 2800), **Ford Amphitheatre** (tel: 323-461 3673), **Alex Theatre** (216 N. Brand Boulevard, Glendale, tel: 818-243 2539, www.alextheatre.org) and **Carpenter Performing Arts Center** (6200 Atherton Boulevard, Long Beach, tel. 562-985 4274, www.carpenterarts.org) also stage dance performances semi-regularly. Contact each venue for a calendar of events.

Opera

The Los Angeles Opera, currently directed by maestro Plácido Domingo, holds regular performances at the **Dorothy Chandler Pavilion** in Downtown's Music Center (135 N. Grand Avenue, tel: 213-972 8001, www.laopera.com). Productions are varied, from adaptations of classics like Puccini's *Madama Butterfly* to innovative creations like *Grendel*.

Music

Given the diversity of LA's ethnic communities, it's no wonder that the city's music scene is just as eclectic. Symphony orchestras, funky blues havens, free salsa concerts – however your musical tastes run, you'll satisfy them somewhere in this lively town.

For classical musical lovers, the 40-member Los Angeles Chamber Orchestra currently alternates between two venues – Glendale's **Alex Theatre** (tel: 818-243 2539) and UCLA's **Royce Hall** (tel: 310-825 4401). Meanwhile, the Los Angeles Philharmonic Association has, for most of the year, a permanent home, the relatively new **Walt Disney Concert Hall** (111 S. Grand Avenue, Downtown, tel: 323-850 2000, www.laphil.com), which also hosts jazz and world music concerts, celebrity and organ recitals and the Los Angeles Master Chorale. In summer, the Philharmonic performs at the **Hollywood Bowl** (2301 N. Highland Avenue, tel: 323-850 2000, www.hollywoodbowl.org), an outdoor amphitheatre nestled in the Hollywood Hills, where nightly classical, jazz, world and pop concerts take place.

Music enthusiasts can enjoy free summer concerts at the **Farmers Market** at 3rd and Fairfax (tel: 323-933 9211, www.farmersmarketla.com) and on the **Santa Monica Pier** (tel: 310-458 8900, www.twilightdance.org). Though not free, the outdoor concerts held at the summer-only **Greek Theatre** in Griffith Park (tel: 323-665 1927, www.greektheatrela.com) and Arcadia's **LA County Arboretum** (301 N. Baldwin Avenue, tel: 626-821 3222, www.arboretum.org) are worth a listen, too.

Top rock bands and solo artists perform at larger venues such as the **Staples Center** (1111 S. Figueroa Street, Downtown, tel: 213-742 7340, www.staplescenter.com), the **Kodak Theatre** in the Hollywood & Highland Center (tel: 323-308 6300) and the **Gibson Amphitheatre** at Universal CityWalk (tel: 818-622 4440; www.citywalkhollywood.com).

Art

Los Angeles has a thriving art scene, with hundreds of public art displays, art galleries and art museums spread throughout the city's diverse neighborhoods and beyond. As with restaurants, clubs and boutiques, galleries can appear and disappear quite frequently, so consult regional tourist information offices for up-to-date listings.

Public art covers a wide spectrum in this city, from the Electric Fountain in Beverly Gardens Park to the stained glass windows beneath the Cathedral of Our Lady of the Angels. Three unique displays worth seeing are **Farmer John's** pastoral murals in Vernon (3049 E. Vernon Avenue), **Watts Towers of Simon Rodia State Historic Park** (1765 E. 107th Street, tel: 213-847 4646) and the **Franklin D. Murphy Sculpture Garden** on UCLA's campus.

As for galleries, you'll find clusters of showrooms – featuring antiques, folk art, modern art, painting, sculpture, ceramics, photography, jewelry, textiles, multimedia and other creations – in places like **Chinatown** (tel: 213-680 0243, www.chinatownla.com) and Santa Monica's **Bergamot Station Arts Center** (2525 Michigan Avenue, www.bergamotstation.com), which includes the **Santa Monica Museum of Art**. You'll also find rows of unique galleries along roads like **La Brea Avenue** and **Montana Avenue**. In addition, you'll discover bizarre, modern artworks at the **LA Artcore at the Union Center for the Arts** (120 Judge John Aiso Street, tel: 213-617 3274, www.laartcore.org) and **Los Angeles Contemporary Exhibitions** (6522 Hollywood

GETTING TICKETS

You can purchase tickets for live theater, concerts, sports and family events by visiting www.tickets.com or contacting the following agencies:

Al Brooks Tickets
900 Wilshire Boulevard, Suite 104
Tel: 213-626 5863
www.albrooks.com

Front Row Center Tickets Service
1355 Westwood Boulevard, No. 3
Tel: 310-478 0848
www.frctix.com

Ticketmaster
Tower Records, 8844 Sunset Boulevard, West Hollywood
Tel: 213-480 3232
www.ticketmaster.com

UCLA Central Ticket Office
James West Alumni Center, UCLA
Tel: 310-825 2101
www.tickets.ucla.edu

For half-price theater tickets, contact the LA Stage Alliance by calling 213-614 0556 or visiting www.lastagetix.com or www.theatrela.org.

Boulevard, tel: 323-957 1777, www.artleak.org).

The city also has some of the country's best-known museums, including the **Museum of Contemporary Art** (250 S. Grand Avenue, tel: 213-626 6222, www.moca.org), the **LA County Museum of Art** (5905 Wilshire Boulevard, tel: 323-857 6000, www.lacma.org), the **Armand Hammer Museum of Art and Cultural Center** (10899 Wilshire Boulevard, tel: 310-443 7000, www.hammer.ucla.edu) and the **Getty Center** (1200 Getty Center Drive, tel: 310-440 7300, www.getty.edu). Less well known, but also worth visiting are the **Geffen Contemporary at MOCA** (152 N. Central Avenue), the **MOCA Pacific Design Center** (8687 Melrose Avenue) and the **Getty Villa** along the Pacific Coast Highway in Malibu.

NIGHTLIFE

Almost every part of Los Angeles – from West Hollywood to Hermosa Beach – has a vibrant nightlife, with pulsing dance clubs, funky blues venues, first-rate comedy clubs and historic movie palaces. Music clubs, especially, can appear and disappear at will, and although most of those listed here are long-standing joints, it's always advisable to consult up-to-date listings in publications like *Calendar* and *LA Weekly*. Because cover charges, dress codes, reservation policies and show times might vary from place to place, you should always call ahead and check the details.

Bars

From star-studded hotel lounges to low-key neighborhood pubs, LA has an enormous number of options for bar-hoppers. Here are a few notable ones:

Casey's Irish Bar & Grille, 613 S. Grand Avenue, Downtown, tel: 213-629 2353, www.bigcaseys.com. A downtown hideaway for 35 years, this pub transports whisky-swigging patrons to 1930s Chicago.

Cinespace, 6356 Hollywood Boulevard, Hollywood, tel: 323-817 3456, www.cine-space.com. Movie lovers can enjoy eclectic film screenings while sipping martinis.

The Dresden, 1760 N. Vermont Avenue, Los Feliz, tel: 323-665 4294, www.thedresden.com. Six days a week, patrons are treated to the jazz tunes of local icons Marty and Elayne.

The Hideout, 112 W. Channel Road, Santa Monica, tel: 310-429 9920, www.santamonicahideout.com. This 1920s-style martini bar lures karaoke singers, cigar smokers, pool players, dancers and movie stars.

Red Lion Tavern, 2366 Glendale Boulevard, Silverlake, tel: 323-662 5337, www.redliontavern.net.

For late-night sausages and beer, many locals crowd this 40-year-old German institution.

Sharkeez, 52 Pier Avenue, Hermosa Beach, tel: 310-374 7823, www.sharkeezbar.com. Not far from the ocean, this rowdy sports bar and grill offers good grub and drink specials.

Tiki-Ti, 4427 Sunset Boulevard, Silverlake, tel: 323-669 9381, www.tiki-ti.com. This tropical-themed bar tempts regulars with a friendly vibe and exotic drinks.

Nightclubs

Like LA's bars, the city's nightclubs embrace a wide spectrum, from gay hotspots to salsa clubs. Here are a few winners:

The Conga Room, 5364 Wilshire Boulevard, tel: 323-938 1696, www.congaroom.com. For at least three nights a week, dancers groove to salsa, hip-hop, soul and reggae.

The Derby Hollywood, 4500 Los Feliz Boulevard, Los Feliz, tel: 323-663 8979, www.the-derby.com. Made even more famous by the flick *Swingers*, this is *the* place to jitterbug.

Key Club, 9039 Sunset Boulevard, West Hollywood, tel: 310-274 5800, www.keyclub.com. A multi-level venue, this upscale joint has a restaurant, dance floor and stage for live musical acts.

The Mayan, 1038 S. Hill Street, Downtown, tel: 213-746 4674, www.clubmayan.com. This 1920s-era movie theater became a multi-tiered dance club in 1990.

The Roxy Theatre, 9009 Sunset Boulevard, West Hollywood, tel: 310-276 2222, www.theroxyonsunset.com. Live music and famous neighboring clubs lure trendy shakers to the Sunset Strip.

Rumba Room, Universal City-Walk, tel: 818-622 1227, www.rumbaroom.com. Featuring tapas and two full bars, this multi-level, upscale dance club pulses with live salsa and Latin jazz.

The Viper Room, 8852 Sunset Boulevard, West Hollywood, tel: 310-358 1881, www.viperroom.com.

With the vibe of a 1920s-era Harlem jazz club, this hip joint continues to lure famous rock acts. Known by many as the spot where the actor River Phoenix died of a drugs overdose. **Whisky A Go-Go**, 8901 Sunset Boulevard, West Hollywood, tel: 310-652 4202, www.whiskyagogo.com. A famous history and rockin' bands continue to entice dancers and partygoers.

Live Music Venues

B.B. King's Blues Club, Universal CityWalk, tel: 818-622 5464, www.bbkingclubs.com. This world-class blues club offers Southern cuisine and live music seven days a week.
The Cowboy Palace Saloon, 21635 Devonshire Street, Chatsworth, tel: 818-341 0166, www.cowboypalace.com. For over 30 years, this honky-tonk has show-cased live country-western music every night.
Harvelle's, 1432 4th Street, Santa Monica, tel: 310-395 1676, www.harvelles.com. Since 1931, this moody, sexy room invites guests to drink, dance and listen to the hottest jazz, blues, soul and burlesque.
House of Blues Sunset Strip, 8430 Sunset Boulevard, West Hollywood, tel: 323-848 5100, www.hob.com. The funky stage attracts famous rock and blues acts, and the gospel brunch lures the locals.
Knitting Factory, 7021 Hollywood Boulevard, Hollywood, tel: 323-463 0204, www.knittingfactory.

com. Young night owls converge in the Hollywood Galaxy for live jazz and punk.
The Troubadour, 9081 Santa Monica Boulevard, West Hollywood, tel: 310-276 6168, www.troubadour.com. Live rock bands have been jamming at this legendary venue since 1957.
Wiltern LG, 3790 Wilshire Boulevard, tel: 213-388 1400, www.thewiltern.com. An Art Deco movie theater in 1931, this gray-green landmark hosts a wide array of live music shows.

Comedy and Magic

Music isn't all that LA has on tap – comics and magicians get around town too.
The Comedy & Magic Club, 1018 Hermosa Avenue, Hermosa Beach, tel: 310-372 1193, www.comedyandmagicclub.info. Jay Leno, host of *The Tonight Show*, regularly tests new material here.
Comedy Store, 8433 Sunset Boulevard, West Hollywood, tel: 323-656 6225, www.thecomedystore.com. Once the site of Ciro's, this club has featured comic greats like Eddie Murphy and George Carlin.
The Groundlings, 7307 Melrose Avenue, Hollywood, tel: 323-934 4747, www.groundlings.com. For over 25 years, this comedy show-case has nurtured talented comics like Conan O'Brien and Jon Lovitz.
Improv Olympic West, 6366 Hollywood Boulevard, Hollywood, tel: 323-962 7560, www.iowest.com. The West Coast branch of the

famous Chicago venue offers improv. shows and classes.
Laugh Factory, 8001 Sunset Boulevard, Hollywood, tel: 323-656 1336, www.laughfactory.com. With a branch in Long Beach, too, this famous comedy club sur-prises patrons with all-star shows.
Magicopolis, 1418 4th Street, Santa Monica, tel: 310-451 2241, www.magicopolis.com. This classy venue presents shows that blend elements of magic, illusion and laughter.

Movies

As the heart of the world's film-making industry, LA has a num-ber of classic movie palaces plus multiplex theaters in area malls. Some of the city's recently re-novated historic theaters – such as the **Egyptian Theatre** (6712 Hollywood Boulevard, tel: 323-466 3456), **Grauman's Chinese Theatre** (6925 Hollywood Boulevard, tel: 323-464 8111) and **El Capitan Theatre** (6838 Hollywood Boulevard, tel: 818-845 3110) – present first-run films with state-of-the-art equipment.

Several tourist-friendly pedestrian areas have high-end movie theaters as well. **West-wood Village**, adjacent to UCLA, has nine different movie theaters, including the landmark **Mann Bruin** (948 Broxton Avenue, tel: 310-208 8998) and **Mann Village** (961 Broxton Avenue, tel: 310-208 5576). Santa Monica's **Third Street Promenade** features perhaps a dozen movie screens in the three blocks between Broadway and Wilshire Boulevard. **Universal CityWalk** contains an 18-screen multiplex plus an IMAX theater, and **Downtown Disney** has a dozen 1920s-style AMC movie theaters.

Most local malls, such as the **Beverly Center** and **Sherman Oaks Galleria**, have multi-screen movie complexes nowadays. Con-sult the *Los Angeles Times* for movie listings, show times and

BELOW: the Blues Brothers tour Los Angeles.

theater addresses. To save time, you can purchase tickets through websites like www.fandango.com and www.movietickets.com.

KIDS

Anaheim's theme parks and Valencia's roller coasters are not the only offerings tailored to children and teenagers. The Los Angeles area has a host of family-oriented activities and attractions, such as those listed below.

Activities

Bob Baker Marionette Theater
1345 W. 1st Street
Tel: 213-250 9995.
www.bobbakermarionettes.com
Since 1961, kids have come here to view puppet shows and buy their own marionettes.
Los Angeles Central Library
630 W. 5th Street, Downtown
Tel: 213-228 7000.
www.lapl.org
Little kids enjoy family storytime; teenagers meet for the graphic novel book club.
Santa Monica Pier
Ocean and Colorado avenues, Santa Monica
Tel: 310-458 8900.
www.santamonicapier.org
The carousel, arcade, amusement park, aquarium, artists and vendors will occupy visitors for hours.
Shoreline Village
429 Shoreline Village Drive, Long Beach
Tel: 562-435 2668.
www.shorelinevillage.com
You'll find hot dogs, ice cream, surrey carts, live bands, a video arcade and more.

Museums for Kids

California ScienCenter
Exposition Park, Downtown
Tel: 323-724 3623.
www.californiasciencecenter.org
Besides an IMAX theater, there are hands-on exhibits about

inventions, space and biology.
Kidspace Children's Museum
480 N. Arroyo Boulevard, Pasadena
Tel: 626-449 9144.
www.kidspacemuseum.org
Kids will encounter climbing towers, a kaleidoscopic tunnel, a dig site and more.
Museum of Television & Radio
465 N. Beverly Drive, Beverly Hills
Tel: 310-786 1000.
www.mtr.org
Kids can watch family films and re-create an old-time radio drama.
Natural History Museum of LA County
Exposition Park, Downtown
Tel: 213-763 3466.
www.nhm.org
Dinosaur models, animated birds, gold exhibits, an insect zoo and other treasures.
Page Museum at the La Brea Tar Pits
5801 Wilshire Boulevard, Los Angeles
Tel: 323-934 7243.
www.tarpits.org
Visitors eye the bubbling pools in Hancock Park and observe rescued fossils inside the museum.
Travel Town Museum
5200 Zoo Drive, Griffith Park
Tel: 323-662 5874.
www.traveltown.org
Families can tour historic locomotives and ride a miniature train.

Zoos and Aquariums

Aquarium of the Pacific
100 Aquarium Way, Long Beach
Tel: 562-590 3100.
www.aquariumofpacific.org
Here is the world's largest coral reef exhibit, plus rainbow lorikeets, bamboo sharks and more.
Cabrillo Marine Aquarium
3720 Stephen White Drive, San Pedro
Tel: 310-548 7562.
www.cabrilloaq.org
Experts supervise tide pool tours and the annual grunion run (when small fish called grunions wash up on the shore to reproduce).

Los Angeles Zoo and Botanical Gardens
5333 Zoo Drive, Griffith Park
Tel: 323-644 4200.
www.lazoo.org
Chimpanzees, Komodo dragons, botanical gardens and a children's zoo are just some of the sights.

Beaches

With 72 miles (116 km) of coastline between Malibu and Long Beach, the Los Angeles area has no shortage of beaches. Though they vary greatly, the young and the young-at-heart will find each one special in its own way. West of Malibu, children can enjoy exploring the rocks, caves and cliff-top trails of **Robert H. Meyer Memorial State Beach**, while teenagers usually head to **Zuma Beach** (30000 Pacific Coast Highway) for the volleyball courts. The **Malibu Lagoon State Beach** (23200 Pacific Coast Highway) encourages saltwater fishing, bird-watching, picnicking, tide pool exploration and surfing.

Closer to LA, swimmers and bicyclists will relish the **Santa Monica State Beach** and its 100-year-old pier with its cafés, performers and amusement park. The adjacent **Venice City Beach** offers a living sideshow of artists, jugglers, punks, musclemen and others. Kids will find a playground and calm waters, perfect for swimming, at **Mother's Beach** in Marina del Rey.

En route to the South Bay, families can enjoy picnics and barbecues at **Dockweiler State Beach** before seeking out the aquarium of **Manhattan Beach**, the boogie board rentals of **Hermosa Beach** and the water sports of **Redondo Beach**. The curious can watch the seasonal gray whale migration, explore tide pools and attempt windsurfing at **Cabrillo Beach**, and snorkelers will relish the underwater kelp forests and shipwrecks off the beaches of **Santa Catalina Island**.

For further information, visit www.lacounty.info or call the **LA County Department of Beaches and Harbors** at 310-305 9503. You can also visit www.parks.ca.gov to learn about California's state parks and beaches.

Parks

Southern California has countless city, amusement and water parks. **Griffith Park** (tel: 323-913 4688, www.laparks.org), for instance, can keep kids occupied all day long with its picnic tables, merry-go-round, summertime pool, hiking and horseback-riding trails, children's zoo and railroad museum.

North of LA, **Universal Studios Hollywood** (tel: 800-864 8377, www.universalstudios.com) thrills kids, teenagers and their families with movie-themed rides and a backlot studio tour. Down south in Carlsbad, **LEGOLAND California** (tel: 760-918 5346, www.lego.com) offers over 50 rides, shows and attractions, including miniature LEGO-constructed versions of famous US landmarks. With its steep slides and lazy river, **Raging Waters** in San Dimas (tel: 909-802 2200, www.ragingwaters.com), California's largest water park, rivals those in Valencia and Buena Park.

EVENTS

With Angelenos' varied interests and ethnicities, it's no wonder that LA and its surrounding cities offer a wide assortment of fairs, festivals and special events. Here are just a few:

January

Big Boat Show, Marina del Rey, tel: 310-301 9019.
Chinese New Year (sometimes in February), Chinatown, tel: 213-617 0396.
Rose Parade and Bowl Game, Pasadena, tel: 626-449 4100.

February

Queen Mary Scottish Festival & Games, Long Beach, tel: 562-435 3511.
Riverside County Fair and **National Date Festival**, tel: 760-863 8247.
Southwest Arts Festival, Indio, tel: 760-347 0676.

March

Blessing of the Animals, Olvera Street, tel: 213-485 6855.
Dana Point Festival of Whales, tel: 949-472 7888.
Los Angeles Marathon, throughout LA, tel: 310-444 5544.
St. Patrick's Day festivities, Farmers Market, tel: 323-933 9211.

April

California Poppy Festival, Lancaster, tel: 661-723 6077.
Los Angeles Times Festival of Books, UCLA Campus, tel: 800-528 4637.
Renaissance Pleasure Faire, Irwindale, tel: 626-969 4750.
Toyota Grand Prix of Long Beach, tel: 562-981 2600.

May

Cinco de Mayo, Olvera Street, tel: 213-485 6855.
Duck-a-Thon, Huntington Beach, tel: 714-375 0790.
Fiesta Hermosa! (also in September), Hermosa Beach, tel: 310-376 0951.
Garden Grove Strawberry Festival, tel: 714-638 0981.

June

Art & Design Walk, West Hollywood, tel: 310-289 2534.
Los Angeles Film Festival, West Hollywood, tel: 310-432 1240.
LA Pride Festival and Parade, West Hollywood, tel: 323-969 8302.
Playboy Jazz Festival, Hollywood Bowl, tel: 323-850 2050.

July

Independence Day fireworks, Marina del Rey, tel: 310-305 9545.
Lotus Festival, Echo Park, tel: 213-485 1310.
Pageant of the Masters and **Festival of Arts**, Laguna Beach, tel: 949-497 6582.

August

International Surf Festival, South Bay, tel: 310-376 0951.
Nisei Week Japanese Festival, Little Tokyo, tel: 213-687 7193.
Sunset Junction Street Fair, Silverlake, tel: 323-661 7771.

September

Abbot Kinney Boulevard Street Festival, Venice, tel: 310-396 3772.
LA County Fair, Pomona's Fairplex, tel: 909-623 3111.
Lobster Festival, San Pedro, tel: 310-798 7478.
Oktoberfest at Alpine Village, Torrance, tel: 310-327 4384.
Watts Towers Day of the Drum Festival and **Simon Rodia Jazz Festival**, 107th Street, tel: 213-847 4646.

October

Affaire in the Gardens Art Show, Beverly Hills, tel: 310-550 4796.
Edge of the World Theater Festival, various LA venues, tel: 310-281 7920.
West Hollywood Halloween Costume Carnaval, tel: 310-289 2525.

November

Beverly Hills Garden & Design Showcase, Greystone Estate, tel: 310 550 4796.
Doo Dah Parade, Pasadena, tel: 626-205 4029.
Hollywood Christmas Parade, Hollywood Boulevard, tel: 323-469 2337.

December

Christmas Candlelight Tours, Rancho Los Cerritos, Long Beach, tel: 562-570 1755.
Hanukkah Family Festival, Skirball Cultural Center, tel: 310-440 4500.
Holiday Boat Parade, Marina del Rey, tel: 310-670 7130.

SHOPPING

What to Buy

Many visitors head to Los Angeles specifically for its shopping opportunities. Between Downtown's Fashion District and West Hollywood's Avenues of Art & Design, some intrepid shoppers consider LA to be as significant to the worlds of fashion and art as Paris, New York and Milan. But not every shopping district is like wealth-conscious Rodeo Drive. If you look in the right places, you're bound to find whatever you seek, at the price you're willing to spend.

Downtown LA is actually a fantastic place to buy apparel, jewelry and flowers at discount prices. Although the 90-block **LA Fashion District** (www.fashiondistrict.org) focuses most of its

BELOW: Rodeo Drive.

business on professional wholesalers, bargain-hunting consumers will find over 1,000 stores that sell handbags, shoes, hats, jewelry, prom dresses, textiles and clothes for men, women and children for 30 to 70 percent off the standard retail prices. The nearby **LA Flower Market** (www.laflowerdistrict.com), which takes place every morning except Sunday, is by far America's largest wholesale and retail floral selection.

LA County's frequent **farmers' markets** can also present terrific bargains, allowing buyers to save money on produce, nuts, baked goods and other delicacies by purchasing them directly from the farmers and bakers. Although most farmers' markets take place on Saturday and Sunday mornings, one occurs somewhere every day, and some cities – such as Hollywood, Santa Monica and Pasadena – hold more than one each week. Visit www.farmernet.com for the complete listings of every certified farmers' market in Southern California, and, in the meantime, feel free to visit Downtown's **Grand Central Market** (317 S. Broadway, tel: 213-624 9496) or the **Original Farmers' Market** (6333 W. 3rd Street, tel: 323-933 9211), both open every day.

Where to Buy

Although LA-area malls and boutiques offer the same name brands available in other major US cities, certain emporiums are fairly unique to the City of Angels, or at least to California. In West Hollywood, there are a number of gay-focused shops such as **A Different Light Bookstore** (8853 Santa Monica Boulevard), which features a definitive collection of gay, lesbian and transgender literature. Hollywood, meanwhile, houses several film-oriented shops, such as **Hollywood Book and Poster Company** (6562 Hollywood Boulevard). LA is also the sort of town where pet owners

flock to **Chateau Marmutt** (8128 W. 3rd Street) for designer squeakers and all kinds of dog care services. Athletes can purchase snowboards and surfboards from **Olympus Boards** (1117 Aviation Boulevard, Hermosa Beach). And, of course, cinephiles can buy movie memorabilia from stores like **It's A Wrap Production Wardrobe Sales** (3315 W. Magnolia Boulevard, Burbank) or **Star Wares Collectibles** (www.starwares.com).

Of course, most fashionistas head for LA's renowned **Rodeo Drive**, which, though it attracts more window-shoppers than buyers, presents world-class shops like Prada, Gucci, Chanel and Cartier. The relatively new **Two Rodeo**, modeled after a cobblestoned European village, has upscale boutiques like Tiffany & Co, and the nearby **Department Store Row** houses famous emporiums like Barneys New York, Saks Fifth Avenue, Neiman Marcus and Robinsons-May.

Many of Los Angeles' shoppers flock to the county's numerous shopping centers and mega-malls, such as **Macy's Plaza** in the downtown area, **Santa Monica Place** and Pasadena's **Paseo Colorado**, but for more unusual items, you might want to stroll through LA's assorted shopping neighborhoods. **Chinatown**, for instance, proffers traditional herbs, antiques, jade figurines, kimonos and ginseng while West Hollywood's **Avenues of Art & Design** present hundreds of art galleries, antique shops, home furnishing stores, wine emporiums and interior design showrooms. **Melrose Avenue** has a variety of upscale fashion boutiques and vintage clothing shops as well as the **Heritage Book Shop** (8540 Melrose Avenue, tel: 310-652 9486), a rare bookstore since 1963. Santa Monica's **Third Street Promenade** attracts tourists with familiar names like Urban Outfitters and Brookstone and

Main Street with its one-of-a-kind items, while Universal City-Walk lures them with chain stores and collections of Native American jewelry, Dodgers souvenirs and kitchen magnets. Meanwhile, curiosity-seekers will find arty housewares and apparel along Santa Monica's Montana Avenue, antiques and fine art on Venice's Abbot Kinney Boulevard and gourmet cheeses and bondage gear (though not in the same shop) at Silverlake's Sunset Junction.

Antiques

AK 11, 1114 Abbot Kinney Boulevard, Venice, tel: 310-399 1453.
Anne Hauck Art Deco, 8738 Melrose Avenue, West Hollywood, tel: 310 659 3606.
Christie's, 360 N. Camden Drive, Beverly Hills, tel: 310-385 2600.
Ming Mai Gallery, 1335 4th Street, Santa Monica, tel: 310-458 3903.

Apparel

Women's Clothes
Bebe, 319 N. Beverly Drive, Beverly Hills, tel: 310-271 2338.
Dior, 309 N. Rodeo Drive, Beverly Hills, tel: 310-859 4700.
Frederick's of Hollywood, 6751 Hollywood Boulevard, Hollywood, tel: 323-957 5953.
Fred Segal, 500 Broadway, Santa Monica, tel: 310-458 9940.
Nicole Miller, 8633 Sunset Boulevard, West Hollywood, tel: 310-652 1629.

Men's Clothes
American Rag, 150 S. La Brea Avenue, tel: 323-935 3154.
Avi's Place, 7527 Melrose Avenue, tel: 323-655 7247.
Barneys New York, 9570 Wilshire Boulevard, Beverly Hills, tel: 310-276 4400.
Lisa Kline Men, 123 S. Robertson Boulevard, tel: 310-385 7113.

For Kids
Pipsqueak, 8213 W. 3rd Street, tel: 323-653 3250.

Ragg Tattoo, 199 S. Beverly Drive, Beverly Hills, tel: 310-271 5423.
This Little Piggy Wears Cotton, 309 Wilshire Boulevard, Santa Monica, tel: 310-260 2727.

Cameras, Computers and Electronics

Apple Store, The Grove, tel: 323-965 8400.
Fry's Electronics, 2311 N. Hollywood Way, Burbank, tel: 818-526 8100.
Samy's Camera, 431 S. Fairfax Avenue, tel: 323-938 2420.

Music

Amoeba Music, 6400 Sunset Boulevard, Hollywood, tel: 323-245 6400.
Big Band CD Store, 9288 Kinglet Drive, tel: 310-858 1992.
Reggae Taz Records, 5080 W. Pico Boulevard, tel: 323-525 3101.
Virgin Megastore, 8000 Sunset Boulevard, Hollywood, tel: 323-650 8666.

Sports Equipment and Clothes

Beverly Hills Bike Shop, 854 S. Robertson Boulevard, tel: 310-275 2453.
Bodies in Motion, 12100 Olympic Boulevard, West LA, tel: 310-836 8000.
NikeWomen, The Grove, tel: 323-954 0450.
Sportmart, 1919 S. Sepulveda Boulevard, West LA, tel: 310-312 9600.

Toys

American Girl Place, The Grove, tel: 877-247 5223.
Meltdown Comics & Collectibles, 7522 Sunset Boulevard, Hollywood, tel: 323-851 7223.
Puzzle Zoo, 1413 Third Street Promenade, Santa Monica, tel: 310-393 9201.
Tom's Toys, 437 N. Beverly Drive, Beverly Hills, tel: 310-247 9822.
The Wound & Wound Toy Co, Universal CityWalk, tel: 818-509 8129.

CLOTHES CHART

The chart listed below gives a comparison of United States, European and United Kingdom clothing sizes. It is always a good idea, however, to try on any article before buying it, as sizes between manufacturers can vary enormously.

● **Women's Dresses/Suits**

US	Continental	UK
6	38/34N	8/30
8	40/36N	10/32
10	42/38N	12/34
12	44/40N	14/36
14	46/42N	16/38
16	48/44N	18/40

● **Women's Shoes**

US	Continental	UK
4½	36	3
5½	37	4
6½	38	5
7½	39	6
8½	40	7
9½	41	8
10½	42	9

● **Men's Suits**

US	Continental	UK
34	44	34
—	46	36
38	48	38
—	50	40
42	52	42
—	54	44
46	56	46

● **Men's Shirts**

US	Continental	UK
14	36	14
14½	37	14½
15	38	15
15½	39	15½
16	40	16
16½	41	16½
17	42	17

● **Men's Shoes**

US	Continental	UK
6½	—	6
7½	40	7
8½	41	8
9½	42	9
10½	43	10
11½	44	11

TRANSPORTATION

ACCOMMODATION

ACTIVITIES

A-Z

SPAS

Despite its smoggy atmosphere, LA is a very health-conscious town, with a multitude of juice bars, vegetarian restaurants, fitness clubs, yoga studios and beachside parks to keep residents looking and feeling young. In addition, many Angelenos, especially movie stars, rely on the city's numerous day spas to achieve the ultimate in relaxation and rejuvenation. Although you'll find most spas by visiting LA's luxury hotels and prowling upscale areas like West Hollywood and Beverly Hills, the following establishments will get you started:

Checkers Spa
535 S. Grand Avenue, Downtown
Tel: 213-300 0456.
www.hiltoncheckers.com
Inside the Hilton hotel, this spa offers massage treatments, body wraps, facials, manicures and access to the hotel's rooftop pool, jacuzzi and exercise facility.

Georgette Klinger
131 S. Rodeo Drive, Beverly Hills
Tel: 310-274 6347.
www.georgetteklinger.com
Since 1941, Georgette Klinger spas around the country have been perfecting their treatments – from make-up lessons and teen facials to pregnancy massages.

l.a. vie l'orange hand + foot spa
638 1/2 N. Robertson Boulevard, West Hollywood
Tel: 310-289 2501.
www.lavielorange.com
Supposedly popular with Oprah Winfrey, Sharon Stone and Mandy Moore, this is the first high-end day spa to focus exclusively on patrons' extremities.

Spa 415
415 No. Crescent Drive, Beverly Hills
Tel: 310-276 8010.
www.spa415.com
One of the best in the city, Spa 415 specializes in providing the latest technologically advanced procedures and products.

SPORTS

Participant Sports

Bicycling and Skating

Bicyclists can explore the **Santa Monica Mountains National Recreation Area** (tel: 805-370 2301, www.nps.gov/samo), one of the world's largest urban wilderness areas and home to miles of biking trails. In addition, there are several different bike routes throughout LA County, in places like Griffith Park, Long Beach and Pasadena, and towns like Santa Monica and Venice have several shops that rent bicycles and rollerblades. The **South Bay Bike Trail**, for instance, guides bicyclists along the coast from Marina del Rey to the Palos Verdes Peninsula. Visit www.labikepaths.com for more information.

Golf

There are numerous golf courses, both public and private. In the greater Los Angeles area, golfers will find the **Rancho Park Golf Club** (10460 W. Pico Boulevard, tel: 310-838 7373, www.rpgc.org) south of Beverly Hills, the **Brookside Men's Golf Club** (1133 Rosemont Avenue, tel: 626-585 3594, www.brookside mensgolfclub.com) in Pasadena and four golf courses in **Griffith Park** (tel: 323-913 4688).

Hiking

Between Griffith Park near Hollywood, Malibu Creek State Park and the countless state beaches, state parks and county parks that pepper Los Angeles County, hikers have hundreds of miles of trails to explore. For further information, contact the **LA County Department of Beaches and Harbors** (tel: 310-305 9503, www.lacounty.info) and the **California Department of Parks & Recreation** (tel: 916-653 6995, www.parks.ca.gov).

Horseback Riding

Adventurous equestrians can tackle the rugged 70-mile (113-km) **Backbone Trail** through the Santa Monica Mountains, from Point Mugu State Park to Will Rogers State Historic Park. Less experienced riders can rent horses from several area stables, such as the **LA Equestrian Center** (480 Riverside Drive, Burbank, tel: 818-840 9063, www.la-equestriancenter.com) and enjoy the picturesque trails in **Griffith Park**.

Water Sports

With the Pacific Ocean so close, it probably comes as no surprise that surfing, sailing, windsurfing and other water sports are very popular pastimes. Based in Marina del Rey, **Marina Boat Rentals** (13719 Fiji Way, tel: 310-574 2822) has power boats, sailboats and jet skis. At the **Redondo Beach Marina** (tel: 310-909 3179), people can rent pedal boats and kayaks.

Spectator Sports

Baseball

The professional baseball season runs from April to late September, with the World Series continuing until mid-October; Southern California has some of the US's finest baseball teams. The **Los Angeles Dodgers** play at Dodger Stadium (1000 Elysian Park Avenue, tel: 323-224 1448, www.dodgers.com); the **Los Angeles Angels** play at Angel Stadium (2000 Gene Autry Way, tel: 888-796 4256, www.angelsbaseball.com).

Basketball

The regular National Basketball Association (NBA) season runs from October through April, with championship playoffs continuing in June. The **Los Angeles Lakers**, the **Los Angeles Clippers** and the all-female **Los Angeles Sparks**, a WNBA team, play at the STAPLES Center (1111 S. Figueroa Street, tel: 213-742 7340, www.staplescenter.com) in downtown LA.

Football

The National Football League (NFL) season begins in September and ends in December. There are pre-season games in August and post-season playoffs in January. Although LA does not currently have a professional football team, it does have an Arena Football League team, the **Los Angeles Avengers** (tel: 888-283 6437, www.laavengers.com), who play at the STAPLES Center. In addition, many Angelenos regularly flock to **USC Trojans football games** (tel: 213-740 4672) at the Los Angeles Memorial Coliseum in Exposition Park and to **UCLA Bruins football games** (tel: 310-825 2101) at Pasadena's famous Rose Bowl.

Hockey

The professional hockey season usually runs from October to April, and the **Los Angeles Kings** (tel: 213-742 7100, www.lakings.com) call the STAPLES Center home.

Soccer

More popular in Europe, soccer has been steadily gaining interest in the US. From April to October, the **Los Angeles Galaxy** (tel: 310-630 2200, www.lagalaxy.com) face other professional US teams in Major League Soccer (MLS), often in the relatively new Home Depot Center (18400 Avalon Boulevard) in Carson.

TOURS AND TAPINGS

If you feel overwhelmed by the sheer size of Los Angeles, or are not quite ready to tackle the freeways without pretty good orientation, a sightseeing tour will probably help. Here are a few of the city's best:

Architours
Tel: 323-294 5821.
www.architours.com
Lovers of architecture, art and design will appreciate these customized walking and driving tours of downtown LA, Pasadena and other historic areas.

Catalina Adventure Tours
Tel: 310-510 2888.
www.catalinaadventuretours.com
Tourists can explore Catalina Island's harbor, city of Avalon and inland wilderness.

LA Tours
Tel: 323-960 0300.
www.lacitytours.com
You'll spend half the day touring beaches, Olvera Street, Hollywood sites and the Sunset Strip.

Los Angeles Conservancy
Tel: 213-623 2489.
www.laconservancy.org
Docents guide history buffs through LA's City Hall, the Biltmore Hotel, Union Station and other landmarks.

Red Line Tours
Tel: 323-402 1074.
www.redlinetours.com
LA's only daily walking tour company offers "edutainment" excursions through Hollywood and Downtown.

Starline Tours
Tel: 323-463 3333.
www.starlinetours.com
An LA tour company since 1935, it now offers everything from Tijuana shopping adventures to haunted Hollywood tours. If you're curious about the film and television studios located around LA County, contact each of these for details:

NBC Studio Tour
3000 W. Alameda Avenue, Burbank
Tel: 818-840 3537.
www.nbc.com
TV enthusiasts take a 70-minute excursion through a working TV studio and possibly view live tapings.

Sony Pictures Studio Tour
Sony Pictures Plaza, Culver City
Tel: 323-520 8687.
www.sonypicturesstudios.com
Sony offers a 90-minute walking tour Monday to Friday. The "yellow brick road" started here.

Universal VIP Experience
100 Universal City Plaza, Universal City
Tel: 818-622 5120.
www.universalstudios.com

In addition to enjoying the theme park, VIP visitors can explore a prop warehouse, a working sound stage, sound mixing rooms and legendary movie sets. Reservations are required.

Warner Brothers VIP Studio Tour
3400 Riverside Drive, Burbank
Tel: 818-972 8687.
www.wbstudiotour.com
Guides lead small groups through backlot streets, working sound stages, craft shops and recognizable sets. The tour ends at a prop-filled museum.

LIVE TV SHOWS

Although strangers are never allowed on film and television sets without prior authorization, visitors can join a live studio audience for several TV shows, mostly prime-time sitcoms, at 20th Century Fox Studios, CBS Studio Center, Sony Pictures Studios, Sunset-Gower Studios, Warner Bros. Studios and other lots. Contact **Audiences Unlimited, Inc.** (tel: 818-753 3470, www.tvtickets.com) for schedules and free show tickets. In addition, you can watch free tapings of the **Dr. Phil** show at Paramount Studios (tel: 323-956 1777), **Hollywood Squares** and **The Price Is Right** at CBS TV City (7800 Beverly Boulevard, tel: 323-575 2624), **JEOPARDY!** at Sony Pictures Studios (tel: 800-482 9840, www.jeopardy.com) and **Jimmy Kimmel Live!** at the El Capitan Entertainment Center (6840 Hollywood Boulevard, tel: 866 546 6984). For tickets to **The Tonight Show with Jay Leno** at NBC, send a self-addressed, stamped envelope and a brief letter, listing at least four desired dates, to 3000 W. Alameda Avenue, Burbank, CA 91523. A limited number of tickets are also available at Universal Studios.

A-Z

A-Z: A SUMMARY OF PRACTICAL INFORMATION, ARRANGED ALPHABETICALLY

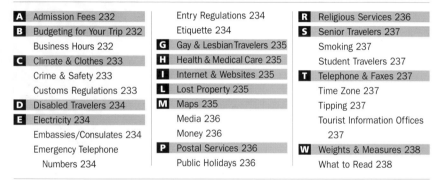

A dmission Fees

Fees for most LA museums range from $5 to $15 per adult. Special exhibitions usually cost extra, but many museums have free general admission on certain days each month. Others, like the Museum of Contemporary Art (MOCA), offer free admission on Thursday evenings. Some attractions, like the Getty Center, are always free. Plays, concerts, sporting events and studio tours are often expensive, and theme park tickets cost $45–60 per adult. You can sometimes get free tickets to live TV shows, especially sitcoms, if you call in advance *(see page 231).*

B udgeting for Your Trip

Your traveling budget depends on your plans, so research your trip well in advance and take advantage of Internet deals on airline travel, hotel rooms and theme park tickets. Besides your budget for shopping, tours, attractions and transportation to LA, you should know what to expect in regards to lodging, meals and local transportation before you arrive.

For accommodations, you might pay anywhere from $60 for a Downtown-area motel to more than $1,500 for an oceanfront suite in Santa Monica. Although most hotels offer complimentary breakfast, you'll be on your own

for lunch and dinner, which can range from $3 hot dogs to a traditional $140 French meal. The city also offers a wide spectrum of transportation choices, from $3 all-day Metro bus passes to car rentals costing $35 or more per day.

Business Hours

Although film shoots might be in progress at any given time, most businesses are open 9am–5pm on weekdays, with many of the city's ubiquitous shopping malls open as late as 9pm. Many stores and some offices are open on Saturday, and some supermarkets and restaurants stay open 24 hours daily, as do Union Station and LAX. Banks and post offices often remain open until 5.30pm on weekdays, some are open on Saturday and almost all are closed on Sunday. Theme parks have longer hours in summer.

C limate & Clothes

The urban area has a pleasantly sunny climate with relatively low humidity throughout the year and an annual average of 329 days of sunshine. The San Fernando and San Gabriel valleys tend to have higher temperatures and more humidity in summer than idyllic coastal towns like Malibu.

Los Angeles is one of the few places in the world where you can ski in the morning and surf in the afternoon. It is not uncommon for the temperature to vary 30–40°F (16.7–22.2°C) as you travel from mountains to deserts to beaches.

There is no drastic change of seasons, however. Each one seems to bleed almost imperceptibly into the next, with the only difference being that you can expect rain for the first few months of the year.

When to Visit

Los Angeles is very pleasant May through October, when the daytime temperature rarely drops below 72°F (22.2°C). From November through April, daytime temperatures often exceed 65°F (18.3°C). In summer, the humidity is usually low outside the valleys, but the famous LA smog is at its worst.

What to Wear

Los Angeles attire is casual, especially in summer and near the beaches. So if you opt for skimpy clothing in the daytime, bring along sunscreen, but nude sunbathing is generally discouraged. For sightseeing, loose cotton clothes and comfortable shoes are recommended, and LA-area shops sell plenty of both. A few restaurants require fine attire, but most don't. The

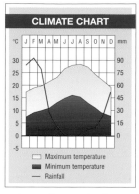

CLIMATE CHART

- ☐ Maximum temperature
- ■ Minimum temperature
- — Rainfall

moderate climate makes heavy clothing unnecessary, but light jackets might be needed for summer evenings and wool coats might be required during the winter or in the mountains. Pack rain gear in winter and spring.

Crime & Safety

Los Angeles, like most big cities, has its share of crime. Despite tourist-friendly neighborhoods like Hollywood, some areas can be dangerous, and visitors should not be lulled into a false sense of security.

Common sense is your most effective weapon, so avoid walking alone at night, never leave small children by themselves and try not to wander into deserted regions. Women especially should travel in groups, avoid slum districts, stay alert in less-populated areas and gravitate towards uniformed officials. All travelers should avoid ostentatious displays of wealth, keep an eye on their belongings, lock their cars at all times and consider securing valuables in hotel safes.

If driving, acquire directions to your destination beforehand and never pick up strangers. Always be aware of your environs, and lock your car doors if traveling through remote areas. If you get lost in a bad section, try to reach a main road quickly, and if you have trouble on the road, stay

inside your locked car, turn on your hazard lights and raise the hood to alert passing police.

If you do happen to run into trouble and you have access to a cell or pay phone, do not hesitate to dial **911**. The operator will connect you with the emergency service that you require: police, ambulance or fire.

Customs Regulations

All people entering the country must go through US Customs, whether or not they have anything to declare. To prevent delays at customs, be prepared to open your luggage for inspection and consider the following restrictions:
• Personal items are acceptable, but you must declare any purchases, gifts, inherited items and duty-free products acquired abroad.
• Depending on your country of origin, you may be allowed a duty-free exemption of $200 to $1600, plus a certain amount of tax-free imported alcohol and tobacco (except Cuban cigars).
• Although baked and canned goods, candy, cheese, fish and condiments are generally admissible, produce and meat are often restricted from entering the US.
• Items like firearms, narcotics, drug paraphernalia and some cultural artifacts are not permitted.
• Dogs, cats and other pets free of parasites and diseases are admissible, although California prohibits certain animals. The US does not quarantine pets but requires proof that dogs have received a rabies shot 30 to 365 days prior to arrival.
• Automobiles may be driven into the US if intended for the personal use of the visitor and guests.
• For up-to-date US Customs and Border Protection regulations, visit www.customs.ustreas.gov or call 202-354 1000, and visit www.usda.gov for the US Department of Agriculture's import guidelines.

D isabled Travelers

Los Angeles is one of the world's most accessible cities. Many buildings – especially airport terminals and hotels – are equipped with handicapped-accessible ramps, doorways, elevators and bathrooms. To obtain information about the services and facilities that LAX offers for disabled travelers, dial the **Public Relations Division** (tel: 310-646 5260) or **Travelers Aid** (tel: 310-646 2270).

Amtrak (tel: 877-268 7252) offers discounted tickets and accessible bedrooms, and LA's public transportation also makes considerations for disabled passengers. The **MTA** operates Metro buses equipped with driver-controlled wheelchair lifts, offers reduced fares and provides visual aids such as Braille-encoded "Metro Flash Books" for signalling the correct bus. For schedules, call 213-922 7023.

For other information regarding LA County's transportation resources and disabled services, contact the non-profit information line (tel: 211) or the **LA County Commission on Disabilities** (tel: 213-974 1053).

E lectricity

The United States uses 110 volts A/C. European appliances, such as hair dryers, will require a voltage adaptor, which is easy to purchase from local stores.

Embassies & Consulates

Foreign visitors can find listings for home country representatives in LA's local telephone books, available in libraries and post offices. Alternatively, call "Information" at **411** or consider the following:
Australian Consulate-General
2049 Century Park East, Century City, tel: 310-229 4800.
British Consulate-General
11766 Wilshire Boulevard, Los Angeles, tel: 310-481 0031.
Canadian Consulate

550 S. Hope Street, Los Angeles, tel: 213-346 2700.
Irish Honorary Consul
751 Seadrift Drive, Huntington Beach, tel: 714-658 9832.
New Zealand Consulate-General
2425 Olympic Boulevard, Santa Monica, tel: 310-566 6555.
South African Consulate-General
6300 Wilshire Boulevard, Los Angeles, tel: 323-651 0902.

Emergency Telephone Numbers

For all emergencies requiring police, fire or ambulance, dial **911** or **0** for the operator. For dental emergencies, visit www.1800dentist.com or call 800-336 8478 to find qualified dentists in your area. Regarding sexual crimes, phone the **LA Commission on Assaults Against Women** (tel: 213-626 3393) or the **National Rape Crisis Center Hotline** (tel: 800-656 4673). For 24-hour pharmacies throughout LA, visit www.savon.com or stop by 6360 W. 3rd Street in Los Angeles (tel: 323-937 3019).

Entry Regulations

Generally, most foreign visitors will need a valid passport and visa to enter the US, although some international visitors will

only need a valid passport and a return ticket for less than a 90-day stay. Visas can be obtained from travel agents or US embassies in your home country. If you lose your visa, you can obtain one from the consulate. Extensions can be granted by various service centers of the **US Citizenship and Immigration Services** (tel: 800-870 3676; www.uscis.gov).

Immigration officers will set the length of stay (maximum six months) and might verify that you have sufficient money, hotel confirmations or invitations. Due to recent security alterations, non-US citizens might need to produce a photo ID when traveling within the US, so always have your passport handy.

Presently, British and Canadian citizens, certain government officials and British subjects from Bermuda or Canada can gain easier access to the US. But by 2008, according to recent anti-terrorism legislation, travelers from the Caribbean, Bermuda, Panama, Mexico and Canada must have a passport or other secure document. For US entry regulations, visit http://travel.state.gov/visa/index.html or call the Department of State's Bureau of Consular Affairs at 202-663 1225.

Etiquette

Far from homogenous, Los Angeles is an enormous, multi-cultural city, crammed with more people than most visitors are accustomed to seeing, and its busy freeways can be a real headache to strangers. If you hope to blend in with native Angelenos, it's important to keep an open mind. After all, you're just as likely to encounter snotty fashionistas in Beverly Hills as laid-back sun-seekers in Santa Monica. So, just enjoy the year-round sunshine, adjust to the vibe of each neighborhood and accept that you'll never experience everything in one trip.

G ay & Lesbian Travelers

Overall, gay and lesbian travelers are welcome in Los Angeles, especially in areas like **West Hollywood**, which contains Southern California's largest homosexual population, has several same-sex nightclubs, bookstores and hotels and sponsors LA's annual Gay Pride Parade. Visit www.visitwestholly-wood.com for more information and check out the website www.oneinstitute.org for details about the **ONE National Gay & Lesbian Archives** (909 W. Adams Boulevard, tel: 213-741 0094), the world's largest research library on gay, lesbian, bisexual and transgendered issues.

H ealth & Medical Care

Medical facilities in major US cities can be excellent but expensive, and foreign visitors must pay hospital and doctors' fees in cash or by credit card right away. Travelers should always have proper identification, a copy of any frequently required prescriptions and comprehensive travel insurance to cover any emergencies. To find the addresses of physicians, dentists, hospitals, 24-hour emergency rooms, drugstores or supermarket pharmacies, consult the *Yellow Pages* directory.

Major Hospitals

California Hospital Medical Center, 1401 S. Grand Avenue (Downtown), tel: 213-748 2411
Cedars-Sinai Medical Center, 8700 Beverly Boulevard (Beverly Hills), tel: 310-423 3277
Saint John's Health Center, 1328 22nd Street (Santa Monica), tel: 310-829 5511
UCLA Medical Center, 10833 Le Conte Avenue (West LA), tel: 310-825 8518
LAC+USC Medical Center, 1200 N. State Street (East LA), tel: 323-226 2622

CITY WEBSITES

Several parts of LA have their own websites, listed under "Tourist Information Offices." Other websites, which provide helpful information, include:
www.losangeles.citysearch.com for reviews of restaurants, shops, arts and entertainment events.
www.ci.la.ca.us, the city's official website, contains news items, mayoral updates and agency info.
www.seemyla.com, offers LA INC.'s selection of accommodations, activities and tips for travelers.
www.la.com lists most local events, area attractions, spas, hotels, eateries, clubs and shops.
www.calendarlive.com for current info about LA's museums, festivals, concerts, plays and attractions.

I nternet & Websites

WIFI (wireless Internet access) is available in many coffee shops, some hotel rooms and several local branches of **FedEx/ Kinko's**, including a downtown location at 835 Wilshire Boulevard (tel. 213-892 1700). Visit www.fedex.com for more locations. In addition, many LA libraries contain computers, from which you can send e-mail. Visit Downtown's **Central Library** (tel: 213-228 7000) at 630 W. 5th Street or check out www.lapl.org to find the branch nearest you. LA also has a number of Internet cafés, including **psychobabble coffee house** at 1866 N. Vermont Avenue (tel: 323-664 7500).

L ost Property

Retrieving lost property is highly improbable, but a charitable individual might turn over found items to the nearest police precinct or to an in-house lost-

and-found office at local hotels, restaurants, malls and transportation hubs. If you happen to lose any valuables, file a report at the local police department, which will inform you if your lost goods are returned.

Most airlines and transportation companies have insurance for lost customer luggage; when purchasing tickets, ask about the company's insurance policy and make sure your luggage items all have identification tags. If your luggage is misplaced during a flight or accidentally left at the airport and turned into LAX's Lost and Found department, an airport official can usually bring it to you.

To inquire about items left at LAX, contact **Lost and Found** at 5600 W. Century Boulevard (tel: 310-417 0440). If something's lost on public transportation, contact the **MTA** at 323-937 8920.

Lost Credit Cards

Lost or Stolen Credit Cards
All 1-800 calls are free of charge:
American Express: 800-528-4800
Discover Card: 800-347-2683
MasterCard: 800-622-7747
Visa: 800-847-2911

M aps

Tourists can receive a variety of Los Angeles maps from **MTA** (transportation maps; tel: 800-266 6883), **LA INC.** (tel: 213-689 8822) and individual visitor bureaus. In addition, the **Automobile Club of Southern California** (tel: 213-741 3686), with various branches in the area, offers assorted street maps of LA plus maps of California and Mexico. It's worth joining if you plan to drive within Los Angeles, because the cost of being towed away once by traffic wardens could be less than the annual membership fee.

The serious urban explorer should purchase two maps. The **Insight Flexi Map: Los Angeles**, a laminated, easy-to-fold map, combines detailed cartography with essential information. The **Thomas Guide**, meanwhile, is a book of detailed maps that chart every street in Los Angeles. Both can be found at many local book-stores, drugstores, gas stations and office supply outlets.

Media

Television and Radio

Television and radio are invaluable sources of up-to-the-minute information about weather, road conditions and current events, and it's now

PUBLIC HOLIDAYS

The US has gradually shifted most of its public holidays to the closest Monday, thereby creating a number of three-day weekends. Memorial Day and Labor Day are probably the most popular, attracting many people to California. Many government offices, museums, banks and post offices are closed on national holidays, while shops and malls usually hold some of the year's best sales then.

If a fixed holiday falls on a Sunday, the following Monday usually counts as the holiday. Fixed holidays are as follows:
New Year's Day: January 1
Independence Day: July 4
Veterans' Day: November 11
Christmas Day: December 25
Other major US holidays include:
Martin Luther King Jr Day: 3rd Monday in January
Presidents' Day: 3rd Monday in February
Memorial Day: last Monday in May
Labor Day: 1st Monday in September
Columbus Day: 2nd Monday in October
Thanksgiving: 4th Thursday in November

almost standard for decent hotels and motels to include TVs, plus basic cable stations, in every room.

With XM satellite radio and cable TV, there are hundreds of radio and television channels serving Angelenos. The three major television networks – CBS, NBC and ABC – all have studios and/or offices here, and the main TV channels include **CBS** (2), **NBC** (4), **WB** (5), **ABC** (7), **FOX** (11) and **UPN** (13). There are also several Public Broad-casting System (**PBS**) and Spanish-language channels.

Newspapers and Magazines

The Los Angeles Times (www.latimes.com) is one of Amer-ica's most widely-read papers. There are several editions, and the Times' Thursday "Calendar" supplement is a terrific entertain-ment section that tells you most of what's hot and happening. The LA Weekly, the city's free alterna-tive newspaper, is an excellent source for up-to-date information on area clubs and events. Also, Los Angeles and Beverly Hills magazines, both monthly periodi-cals, present articles on South-ern California culture, plus restaurant listings.

Money

Foreign visitors should travel with a small amount of US currency (cash and coins), a credit card (Visa, MasterCard, American Express, Discover, etc.) and travelers' checks in US-dollar amounts. If lost or stolen, most travelers' checks can be replaced. With proper identifica-tion, you can cash them in some banks and use them in most establishments, where you will receive change in cash. Note that LA County imposes a sales tax of 8.25%, and hotels charge a 14% transient occupancy tax.

Credit and debit cards are accepted practically everywhere, though not all cards at all places.

For a fee, you can withdraw money from bank tellers during business hours and from most 24-hour automatic teller machines (ATMS) as long as you have a personal identification number (PIN). If you use a credit card for car rentals, hotel book-ings or hospital admittance, you will not have to leave a deposit.

There is no limit to the amount of currency that may be imported or exported, but you must declare any amount over $10,000. Although it's more convenient in other cities, you can exchange foreign currencies at LAX or in a few of LA's larger banks, but be sure to bring your passport with you. In addition, you can exchange currencies and purchase travelers' checks at the **American Express Travel Service** (tel: 310-659 1682) at 8493 W. 3rd Street.

P ostal Services

Post offices open by 9am and usually close around 5pm on weekdays. Many of them are also open on Saturday, and almost all are closed on Sunday. If you don't know where you'll be stay-ing, you can have mail addressed to General Delivery at a specific post office and pick it up in person with proper identification. In LA, the **Airport Station** (tel: 310-649 7490) at 9029 Airport Boulevard is open daily 7am–11pm. Visit www.usps.com for specific locations, hours and services of post offices through-out the city.

R eligious Services

Los Angeles is a very religious town, containing an enormous number of Catholics, Jews, Protestants, Buddhists, Hindus and Muslims, among others. Thousands of cathedrals, churches, synagogues, temples and mosques are scattered throughout LA County. Consult the Yellow Pages for the nearest house of worship.

Senior Travelers

Movie theaters and restaurants typically offer discounts to senior citizens with proper photo IDs. Anyone 62 years old or older can also qualify for a Metro Senior ID card, which provides discounts on Metro buses and trains; call 213-680 0054 for details about reduced fares. To obtain information about the services that LAX offers elderly travelers, dial **Travelers Aid** (tel: 310-646 2270).

Smoking

There is currently a no-smoking law in effect in virtually all Los Angeles bars, restaurants and offices. Be sure to request a smoking room if you smoke when booking a place to stay.

Student Travelers

With a current school ID, a student traveler can take advantage of discounts at movie theaters and on Metro public transportation.

Telephone & Faxes

Given its enormous size, Los Angeles has numerous area codes to accommodate its countless fax lines, modems and cell phones. Although this list of telephone prefixes is current, it's still a good idea to check with the operator (**0**) when in doubt:
Downtown LA – **213**
Hollywood and West Hollywood – **323**
Beverly Hills and Santa Monica – **310**
Burbank – **818**
Pasadena – **626**
Long Beach – **562**
Anaheim – **714**
Valencia – **661**
  Toll-free numbers are prefixed by **800**, **888**, **877** or **866** and, after dialing **1** first, can be used to contact many hotels, airlines, cruise lines and car rental companies. To make a long-distance call within the US, dial **0** for the

operator or simply dial the number directly, using 1, the area code and the local seven-digit number. For a hefty price, you can usually dial local and long distance numbers from hotel rooms, but it's cheaper to buy a phone card, available in most drugstores, and use one of the city's ubiquitous public phones, often found in hotel lobbies, restaurants, malls and gas stations.

  Cell phone usage is widespread in LA, and travelers should consider purchasing one, especially if you're planning to stay a while. Cell phones are handy in emergency situations or remote areas.

  Most major hotels offer **fax services**, and faxes can also be sent from numerous branches of **FedEx/Kinko's** (see the *Yellow Pages* for locations). Also, **Western Union** (tel: 800-325 6000) will take telegram messages and orders to wire money over the telephone.

Time Zone

California is contained within the Pacific Standard Time zone (PST), which is two hours behind Chicago, three hours behind New York and eight hours behind London. On the first Sunday in April, the clock is moved ahead one hour for Daylight Savings Time. On the last Sunday in October, the clock is moved back one hour to return to Standard Time.

Tipping

Most Angelenos in the service industries rely on tips to compensate for poor hourly salaries. So, unless service is truly horrendous, you should expect to tip everyone from porters to waiters.

  In restaurants, it is customary to leave a sum equivalent to about 15 percent of the bill. For groups of six or more, the bill usually includes an automatic gratuity. You should also plan on paying 15 percent of the bill to

International calls: 011 (international access code) plus the country code, city code and local number
Directory help: 411 or 555-1212 (preceded by 1-800 or a specific area code)
Emergencies: 0 or 911
Current weather: 213-554 1212
Freeway conditions: 800-427 7623

bartenders, room-service waiters, taxi drivers and hairdressers. Hotel doormen should receive $1 for hailing you a cab, hotel porters should earn $1–2 for each item of luggage and restroom attendants should garner at least 50¢ for assisting you. When you check out of your hotel, you should leave the maids $1–2 for each day of your stay.

Tourist Information Offices

LA INC., the city's convention and visitors bureau, provides various itineraries, an official visitor guide called *LA Now* and a website, www.seemyla.com, listing selected hotels, restaurants, nightclubs, museums, shops and activities. Visitors are welcome at the **Downtown Los Angeles Visitor Information Center** (tel: 213-689 8822) at 685 Figueroa Street and at the **Hollywood Visitor Information Center** (tel: 323-467 6412) in the Hollywood & Highland Center.

  Given LA's enormous size, out-of-towners will find that many areas have their own tourist offices. Contact the **Hollywood Chamber of Commerce** (tel: 323 469 8311; www.hollywoodchamber. net) to learn about the next dedication ceremony on the Hollywood Walk of Fame. For information about WeHo's annual events and trendy restaurants, stop by the **West Hollywood Convention & Visitors Bureau** (tel: 310-289

2525; www.visitwesthollywood.com) inside the Pacific Design Center at 8687 Melrose Avenue. The **Beverly Hills Conference and Visitors Bureau** (tel: 310-248 1015; www.beverlyhillsbehere.com), at 239 S. Beverly Drive, offers visitor guides and private walking tours.

For information about dining, shopping, cultural and recreational activities in LA's beachside communities, visit the **Santa Monica Visitor Information Center** (tel: 310-319 6263; www.santa monica.com) at 1920 Main Street, the **Marina del Rey Visitor Information Center** (tel: 310-305 9545; www.visitthemarina.com) at 4701 Admiralty Way and the **Long Beach Area Convention & Visitors Bureau** (tel: 562-436 3645; www.visitlongbeach.com) at 1 World Trade Center. Visitors to Santa Catalina Island can gain free information about island activities, lodging and dining at the **Catalina Island Chamber of Commerce & Visitors Bureau** (tel: 310-510 1520; www.catalina.com) in Avalon. Tourists can obtain details about the Rose Bowl at the **Pasadena Convention & Visitors Bureau** (tel: 626-795 9311; www.pasadena cal.com) at 171 S. Los Robles Avenue and access information about Orange County's theme

parks at the **Anaheim/Orange County Visitor & Convention Bureau** (tel: 714-765 8888; www.anaheimoc.org) at 800 W. Katella Avenue.

W eights & Measures

The United States uses the Imperial system of weights and measures. The Metric system is rarely used, so the following conversions are helpful for Europeans:
1 inch = 2.54 cm
1 foot = 0.3048 m
1 mile = 1.609 km
1 acre = 0.405 hectares
1 quart = 0.946 liter
1 ounce = 28.35 grams
1 pound = 0.454 kg

What to Read

Barbie Loves LA: America's Favorite Doll Sees the Sites by Greg LaVoi, Angel City Press, 2004.
The Big Sleep by Raymond Chandler, Knopf, 1939.
The Day of the Locust by Nathanael West, Random House, 1939.
Devil in a Blue Dress by Walter Mosley, W.W. Norton & Company, 1990.
The Encyclopedia of Hollywood by Scott and Barbara Siegel, Checkmark Books, 2004.
Hollywood Haunted: A Ghostly Tour of Filmland by Laurie Jacobson and Marc Wanamaker, Angel City Press, 1999.
Hollywood, Interrupted: Insanity Chic in Babylon – The Case Against Celebrity by Andrew Breitbart and Mark Ebner, John Wiley & Sons, 2004.
Hollywood Urban Legends: The Truth Behind All Those Delightfully Persistent Myths of Films, Television, and Music by Richard Roeper, New Page Books, 2001.
Inside Rodeo Drive: The Stores – the Stars – the Stories by Scott Huver and Mia Kaczinski Dunn, Angel City Press, 2001.
LA City Limits: African American Los Angeles from the Great Depression to the Present by

Josh Sides, University of California Press, 2004.
Landmark LA: Historic-Cultural Landmarks of Los Angeles edited by Jeffrey Herr, Angel City Press, 2002.
Los Angeles Stories: Great Writers on the City edited by John Miller, Chronicle Books, 1991.
The Los Angeles Watts Towers by Bud and Arloa Goldstone, J. Paul Getty Trust Publications, 1997.
Movie Star Homes: The Famous to the Forgotten by Judy Artunian and Mike Oldham, Santa Monica Press, 2004.
Natural Los Angeles by Bill Thomas, Perennial Library, 1989.
Santa Monica Mountains: Range of Majesty from the Sea to the City by Tom Gamache and Matthew Jaffe, Angel City Press, 2005.
Street Gallery: Guide to 1000 Los Angeles Murals by Robin J. Dunitz, RJD Enterprises, 1998.
This is Hollywood: An Unusual Movieland Guide by Kenneth Schessler, 2002.
UCLA vs USC: 75 Years of the Greatest Rivalry in Sports by Lonnie White, Los Angeles Times Books, 2004.
Venice of America: Coney Island of the Pacific by Jeffrey Stanton, Donahue Publishing Company, 1987.
Walk Los Angeles: Adventures on the Urban Edge by John McKinney, Olympus Press, 1992.
Whitewashed Adobe: The Rise of Los Angeles and the Remaking of Its Mexican Past by William Deverell, University of California Press, 2004.

Other Insight Guides

Insight Guide: California Captures the energy and excitement of America's Golden State.

LOS ANGELES STREET ATLAS

The key map shows the area of Los Angeles covered by the atlas section. An index of street names and places of interest shown on the maps can be found on the following pages. For each entry there is a page number and grid reference.

Map Legend

▰▰▰ Freeway with Exit	✝✝ Church (ruins)		Freeway	Ⓜ	Metro
▰▰▰ Freeway (under construction)	✝ Monastery		Divided Highway	🚌	Bus Station
▰▰▰ Divided Highway	🏰🏯 Castle (ruins)	}	Main Roads	❶	Tourist Information
Main Road	∴ Archeological Site			✉	Post Office
Secondary Road	∩ Cave	}	Minor Roads	✝	Cathedral/Church
Minor road	★ Place of Interest			☾	Mosque
Track	⌂ Mansion/Stately Home		Footpath	✡	Synagogue
International Boundary	※ Viewpoint		Railroad	👤	Statue/Monument
State Boundary	🏖 Beach		Pedestrian Area	🏛	Tower
National Park/Reserve	✈ Airport		Important Building		
			Park		

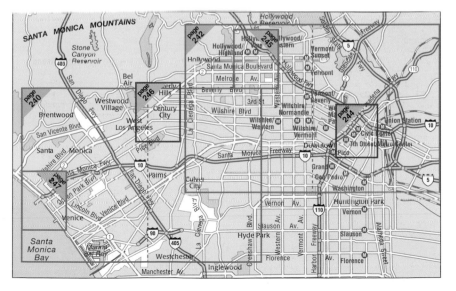

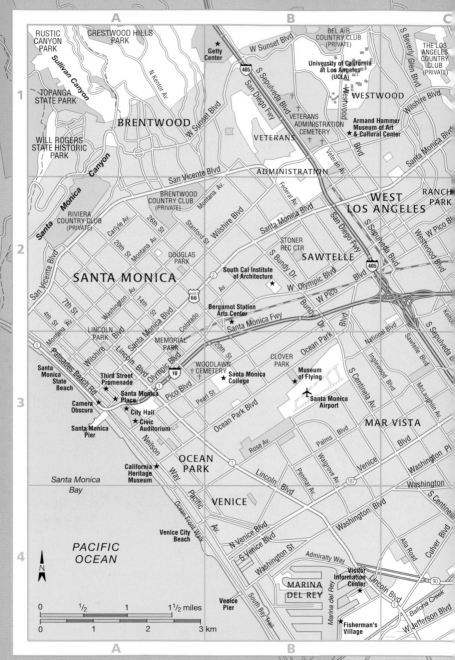

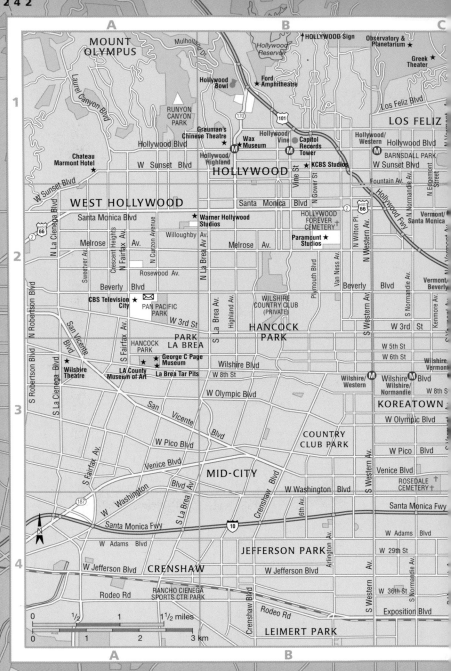

A

MOUNT OLYMPUS

Mulholland Dr

Laurel Canyon Blvd

Hollywood Reservoir

★ HOLLYWOOD Sign

Observatory & Planetarium ★

Greek Theater ★

Hollywood Bowl

Ford ★ Amphitheatre

1

RUNYON CANYON PARK

Los Feliz Blvd

LOS FELIZ

Grauman's Chinese Theatre

Hollywood/ Vine

Capitol Records Tower

Hollywood/ Western

Hollywood Blvd

Hollywood Blvd ★

Wax Museum

Ⓜ

Ⓜ

Ⓜ

Hollywood Blvd

BARNSDALL PARK

Chateau Marmont Hotel ★

W Sunset Blvd

Hollywood/ Highland

HOLLYWOOD

★ KCBS Studios

W Sunset Blvd

N Edgemont Street

W Sunset Blvd

Fountain Av.

WEST HOLLYWOOD

Santa Monica Blvd

N Normandie Av.

Vermont/ Santa Monica

HIST 66

N La Cienega Blvd

Santa Monica Blvd

N Curzon Avenue

★ Warner Hollywood Studios

HIST 66

2

2

Hollywood Fwy

Melrose

Willoughby Av.

Melrose Av.

HOLLYWOOD FOREVER CEMETERY ✝

N Western Av.

Vermont/ Santa Monica

Sweetzer Av.

Crescent Heights

N Fairfax Av.

N La Brea Av.

★ Paramount Studios

2

Rosewood Av.

Beverly Blvd

S Fairfax Av.

Van Ness Av.

Plymouth Av.

Beverly Blvd

S Western Av.

S Normandie Av.

Vermont/ Beverly

Kenmore Av.

CBS Television City ★ ✉

PAN PACIFIC PARK

W 3rd St

S La Brea Av.

Highland Av.

WILSHIRE COUNTRY CLUB (PRIVATE)

W 3rd St

N Robertson Blvd

San Vicente Blvd

HANCOCK PARK

PARK LA BREA

HANCOCK PARK

W 5th St

W 6th St

Wilshire/ Vermont

Wilshire Theatre

George C Page ★ Museum

Wilshire Blvd

Ⓜ

Ⓜ

Wilshire Blvd

S Robertson Blvd

S La Cienega Blvd

S Fairfax Av.

LA County Museum of Art ★

La Brea Tar Pits

W 8th St

Wilshire/ Western

Wilshire/ Normandie

W 8th St

3

San Vicente Blvd

W Olympic Blvd

KOREATOWN

W Olympic Blvd

W Pico Blvd

COUNTRY CLUB PARK

W Olympic Blvd

Venice Blvd

W Pico Blvd

S Western Av.

Venice Blvd

ROSEDALE CEMETERY ✝

S La Brea Av.

Blvd

MID-CITY

Crenshaw Blvd

W Washington Blvd

Santa Monica Fwy

187

W Washington

16th Av.

Arlington Av.

Santa Monica Fwy

Santa Monica Fwy

10

W Adams Blvd

W Adams Blvd

JEFFERSON PARK

W 29th St

4

W Jefferson Blvd

CRENSHAW

W Jefferson Blvd

S Western Av.

W 36th St

S Normandie Av.

Rodeo Rd

RANCHO CIENEGA SPORTS CTR PARK

Crenshaw Blvd

Rodeo Rd

Exposition Blvd

LEIMERT PARK

0   ½   1   1½ miles

0   1   2   3 km

A   **B**   **C**

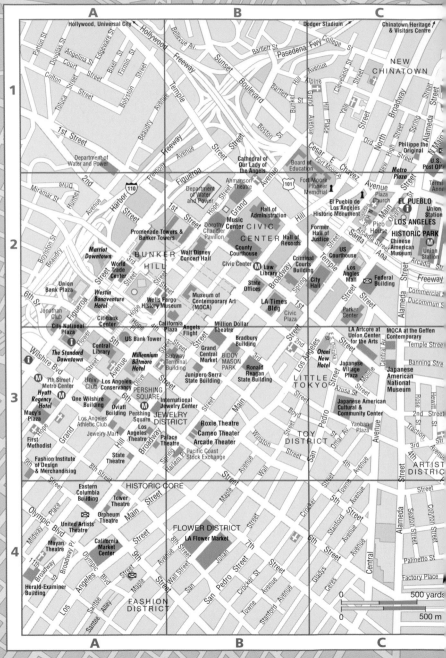

HOLLYWOOD HILLS

Hollywood Reservoir

Hollywood Bowl

Ford Amphitheatre

Cahuenga Blvd West

Cahuenga Boulevard East

Hollywood Heritage Museum

Camrose Dr.

Hollywood Freeway

Holly Drive

North Beachwood Drive

Hollyridge Drive

Canyon Drive

Foothill Drive

Hillcrest Road

SCENIC GARDENS

North Highlands Av.

Franklin Avenue

Franklin Avenue

N Van Ness Av.

Taft Avenue

North Wilton Place

Renaissance Hollywood Hotel

Franklin Av.

Hollywood & Highland Center Complex

Grauman's Chinese Theatre

Wax Museum

Yucca Street

Whitley Av.

Ivar Av.

Yucca Street

Capitol Records Tower

Carlos Av.

Hollywood Roosevelt Hotel

El Capitan Theater

Hollywood/ Highland

Walk of Fame

Hawthorn Av.

Egyptian Theatre

N Las Palmas

LA Contemporary Exhibitions

Selma Avenue

North Cahuenga Boulevard

N Wilcox Avenue

Hollywood/ Vine

Vine Street

Pantages Theatre

Hollywood Boulevard

Carlton Way

N Argyle Avenue

Selma Avenue

N El Centro Avenue

Hollywood Palladium

Hollywood High School

HOLLYWOOD

W Sunset Boulevard

Cinerama Dome

W Sunset Boulevard

Sunset-Gower Studios

De Longpre Avenue

N Highlands Avenue

N Orange Drive

Cherokee Avenue

N June St.

DE LONGPRE PARK

North Seward Street

N Wilcox Avenue

Cole Avenue

De Longpre Avenue

Homewood Av.

Fountain Avenue

Gordon Street

Tamarind Av.

N Bronson Avenue

N Van Ness Av.

La Mirada Av.

Fountain Avenue

N McCadden Place

N Las Palmas Avenue

Lexington Avenue

Lexington Avenue

Virginia Av.

Hudson Theatre

Hollywood Recreation Center

Santa Monica Boulevard

Santa Monica Boulevard

Eleanor Avenue

Abbey of the Psalms

Clark Mausoleum

Romaine Street

Romaine Street

HOLLYWOOD FOREVER CEMETERY

N Gower Street

N Ridgewood Place

Willoughby Avenue

Willoughby Ave.

Cathedral Mausoleum

Waring Avenue

Seward Street

N Hudson Avenue

N Wilcox Avenue

Cole Avenue

N Lillian Av.

North Cahuenga Boulevard

N El Centro Avenue

Vine Street

N Van Ness Av.

N Wilton Place

Paramount Studios

Waring Avenue

Camerford Av.

Astroburger

Melrose Avenue

Melrose Avenue

N Irving Blvd

N Bronson Street

Clinton Street

Clinton Street

Rosewood Avenue

WILSHIRE COUNTRY CLUB

N Cherokee Av.

N June St.

N Rosemore Av.

N Arden Blvd

N Gower Street

0   500 yards

0   500 m

WILL ROGERS MEMORIAL PARK

West Sunset Boulevard

Greenway Drive

Lomitas Avenue

Whittier Drive

North Roxborough Drive

North Bedford Drive

North Campden Drive

North Rodeo Drive

North Beverly Drive

Elevado Avenue

Canon Drive

North Crescent Drive

North Alpine Drive

North Rexford Drive

Foothill Road

N Elm Drive

N Maple Drive

N Palm Drive

HWY 66

Santa Monica Boulevard

Carmelita Avenue

BEVERLY HILLS

GARDENS

Library

West 3rd Street

Beverley Hills Civic Center

Burton Way

THE LOS ANGELES COUNTRY CLUB

North Linden Drive

Walden Drive

Trenton Drive

Wilshire Boulevard

BEVERLY

Museum of Television & Radio

N Crescent Drive

Canon Drive

N Rodeo Drive

Little Santa Monica Boulevard

Way

Two Rodeo

Brighton Way

Dayton

North Rexford Drive

North Elm Drive

THE GOLDEN TRIANGLE

Department Store Row

Wilshire Boulevard

Beverly Hilton Hotel

HWY 66

Durant Drive

South Moreno Drive

Regent Beverly Wilshire

Charleville Boulevard

S Lasky Drive

South Spalding Drive

South Linden Drive

South McCarty Drive

South Roxbury Drive

South Bedford Drive

S Peck Dr

Gregory Way

S Camden Dr.

South Rodeo Drive

S El Camino Drive

South Beverly Drive

South Reeves Drive

South Canon Drive

South Crescent Drive

South Elm Drive

South Rexford Drive

Beverley Hills High School

Comstock Drive

Comstock Avenue

Ensley Av.

Santa Monica

Santa Monica Boulevard

Little Santa Monica Boulevard

CENTURY CITY

Century City Center

Century Park West

Constellation Boulevard

Century Park East

Avenue of the Stars

Shubert Theatre

Century Plaza Hyatt

ABC Entertainment Center

Galaxy Way

Heath Avenue

S Spalding Drive

ROXBURY PARK

West Olympic Boulevard

S Roxbury Drive

S Castello Avenue

Avalon Hotel

S Beverly Drive

West Pico Boulevard

Reeves St.

Alcott Street

Comstock Avenue

Benecia Avenue

Fox Hills West Drive

Mississippi Av.

Century Park West

Empyrean Way

Museum of Tolerance

Roxbury Drive

Cashio Street

Rexford Drive

South Beverly Glen Boulevard

West Olympic Boulevard

Patricia Avenue

Tennessee Avenue

Keswick Avenue

Ilona Avenue

Kerwood Avenue

Almayo Avenue

Fox Hills West Drive

20th Century Fox Studios

West Pico Boulevard

Motor Avenue

HILLCREST COUNTRY CLUB

Roxbury Drive

Beverly Drive

Monte Mar

Kirkside Rd

Oakmore Rd

Cresta Drive

S Beverly Drive

N

0   500 yards

0   500 m

CHEVIOT HILLS PARK

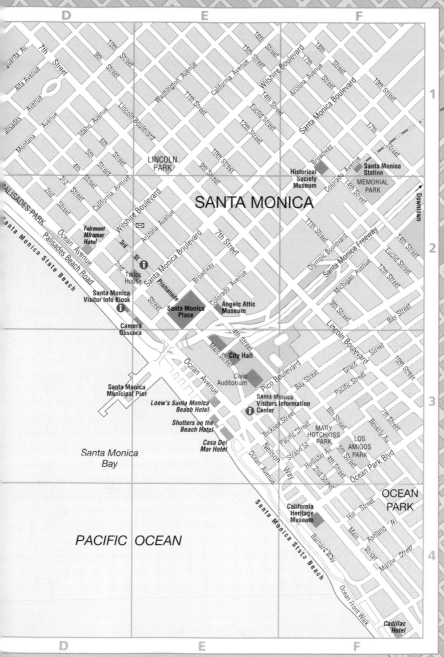

STREET INDEX

ART & PHOTO CREDITS

Corbis 39, 173
Donna Dailey 197, 202, 203
Department of Water & Power 189
Mark Downey 4B, 160TL
David Dunai 6T, 6B, 9CL, 33, 38,
44, 45, 72, 73, 76TL, 78TL, 79,
80, 82TL, 86, 87, 89, 89TR, 90,
91, 92, 92TL, 93, 104, 105,
107BR, 108BR, 109BL, 109BR,
120TL, 122, 124, 126TL, 131,
134TL, 137TR, 138TL, 138, 155,
165, 166TL, 167BR, 168, 179,
183TR, 184TL, 188TL
The El Capitan Theatre Company
107TR
Glyn Genin 154TL, 175TR, 198,
206, 207TR
Getty Images 30, 106
J. Paul Getty Center 56
J. Paul Getty Trust 8B
Hollywood & Highland 108BL
Hotel Bel-Air 141, 147, 219
Catherine Karnow 1, 2/3, 3, 4T,
5, 7T, 7B, 9TR, 10/11, 12/13,
14, 17, 31, 32, 34/35, 36, 37,
40, 41, 42, 46, 47, 49, 51, 52,
53, 62, 64/65, 66/67, 68, 76,
77, 78, 80TL, 81, 84, 87TR, 88,
94TL, 95, 96, 96TL, 97, 100,
101, 103, 105TR, 109TR, 111,
112, 113, 118, 121, 133, 134TL,
125, 130, 133, 136, 137, 140,
142TL, 143, 144, 145, 145TR,
146BR, 146BL, 146TL, 150, 151,
153, 153TR, 154, 156, 157,
157TR, 158, 160, 161, 164,
170, 172, 174, 176/177, 178,
181TR, 182, 183, 185, 186,
192, 195, 195TR, 196, 196TL,
199, 199TR, 200, 201, 202TL,
204, 208, 208TL, 210, 211TR,
213, 215, 225, 228, 234, 238
**Catherine Karnow/Museum of
Neon Art** 81TR

L.A Inc/David C. Miller 63
L.A Inc/African Marketplace Inc
82
L.A Inc/USC 85
L.A Inc/Skirball Center 171
Melba Levick 19, 188, 193
David Livingston/Getty Images
184
Jim Mendenhall 133TR
**Jim Mendenhall/Los Angeles
Convention & Visitors Bureau** 135
The Packing House 22,
Carole Pearlman 43, 110TL
Petersen Automotive Museum 48
Sara Remington 8T, 75, 83,
93TR, 98, 99, 102TL, 112TL,
114, 115, 119, 123TR, 128,
129, 134, 139, 143TR, 159,
159TR, 162, 163, 167BL, 168TL,
171TR, 172TL, 180TL, 185TR,
187TR, 200TL, 205
**Research, Natural History
Museum of L.A County** 20, 21,
23, 24, 25, 26
Rex Features 29, 107BL, 209
The Ronald Grant Archive 50
Southwest Museum 16, 18,
Spectrum Colour Library 207, 211
Topham Picturepoint 28
Joseph F. Viesti 187
B. Vikander/Art Directors Trip 94
Michael Webb 57, 58, 59, 60,
61, 169
**West Hollywood Convention &
Visitors Bureau** 121TR, 126, 127
M. Wilson/Trip 108TL

PICTURE SPREADS

Pages 54/55 Alan
Becker/Imagebank/Getty Images
54BC, Alberto
Incrocci/Imagebank/Getty Images
54/55C, Anthony Johnson/

Imagebank/Getty Images 55BL,
Steve Orubman/Imagebank 55C,
Rex Features 54CR, 55BR,
Topham Picturepoint 55TR, Roy
Wieman/Imagebank/Getty Images
54CL

Pages 116/117 David Dunai
116BL, 117BL, H. Garcety/Art
Directors Trip 116/117C, Ronald
Grant Archive 117CL, Catherine
Karnow 116CL, Rex Features
116BR, 117TR, 117CR

Pages 148/149 Tom Boncr/J.
Paul Getty Trust and Richard
Meier & Partners 148CL, Hulton
Deutsch/Getty Center 149TR, The
Getty Institute for the History of
Art & the Humanities 148CR, J.
Paul Getty Museum 148BR,
149CL, 149BR, J. Paul Getty Trust
148/149C

Pages 190/191 The Ronald Grant
Archive 190CR, 191TR, 191CR,
Robert Harding Picture Library
191BL, Catherine Karnow 190CL,
190/191C, Rex Features 190BL,
Universal Studios Hollywood
191BR

Map Production: Phoenix Mapping and
James Macdonald

Production: Linton Donaldson
©2006 Apa Publications GmbH &
Co Verlag KG, Singapore Branch

GENERAL INDEX

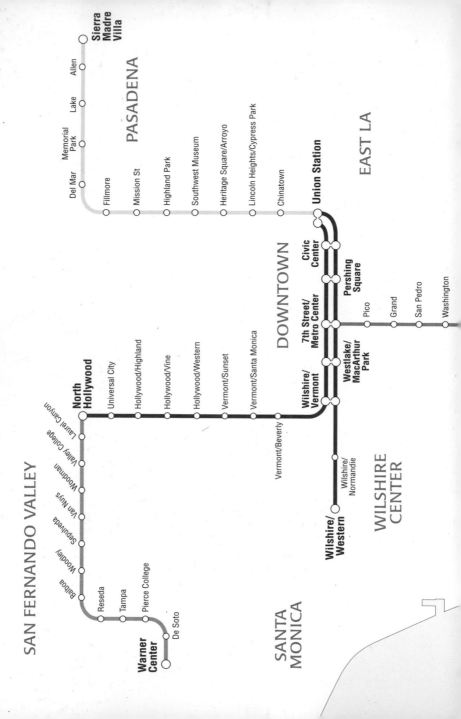